# MIDNIGHT MARQUEE
## Volume 3, Number 1

**Editors**
Gary J. Svehla
Susan Svehla

**Managing Editor**
Richard J. Svehla

**Copy Editor**
Linda J. Walter

**Graphic Design Interior**
Gary J. Svehla

**Cover Design/
Title Page Design**
Susan Svehla

**Contributing Writers**
Anthony Ambrogio, Mark Clark, Erich Kuersten
Jonathan M. Lampley, Michael H. Price,
Cindy Collins Smith, Brian Smith, Bryan Senn,
Gary J. Svehla, Steven Thornton, Robert Tinnell

**Acknowledgments**
John Antosiewicz Photo Archives, Eric Caidin,
Jerry Ohlinger's Movie Material Store,
John E. Parnum Archival Collection
Photofest/Buddy Weiss, Michael H. Price

**Illustrator**
Allen J. Koszowski

**Publisher**
Midnight Marquee Press

Midnight Marquee Vol. 3, No. 1, Number 69/70, First Reprint July 2013
Copyright 2003 © by Gary J. Svehla
Published twice yearly by Midnight Marquee Press at $17 per year. Printed by King Printing, East Lowell, MA.
Return postage must accompany articles and art, if the owner wants them returned. No responsibility is taken for unsolicited material. Editorial views expressed by our contributors are not necessarily those of the publisher. Nothing may be reproduced in any media without written permission of the publisher. Send submissions of articles, letters and art to Gary J. Svehla, 9721 Britinay Lane, Baltimore, MD 21234; web site: http://www.midmar.com; e-mail: mmarquee@aol.com
Letters of comment addressed to Midnight Marquee or Gary or Susan Svehla will be considered for publication unless the writer requests otherwise. Subscription rates: $10 per single copy or $17 per year (shipped U.S. Media Mail). Subscription copies are mailed in sturdy cardboard mailers and will arrive in excellent condition; support MidMar by becoming a direct-mail subscriber. Foreign orders are no longer accepted. Foreign customers please order our products from Amazon.com

# TABLE OF CONTENTS

**3** Marquee Mutterings: Editorial
by Gary J. Svehla

**6** Sounds of Silents
by Steven Thornton

**22** Terror from 1963 and Beyond: Past 40 Years —Top 50 Films
by Gary J. Svehla

**38** *The Spider*: Weaving a Web of Suspense
by Michael H. Price

**46** Things That Came: Significant Horror Movie Trends (1963-2003)

**64** Forum/Against 'Em: *The Wicker Man*
Edited by Anthony Ambrogio

**74** *Return of the Ape Man* —Revisiting the Wartime Savage from a Post-Modern Perspective
by Erich Kuersten

**86** DVD Reviews
by Gary J. Svehla

**123** Grave Diggings [Letters]

# MARQUEE Mutterings

Thirteen-year-old Gary Svehla, who had recently survived the Cuban Missile Crisis (with the help of his favorite horror actors—Karloff, Chaney, Jr. and Lorre—who had just appeared on the *Route 66* TV series), and would experience the Kennedy assassination the following fall, was preparing to enter eighth grade, his second year in the big time junior high wonder years. Gary was an avid reader of *Famous Monsters of Filmland and Castle of Frankenstein*. To him, Forrest J Ackerman and Calvin T. Beck were the true heroes of the horrors. The world outside was frightening—students at Herring Run still underwent "Duck and Tuck" nuclear attack drills, and the prospect of attending eighth grade made young Gary nervous. His old pals the monsters became his security blanket.

*Famous Monsters* was the Holy Grail and within its pages was a wondrous world of gods and monsters waiting to be discovered... reading about them and looking at photos only sparked the imagination. Local theaters—the Earle, the Vilma, the Paramount (young Gary could take the bus to these theaters if father Richard was too busy to drive Gary and his friends)—became the houses of the holy, cathedrals to a fantastic world of fright cinema. In 1963 the Silver Age of Hammer and American International were showing regularly in these theaters, and Gary never missed a horror or science fiction monster show.

Enter Dave Metzler. Kids called him "Metzie" because he lived right next door to another boy his own age, David French, so his buddy was called "Frenchie." David and Gary become fast friends (and even faster enemies... all adolescents have this love/hate thing going) and both boys *loved* horror movies. David, who was more outgoing, loved to draw and constantly showed Gary his pencil and pen-and-ink masterpieces of the classic monsters. David's father owned and managed a beach in Middle River, Maryland, Holly Beach, and David and Gary envisioned writing, starring in and filming an 8mm extravaganza called *Frankenstein vs. The Wolf Man*. Gary, of course, would portray Baron Frankenstein, in white lab coat and Whiffle-cut hair. David, more theatrical and physically daring, would portray the doomed Larry Talbot, the Wolf Man. Our other buddy Keith Vinroe played the Monster in the fight sequences (with David subbing for the fiend in other low-key situations... such as laying prostrate on the lab table). We spent that summer concocting a cinematic masterpiece.

Meanwhile, in the pages of *Famous Monsters* was the tempting and always fascinating *Haunt Ad* section, a fanboy column where fanzines or amateur versions of *Famous Monsters of Filmland* could be advertised and sold. Gary recently received copies of a wonderful offset fanzine, a mini-*FM* but written on a higher intellectual level, called *Horrors of the Screen* (edited by Alexander Soma, another inspiration). Gary soon imagined himself as chief writer and editor (who needed a staff anyway... he could publish his own thoughts and opinions about the movies and stars he loved). However, Gary realized a magazine needed an attractive cover and beautiful interior illustrations. David Metzler was soon called to duty and together the boy geniuses planned the first issue of Gary's fanzine, to be called *Gore Creatures*.

To be quite honest, Gary didn't need David yet (or so he thought), for the first issue contained no art (the first copies contained a totally blank front cover) and was written out in longhand with ball-point pen. At least one or two issues were created, digest-size, in this manner. However, the effort was enough to write a letter to the *Haunt Ad* section of *Famous Monsters*, advertising the first issue of *Gore Creatures* for a hefty 20¢ an issue (or $1.00 for a year's subscription, five issues). Gary's nervous hands trembled when he purchased the new issue of *FM* (he use to walk half a mile down Belair Road to his favorite drugstore that stocked all the monster magazines and comic books) and slowly flipped through the pages to see if the advertisement appeared. Holy Monster Mash! It did. And only a few days passed until the very first order came in the mail, a personal order from the man who started it all, Forry Ackerman, the editor-in-chief and godshead of *Famous Monsters*. Including a crisp dollar bill, Ackerman wrote a brief note referring to "Gore Jelly" and subscribed to the fanzine for one year.

History had been made, the first issue of *Gore Creatures* had been sold, and the summer of '63 never seemed brighter or more fun-filled.

But for Gary, the pressure was on... how could he keep up with production of his fanzine if he had to hand-copy each and every issue (which he was

willing to do, of course)? Enter Joan Jewell, babysitter to Gary's older brother Dickie and best-friend of Gary's mother Ann. Gary, at the tender age of seven, and Joan became best friends. They played "office"— Gary was the boss and Joan was the secretary. He loved it when she read all the sordid news stories from the local newspaper to a wide-eyed Gary riveted by plane crashes, amazing features, murder stories, etc. But Gary at age 13 was now older and more sophisticated, so the play office became a real office, and Joan offered to use carbon paper to type up 20 copies of the magazine for the young entrepreneur to mail out. Since David Metzler (now involved as illustrator) and Gary were planning the second improved issue, now to be printed on hectograph gelatin pads (after Joan typed up the text on special masters), the boys jumped the gun by using the Metzler-created werewolf cover of issue #2 as the cover for these copies of issue #1. Forrest Ackerman received one of the handwritten coverless copies, but 20 lucky people (Dave and I each kept one copy each) received the carbon-copy typed issues and these copies became the official debut of the world's longest-running horror movie magazine. Dave Metzler and Gary, encouraged by Gary's Dad Richard, were enthusiastic about the budding world of journalism and magazine production. Gary was the writer and designer and shipping department (with Richard), and Dave was the cover artist, soon to be interior illustrator as well. Boys being boys, David was only involved the first year or so, but the magazine kept on going and going and going.

In that idyllic summer of 1963, Gary reached out to other monster fans and delivered to them this labor of love, this personal tribute to horror movies and *Famous Monsters* and *Castle of Frankenstein*, never realizing that 40 years later he would still be producing an adult version of his adolescent dream. Amid horror movies on TV, Hammer films and Poe epics in theaters, Castle 8mm home movies in the bedroom and boxes and shelves of books and magazines sprawled all over the bedroom table and floors, this weirdo-boy Gary created his little monster world that reached from the bedroom clear across the country, and one boy's little horror film magazine became a defining moment that created for Gary both an identity and a drumbeating cause that still roars and rumbles to this day.

Forty years after the summer of 1963, the little monster boy still resides comfortably within the maturing Gary, always reminding him of how a love for something can be so strong, so obsessive, that if it be allowed to nurture and grow, that passion can last a lifetime.

Indeed it has!
—Gary J. Svehla

# Midnight Marquee Press Summer Sale
## Take 25% off on orders over $50
### Orders over $100 shipping is FREE!

 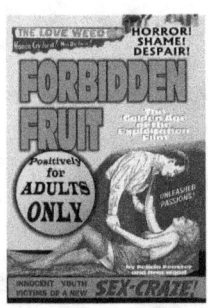   

|  |  |
|---|---|
| **Imogen Hassall** (the bio of the tragic '60s British starlet) | $20 |
| **Spawn of Skull Island** (the making of *King Kong*) $40 | $40 |
| **Lon Chaney, Jr.** (back by popular demand) $20 | $20 |
| **Hollywood's Maddest Doctors**: Lionel Atwill, Colin Clive, George Zucco by Gregory William Mank | $20 |
| **Memories of Hammer** (the FANEX interviews) $35 | $35 |
| **Silent Screams** (fascinating info on silent horror films) | $35 |
| **Forbidden Fruit: The Golden Age of the Exploitation Film** by Felicia Feaster and Bret Wood | $25 |
| **Silver Scream Legends Bela Lugosi** (32 pages photo mag, 16 pages of color, import) | $12 |
| **Forgotten Horrors 3** (another must have for genre film lovers) by Michael H. Price and John Wooley | $20 |
| **Forgotten Horrors 2** | $20 |
| **Forgotten Horrors**: The Definitive Edition (sale price) | $5 |
| **Midnight Marquee 67/68** (lost horrors, overrated/under-rated, DVD reviews; much more) | $10 |
| **Fantastic Journeys**: Sci-Fi Memories (FANEX sci-fi interviews, plus more) | $25 |
| **Attack of the B Queens** (with chapters by Linnea Quigley, Debbie Rochon, Brinke Stevens; Sept. 2003) | $25 |
| **Midnight Marquee 69/70**, 40th Anniversary issue | $10 |
| **Drums O' Terror**: Voodoo in the Cinema (back in print) by Bryan Senn | $25 |

Midnight Marquee Press; 9721 Britinay Lane; Baltimore, MD 21234; 410-665-1198;
www.midmar.com; Mmarquee@aol.com;
25% discount on sales of $50 (not including shipping). All sales final.
SHIPPING $4 for first book, $1 for each additional book.

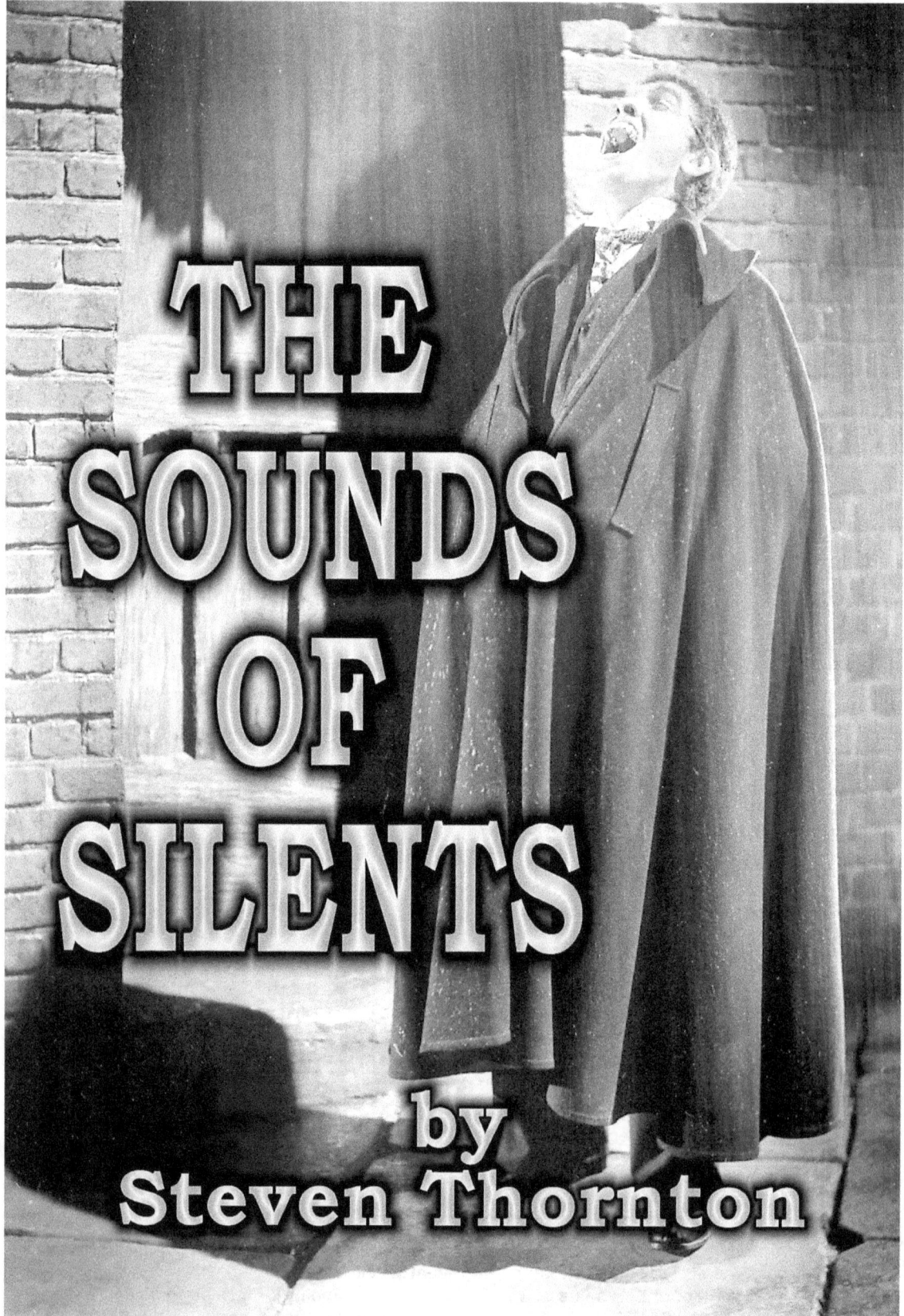

# THE SOUNDS OF SILENTS

### by Steven Thornton

Among longtime fans of fright cinema, the bromide goes largely unchallenged—cinema's Golden Age of horror would never have commenced without the advent of talking film. On the surface, the assumption appears valid. Hollywood's output of horror films, after all, was unquestionably a scattershot affair prior to the 1930s. Even the ones that were produced tend to fall into predictable formulas, with few of the imaginative touches that characterized the genre's later classics. But the truth, to borrow a cinematic reference, may not be quite that black and white.

When one looks closely at that critical period in film history, it becomes clear that a number of factors were at play. Germany's Expressionist cinema had already taken root, establishing the groundwork for the American horror film, both in style and in content. The Nazi menace, which was just beginning to spread its shadow over Europe, chased many of that continent's leading filmmakers and performers to America in search of safe harbor. Technical advances also influenced American filmmaking; panchromatic film stock, specialized camera lenses and improvements in studio lighting gave cinematographers the ability to capture more subtle shadings of black and gray. Yet all of these developments pale in comparison to the cultural calamity that dominated the headlines of that era—the chaos of the Great Depression.

*Dracula* (1931) has uncomfortably long spells of silence which are damning in the new world of sound.

The sudden and devastating deterioration of America's financial climate in the early 1930s echoes the crisis experienced by the German economy in the years following World War I. And in both cases, the medium of cinema served as a safety valve through which the audience could confront its fears of a world gone mad. Whether it was the doppelganger and the fateful legends of German Expressionism or the walking dead and the man-to-monster transformations of Hollywood's Golden Age horrors, the dark terrors expressed via the cinema took on the fury of vengeful gods unleashing their rage against an unsuspecting world. To the legion of the chronically unemployed, this expression of cultural anxiety must have been a coping device every bit as essential as Franklin Roosevelt's eternal optimism.

If it is indeed true that Hollywood's horror cinema was the bastard child of the Great Depression, we should expect that this cinematic catharsis could easily have taken place without the presence of sound. Perhaps, then, it would be enlightening to reevaluate the shockers of the early 1930s, imagining what might have been if the crucial transition to talking film had been delayed. More than just mere speculation, this approach will allow us to observe how sound shaped the genre at various points in its early development. And along the way, we might gain additional insights into the films that form the bedrock of American horror cinema.

Some general background might be helpful to illustrate how haphazard the adaptation of sound to cinema truly was. From Edison onward, early film pioneers envisioned the artistic potential of talking film but were thwarted by two problems—amplification and synchronization. The first issue was addressed by the invention of the vacuum tube and the perfection of the public address system in the late 1910s. Meanwhile, inventors like Lee De Forest were hard at work developing ways to combine filmed action with a simultaneously recorded soundtrack. A number of early efforts were produced using prototype sound/film systems, including D.W. Griffith's *Dream Street* (1921), but none caught the ear of the public. By the mid 1920s, a time when the cinema and the radio were both enjoying growing levels of popularity, few realized that these two entertainment experiences would soon come together in dynamic fashion.

The changeover occurred with astounding rapidity. Warner Bros., after releasing a series of Vitaphone shorts, utilized their new sound-on-disc

Bela Lugosi carries Helen Chandler down the long and winding staircase in *Dracula*, emphasizing the dramatic Gothic sets used in the production.

Bela Lugosi and Dwight Frye from *Dracula*: Silent cinema might have made better use of *Dracula*'s expansive sets.

system for the 1926 John Barrymore feature, *Don Juan*. Then came the watershed moment when Al Jolson vocalized directly to the audience in *The Jazz Singer* (1927). Interestingly enough, both films confirm that the original goal was to use sound as an adjunct, and not a replacement, to silent cinema. Music, sound effects and limited dialogue were to accompany a film, which would remain a largely speechless affair. The primary benefit was in giving secondary movie theaters a way to present films with a full orchestra backing, a practice that hitherto had been limited to premium movie palaces.

All of that changed, however, in 1928. The runaway success of *Lights of New York*, a forgettable crime drama enlivened by a full talking score, caught the attention of filmmakers anxious to latch onto the next big thing. A number of similarly loquacious releases followed and, by year's end, audiences in the large city markets were beginning to thumb their noses at films that did not contain significant talking content. Then ensued the Big Panic as studios rushed to build sound stages, evaluate high-profile (and high-priced) movie stars and rewire theaters from coast to coast to accommodate the requirements of both Vitaphone and the Fox sound-on-film Movietone system. As it was, many studios held out, hoping that the fascination with talkies was but a passing fad. (Among the majors, Universal and MGM were slow to adapt, and minor studios like Mascot were still releasing silent films as late as 1930.) But in spite of these and dozens of other complications, talking cinema had arrived and the movie industry never looked back.

Although the transition was clearly inevitable, the timing of the above events was far from a certainty. Advances in radio and amplification technology, driven in part by the onslaught of World War I, were a hit and miss affair. Likewise, the eventual consolidation on industry-wide standards could have easily taken a back seat to corporate politics and inter studio rivalries. Warner Bros.' aggressive pursuit of talking cinema was a gamble that many thought foolhardy, and the public's enthusiastic embrace of sound was a wild card that no one saw coming. Finally, there was the stock market crash of 1929, which, if it had occurred earlier, would have dried up the cash outlay needed to fund the silent-to-sound transition. Break any link in this interrelated chain and the 1930s, instead of witnessing the dawn of the talkie era, would have experienced a continuation of the cinematic stylings established in the prior decade.

For horror cinema, the implications are profound. Limitations in early sound technology helped define the 1930s horror cycle in ways both good and bad. Even today, film critics routinely cite the creaky qualities or, alternatively, the marvelous atmosphere that characterizes films from this period. Based on the above discussion, it becomes easy to see that things could have been very different.

*Dracula*, talking cinema's first horror classic, seems in many ways to have one foot still set in the silent era. Although visually rich and brimming over with evocative atmosphere, the film's protracted pace and uncomfortably long spells of silence are sins that seem doubly damning in the new world of sound. Some have suggested that this was due, in part, to director Tod Browning's inability to adapt to the requirements of this new cinematic dimension. If true, how might we expect a silent *Dracula* to differ from its talking incarnation?

As fate would have it, a silent version of the Browning/Lugosi *Dracula* does, in fact, reside in the Universal vaults. This cinematic orphan, which differs little from the official release, was prepared during the latter stages of production for rural show houses that had yet to undergo the silent-to-sound conversion. Had Bram Stoker's tale been adapted specifically for the silent screen, however, additional stylistic changes would be evident. The film's stagebound and dialogue-heavy second half would certainly require a retooling to work in a speechless medium. Dracula's confrontations with Van Helsing, Mina's aborted seduction of Harker and the last reel search for the vampire lair are scenes that would have benefited from this approach. This would also have provided an opportunity to more fully utilize the film's spacious standing sets, many of which barely appear in the finished print. An effective orchestral score might have been another plus; silent films were always backed by musical accompaniment, be it full orchestra, solo keyboard or (late in the era) a Movietone soundtrack. Fans of true-life cinema lore will wonder, too, how a *Dracula* devoid of sound would have impacted the troubled fortunes of Bela Lugosi, Hollywood's legendary vampire king. With his salient accent shielded from the ears of the public, perhaps this luckless horror icon could have charted his career path in a more lucrative and sustainable direction.

But a silent *Dracula* might present some drawbacks as well. The richness of the film's dialogue is near and dear to every fan of classic cinema. Would Lugosi's reading of "the children of the night" or "I never drink... wine" deliver the same chill when presented in the truncated black and white of a title card? There is also the matter of *Dracula*'s "sleepwalker" quality. Unique among movie vampire tales,

The three slithering undead "brides" in *Dracula*: Would this unreal, dreamlike world be maintained without its long stretches of silence?

the drawn out passages of Universal's adaptation help create an unreal, dreamlike world in which the presence of the undead is never far away. Whether or not this is an asset is certainly debatable; even today, film fans remain divided on the issue. But it is unlikely that this odd, hypnotic effect could have been sustained without the film's long stretches of silence. Give *Dracula* a non-stop piano backing and its mood is altered radically.

It should be remembered that *Dracula* was a production plagued by budget cuts, studio uncertainty and a director whose command of visual action was never a strong suit. However, it is also reasonable to suggest that the period in which the film was made did much to shape the final product, one that holds up as a flawed yet influential movie classic. Move *Dracula* into the world of the silent cinema and the film, while looking fundamentally the same, might emerge as a very different viewing experience.

Universal's other blockbuster of 1931, *Frankenstein*, is light years ahead of *Dracula* in terms of

Recasting *Frankenstein* (1931) as a silent, James Whale might have emphasized the action-oriented aspects of the story.

its dramatic technique. But the film's basic assets, its haunting theme and Expressionist-influenced visuals, would almost certainly survive a transition to a silent screen version. The real question is how director James Whale would have handled such an intriguing cinematic challenge.

One approach Whale might have chosen would have been to emphasize the action-oriented aspects of the story. Frequent cutting between parallel subplots, a technique that dates back to D.W. Griffith, might have been used to heighten the tension level during the monster's escape and rampage through the countryside. It is tempting, also, to imagine additional episodes that might have been added to accentuate the film's action quota; a more dynamic grave-robbing sequence and the monster's stalking of Fritz are candidates that could have given *Frankenstein* an added visual punch.

But it is also possible that Whale might have chosen to downplay action in favor of atmosphere. Imaginative, stylized visuals, such as those employed by F.W. Murnau in *Faust*, would have been a bold addition to the laboratory creation scene or, equally likely, as a visual device to illustrate Frankenstein's theories of life. This approach would have affected the film in a more significant way, nudging it in the direction of dark fantasy. Since *Frankenstein* was one of the 1930s most influential horror films, this change is one that would have had interesting repercussions.

In either scenario, it might have proven difficult to retain the poetic qualities that elevat *Frankenstein* from graveyard shocker to classic morality tale. Much of this is conveyed through dialogue, especially the confrontations between Henry Frankenstein (Colin Clive) and Dr. Waldman (Edward Van Sloan) and the former's wistful musings about the nature of our universe. Sound also adds to the effectiveness of Boris Karloff's performance; his sympathetic, nonverbal utterances emphasize the degree to which he is cut off from normal human contact. In one aspect, however, sound hampers the illusion of reality. The film's competing American and European accents have always been given attentive viewers a reason to snicker. In the world of silent cinema, *Frankenstein*'s legendary director is the one who might have had the last laugh.

Despite its many rough edges, *Frankenstein* retains a raw power that has helped it endure as a cinema classic. Although James Whale never directed a silent, it is well known that he studied a number of early German thrillers while preparing to adapt Mary Shelley's tale for the screen. The question remains whether Whale, without the dimension of sound, could have found a way to visually express the haunting characteristics that make this film so unique. Take these qualities away and the horror film's most celebrated monster franchise may never have been given the breath of life.

One of the more polished of the early talking horrors was Paramount's 1931 version of *Dr. Jekyll and Mr. Hyde*. Directed by Rouben Mamoulian and featuring Fredric March in the dual title roles, the film expertly fuses the visual splendor of the silent era with the new dynamism of sound. This was no accident on Mamoulian's part. Even in his first film, 1929's *Applause*, he bucked conventional wisdom by filming scenes with a moving camera, a daring move in light of the "bolted to the floor" cinematography favored during the early sound period. Such a freethinking maverick might have enjoyed the freedom for visual expression in a totally speechless medium.

In the released version, stylized camera techniques are used to draw parallels between char-

**Director James Whale might have found it difficult to retain the poetic qualities that elevate *Frankenstein* from graveyard shocker to classic morality tale.**

acters and to help dramatize the story. Diagonal wipes, physical symbolism and striking point-of-view shots are all freely employed, sometimes in ways so obvious that they call attention to themselves. Some of these visual tricks would arguably play better in a silent version, especially the protracted opening sequence as seen through Jekyll's eyes. Other visual touches are presented in less obtrusive fashion, such as the hospital sequences that depict the good doctor as a man of compassion. Then, of course, there is the film's famous transformation sequence, presented as a montage of whirling, overlapping images. In each case, Mamoulian hints at a creative flair that would have been well suited to visual orientation of the silent cinema.

But Mamoulian is equally adept in his application of sound. Dialogue is used to advance the plot in a manner that is especially impressive for the early 1930s. Character relationships benefit from the spoken word as well, most notably the sadistic cat and mouse game between Hyde and the doomed Ivy Pierson (Miriam Hopkins). Hyde's speech, a curious amalgam of Far Eastern and Harlem dialects, is another quirky touch. Even in moments that are primarily visual, sound adds a distinctive punctuation mark. Especially notable in this regard is the lengthy shot of Ivy's leg dangling over the bed, her voice charged with forbidden desire as she tempts Jekyll to "come back... soon."

As evidenced by the 1920 John Barrymore version, a silent rendering of *Dr. Jekyll and Mr. Hyde* would have mandated a more straightforward telling of the tale. The range of emotions expressed by Jekyll—his joy, love, frustration and despair—would need to be depicted in purely visual terms. Hyde's

**Diagonal wipes, physical symbolism and striking point-of-view shots are used in *Dr. Jekyll and Mr. Hyde* (1931).**

Stylized camera techniques are used to draw parallels between characters and to help dramatize the story in *Dr. Jekyll and Mr. Hyde*.

larly despicable yet very real menace. For all his cinematic bag of tricks, Rouben Mamoulian would have found it difficult to accomplish this task as smooth-ly as he does in his 1931 horror masterpiece.

Then there is Carl Dreyer's *Vampyr* (1931). Today, seven decades after its release, critics voice widely differing opinions regarding this early example of Euro-horror. Some see it as a wonder of mood and suggestion, while others simply stare and wonder. The use of dialogue is downplayed in the film to the extent that first time viewers often mistake it as a late period silent. Perhaps it is fitting to explore how the movie's unique atmosphere might be impacted if this, in fact, were the case.

To draw parallels between *Vampyr* and the world of silent cinema simplifies the matter greatly. The film more accurately reflects a pre-Hollywood era in which the familiar conventions of narrative cinema had yet to be established. Movie historians routinely site the many unconventional elements (such as its disjointed story line, deliberate use of non-actors and unique visual motif) that set the film apart in both look and style. These qualities recall a time when moviemakers were inventing the rules of cinema as they went along, creating avenues of expression that would quickly be discarded and forgotten.

outlandish characterization, especially his simian-like appearance late in the film, would probably have been toned down to avoid inducing audience laughter. Another intriguing possibility involves the emphasis on the film's romance angle. Love stories always played well on the silent screen, where the pantomime of an endearing young couple could readily engage the emotions of the audience. With some judicious shifts in story line, it becomes easy to imagine *Jekyll and Hyde* as a tragic romance, rather than the powerful horror film that we know today.

One other important contribution of sound to Paramount's *Dr. Jekyll and Mr. Hyde* is the extent to which it reinforces the human qualities of the film's monster. A beast he is and a beast he remains, but his sadistic tendencies are rooted in recognizable modes of behavior. A silent version of this story would face the challenge of making Hyde a simi-

Given its sketchy dialogue, the film could conceivably translate well and work as a silent. *Vampyr*'s primary episodes play well in visual mode, especially the famous "burial" scene in which Julian West's character has visions of his own entombment. Producer/director Carl Dreyer fills his film with double exposures, moving shadows and other visual tricks that register a suitably eerie impact whether viewed with or without sound. But as is the case with *Dracula*, *Vampyr* uses an abundance of speechless passages to sustain its unique, trance-like quality. Take away the dialogue and the film looses its connection with reality, a thread that is admittedly rather tenuous from the onset.

For many, *Vampyr* remains something of an acquired taste. But it is also unquestionably a landmark in the cinema of suggested horror. All facets of cinematic technique are used to depict a shadow world, one that is neither day nor night, neither alive nor dead. It seems likely that regardless of how we might try and mentally rework it—sound or silent, English language or foreign tongue—it would forever remain something of an enigma.

Although a lesser entry, *Murders in the Rue Morgue* (1932) is also of interest due to its strong parallels to the pre-talkie era. Today the film is remembered largely for the flamboyant performance of Bela Lugosi as crazed evolution proponent Dr. Mirakle. Had the film been released a few years earlier, its striking use of visuals might have been commanded even greater attention.

Carl Dreyer fills *Vampyr* with double exposures, moving shadows and other visual tricks that register a suitably eerie impact.

Reviewers are quick to point out the film's *Caligari*-like set design, a clear homage to the great granddaddy of all horror films. But *Rue Morgue*'s debt to German cinema runs even deeper; the film's odd camera angles, elongated shadows and carnival setting make it clear that director Robert Florey had borrowed heavily from the European horror tradition. Such visual razzmatazz, incidentally, does not always work to the film's advantage. The elaborate garden swing shot or the frozen close-ups during heroine Sidney Fox's abduction are so flashy that viewers are inevitably pulled away from the film, focusing instead on the mechanics of such complicated camera setups.

In contrast to its emphasis on visuals, the film's handling of sound is noticeably clumsy. Long, awkward pauses in dialogue contribute to a sluggish pace, a problem that is endemic among the earliest talkies. Aside from the opening credits, not a note of music is heard to grant relief from the static and lifeless background. An abundance of flowery banter between Fox and romantic lead Leon Waycoff (later to find success as Leon Ames) does the film no benefit either. Many performers of this period seem at a loss in trying to adapt their acting styles to the requirements of the sound cinema. Such is the case with Fox, whose coquettish look and broad acting style are badly out of place in the new world of the talkies.

Another of the film's drawbacks is its awkward dramatic construction, a problem that would still be evident in a silent version. After a promising (and largely visual) opening, the story becomes mired down with incidental episodes that turn its brief

Bela Lugosi as Dr. Mirakle from *Murders in the Rue Morgue*: Incidental episodes turn its brief running time into an endurance test.

addiction and white slavery were among the many taboo topics that were used to spice up plot material. And while the cinema of the Roaring Twenties tended to reflect that period's optimistic mindset, a handful of filmmakers were obsessed with using the medium to explore life's darker side. Chief among them is that poster boy for demented storytelling, Tod Browning. Given the track record from his financially successful collaborations with legendary performer Lon Chaney, Browning certainly could have been in a position to bring *Freaks* to the silent screen. Making it work in that medium, however, is another matter entirely.

The transformation, from a technical standpoint, would have been simple enough. Browning shot *Freaks* in a manner reminiscent of his silents, with minimal camera movement and a preponderance of medium shots. Intertitles are even used at one point to bridge an important scene transition. But sound does make one significant contribution—it reinforces the humanity of the circus clan, disarming our shock at their misshapen appearance. Just a few lines of dialogue from Johnny Eck, Koo Koo or Daisy and Violet Hilton and our revulsion melts into heartbreaking sympathy for these unfortunates to whom life gave the raw-

61-minute running time into an endurance test. Mirakle, the film's most interesting character, is killed far too early, resulting in a finale that is badly anti-climactic. The story's unsavory elements (brutal murders, forced blood transfusions and the eventual goal of gorilla/human mating) also make it the grimmest of the early talking horrors. It's not hard to see that many changes would have been needed to make *Murders in the Rue Morgue* an effective screen thriller in either a sound or silent incarnation.

*Freaks*, Tod Browning's infamous production of 1932, is remembered as the most problematic of the early talking horror films. Given its jaw-dropping use of real world circus performers and its "us against the world" vengeance motif, MGM had little choice but to disown the finished product and consign it to the hell of independent film distribution. Could a story this audacious ever have been filmed in the never-never land of the silent cinema? The answer, perhaps surprisingly, is a qualified yes.

To a casual observer, it might be a revelation to learn of the full breath of subject matter that found its way to the silent screen. Abortion, adultery, drug

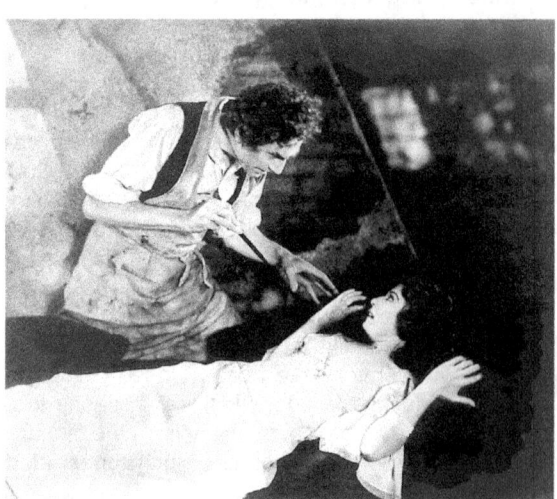

*Murders in the Rue Morgue* (1932) owes a debt to German cinema with odd camera angles.

est of deals. Without sound, Browning would have needed a visual or thematic way to elicit the same degree of empathy for his characters. Although it stretches the limits of credibility, this might have been accomplished by emphasizing the fable-like aspects of the story. The story of Hans' love for the beautiful but treacherous Cleopatra calls to mind the old adage "beauty is only skin deep." A silent version of this story, deprived of the reality that sound dictates, would have had to drive this point home in a less horrific but more commercially acceptable way.

With its nightmare catalog of images, *Freaks* is a natural heir to the Lon Chaney shockers of the 1920s. Chaney's popularity demonstrated that a market for such strong story material did indeed exist, providing that the essential component of audience sympathy was properly established. Perhaps the gambit of using real-life sideshow performers was simply too much for audiences of that era to accept. (One wonders if the use of dwarfs alone was ever given serious consideration.) But if handled with the proper storybook ambiance, the film might have provided a fascinating and unforgettable coda to a chapter of the silent cinema that remains largely forgotten today.

**Hans (Harry Earles) and Cleopatra (Olga Baclanova) from *Freaks* (1932) remind us that beauty is only skin deep.**

The horror film's strongest link between the sound and silent eras is 1932's *White Zombie*. Produced independently by the Halperin brothers and released through United Artists, the film contains many episodes that recall the time when the movies were a purely visual experience. Watching the film today, we get a clear indication of how the horror genre might have evolved if cinema history had taken a different turn.

*White Zombie* uses visuals in two key ways—to advance the plot and to give the film a very deliberate stylistic flair. Images like Legendre (Bela Lugosi) commanding his cadre of zombies, Beaumont's (Robert Frazer) refusal to shake Legendre's hand or the gift of a tainted flower to Madeline (Madge Bellamy) linger in the mind and speak more than any dozen lines of dialogue. Other interludes, such as Legendre's burning of the wax effigy, play out over extended length with effusive musical backing and little or no words. And at other times the camera walks through a corridor, peers from an iron grating or lingers on Lugosi's hypnotic stare, adding a striking look to an otherwise prosaic moment. Such deliberate scene composition was commonplace in the silents, but became a rarity as the conventions of talking cinema became fixed in place.

Sound makes its presence felt in ways both positive and negative. Few films capitalize so successfully on Lugosi's distinctive speech pattern, especially the uncanny emphasis he gives to individual words. Other sound bites that linger in the memory include the ghastly creaking of the sugar mill, the anguished wail of Neil (John Harron) when he discovers Madeline's empty tomb and the unnerving native chant that opens the film. On the detrimental side, the film's dialogue often sounds forced and artificial, especially the romantic interludes between Harron and Bellamy. The spoken word, in fact, often intrudes on the story's fragile mood, adding fuel to the speculation that director Victor Halperin was chiefly concerned with the film's look over all else.

Like most independent productions of its day, *White Zombie* was something of a throwback. The production techniques used in the making of this film seem downright primitive compared to those in use at Hollywood's major studios. But this, in an ironic twist, is a chief reason why the film remains so memorable today. Although its plot meanders and its performances are uneven, *White Zombie*'s visual opulence gives it a sense of style that few horror films of that period can match. As heroine Madge Bellamy says in the film's closing moments, "...I dreamed." Indeed.

*White Zombie* (1932) uses a silent movie technique of having the camera linger on Bela Lugosi's hypnotic stare.

the cadence of a typewriter, also enhances the mood of the film. Supporting characters benefit from this greatly; the personalities of beat cops, ladies of the night and house servants virtually come alive through the use of the spoken word. And note the unsavory voices of Xavier's scientific colleagues. In a silent world, this effect could only have been approximated through the use of visual stereotypes suggesting foreign (and presumably undesirable) origin.

Sound also adds a dimension to the performances of the film's lead players. Atwill's clipped diction quickly establishes him as the film's first red herring, while Lee Tracy's nervous prattle and Fay Wray's sexy aloofness generate romantic sparks in abundance. Hearing this trio, one can easily identify the aural signature that was fast becoming a Warner Bros. trademark. It should also be noted how the film's dialogue conveys a comic yet macabre undercurrent. Any attempt to capture this "whistling in the dark" quality via the use of title cards would likely stun viewers over the head with the subtlety of a sledge hammer.

Meanwhile over at Warner Bros., horror movies were being fitted into a more contemporary framework. The studio that kicked off the sound revolution was creating a niche for itself by utilizing dialogue that had a gritty, streetwise sensibility. While the gangster genre was the primary beneficiary of this approach, the horror film also stood to gain, as evidenced by 1932's *Dr. X*. This Michael Curtiz-directed thriller incorporated sound so deftly that to imagine the film as a silent is to rethink it in its entirety.

Ambient noise and throwaway dialogue is used so freely in *Dr. X* that one scarcely notices it. Such touches as the moan of the Cape Cod wind, the clatter of autopsy instruments and the jolt of Lee Tracy's joy buzzer do much to keep the audience on the edge of its seat. This effect adds to the pace as well, especially in the chaotic aftermath of the sequences in which the "moon killer" murders are restaged. Dialogue, hammered out with

*Dr. X* does provide some memorable visual touches and it is these that a silent version would have to more fully explore. A persistent use of shadows paints the sets in dark,

*White Zombie*'s visual opulence gives it a sense of style that few horror films can match.

menacing imagery. Odd angles and intense close-ups fill the screen, rendering the viewer slightly off kilter. Other visual cues boarder on the comic, such as the bouncing skeletons or the "John Doe" tag attached to Lee Tracy's foot as he hides in the morgue. The weird ambiance of the early two-color process, with its emphasis on red-green, also contributes to an otherworldly look. Once underway, the story settles into "old dark house" mode, a tradition that had a long and venerable history in the silent cinema. Without the transforming element of sound, this film's kinship with *The Bat* and *The Cat and the Canary* would likely be much more apparent.

The initial wave of sound films relied on the flawless elocution of actors who had extensive training in the theater. Before long, however, a new style of performing had evolved, one that drew its inspiration from the rhythms and speech patterns of the everyday life. *Dr. X* takes full advantage of this shift, using it to pull us into the film and persuading

Fay Wray from *Dr. X* (1932) is bathed in a persistent use of shadows painting the sets in dark, menacing imagery.

us to turn a blind eye to the implausible nature of the plot. Sans sound, our willingness to suspend disbelief would have been stretched to the breaking point, a problem that bedevils many horror efforts of the silent era. For *Dr. X*, consequently, sound is an indispensable component, essential in ways that other Golden Age horrors did not require.

James Whale's second horror entry, *The Old Dark House* (1932), is noticeably more polished than his first. Although the film has none of the weighty philosophic implications of *Frankenstein*, its production values are of a higher order, resulting in a pleasing look and a brisk, entertaining pace. And among the improvements is a more sophisticated use of the spoken word.

Dialogue is used to reveal character nuances in a manner reminiscent of the stage (an understandable ploy given Whale's theatrical background). From the opening scene bickering between Philip and Margaret Waverton (Raymond Massey and Gloria Stuart) to the bitter taunting voiced by Horace and Rebecca Femm (Ernest Thesinger and Eva Moore), dialogue gives important insights into character relationships. Verbal cues also yield fascinating details regarding the depraved Femm clan. In addition, words provide Whale with an opportunity to express his affinity for arch, sardonic characters (a trend that he would revisit with relish in *The Invisible Man* and *Bride of Frankenstein*). Finally, there is the pure joy of hearing old pros like Thesinger and Charles Laughton deliver lines that are rife with subtle implications. What movie fan can listen

Lionel Atwill (with Fay Wray) and his use of clipped diction establishes him as a red herring in *Dr. X*.

*The Old Dark House* (1932) stresses the shadows and darkness in a sequence with butler Boris Karloff.

to Horace Femm's mock dinner invitation, "Have a potato!" and not break out in a grin?

Although sound is a critical component of the film's effectiveness, *The Old Dark House* offers plenty for the eyes as well. As implied by the title, the film stresses the shadows and darkness where the story's true horrors lie hidden away. The action, although confined to a few interior sets, never feels cramped, thanks to maze of cascading hallways and interconnecting staircases. Among the individual scenes, the episode in Eva Moore's bedroom is visual standout (the distorted image of her face in the mirror is especially haunting). Notable too is Gloria Stuart's innocent shadow play, an inspired moment that is comic and frightening all at once. This visual touch works so well, it's a wonder no filmmaker ever appropriated it into a silent melodrama.

*The Old Dark House* starts out like any traditional spook house melodrama, but it then reinvents the formula in search of something original. A key factor in this transformation is the way in which sound is used to invite us into the story, giving us characters with whom we readily identify. Although the film falters in its final reel, its use of sound is highly effective. The only real surprise is why it took so long for other filmmakers to emulate Whale's approach.

Paramount pulled off the triple threat of merging elements from horror, science fiction and jungle thrillers in 1933's *Island of Lost Souls.* While not as celebrated as some of his fellow filmmakers, director Erle C. Kenton did a credible job maintaining suspense amid a menacing jungle backdrop. He does, however, struggle with some of the finer points of cinematic technique, including, as pertinent to our discussion, the use of sound.

*Island of Lost Souls* fumbles many opportunities to use sound creatively, a fact that is especially surprising for a film of this late vintage. An absence of background music dates the film and contributes to a ragged sense of pacing. Dialogue is a hit and miss affair; Charles Laughton's voicing of vainglorious Dr. Moreau is menacing and authoritative one minute, but flip and inappropriately giddy the next. As the film's nominal hero, Richard Arlen looks and sounds ill at ease, and Bela Lugosi, the Sayer of the Law, speaks in modulated tones that are hard to decipher. Helping to offset this are a couple of nice audio touches, including the ghastly cries of the manimals in Moreau's House of Pain and their half-human cries of vengeance during the film's gripping conclusion.

Visually, however, the film is a standout. Principal characters are often glimpsed in half shadow, illuminated by an unseen light source. An abundance of white interiors bathe scenes in a shimmering glow, reminiscent of the best of silent cinematography. Eye-catching also are the visual patterns of cages and bars seen throughout the film, images created by jungle foliage, window blinds or crisscrossing wood panel. Touches like these would have been doubly effective in a silent version, where such motifs were frequently used to compliment the action onscreen.

Given its visual orientation, the story offered interesting possibilities for a silent treatment. The film's action scenes and the unsettling ambiance of Moreau's hellish jungle would have translated well, especially if accentuated through the use of tinted film stock. Tinting was a technique commonly used by both major and minor studios to give a film an impressive, arty look. Colors were chosen to reflect time and setting—blue for night scenes, amber for daylight and red for fire. Although its usage began to taper off in the late 1920s, the practice continued until the widespread adaptation of the Fox sound-on-film system, which registered an audible pop in the presence of tinted film. (Various two-strip colors processes were also used during the late silent/early talkie period, but the practice remained a novelty until the development of three-strip Technicolor in the mid 1930s.) Had the exotic locale and shadowy horrors of H.G. Wells' tale been given this treatment, its nightmare world might have been rendered all the more vivid.

*Island of Lost Soul*'s abundance of white creates a shimmering glow, reminiscent of silent cinema.

*Island of Lost Souls* (1932) shows Charles Laughton's voicing of vainglorious Dr. Moreau as menacing, flip and giddy at various moments.

The visual touches seen in *Island of Lost Souls* are indeed effective, even if some of the directorial choices are not entirely original. (One camera shot, that of an enormous growing shadow, was lifted directly from Mamoulian's *Dr. Jekyll and Hyde*.) Kenton and cinematographer Karl Struss use the jungle milieu to good advantage, creating some of the most disturbing visual tableaus of the early sound era. A silent version would have also benefited from their approach, especially when one takes into account the full range of visual tools available to filmmakers during that period. In this case, the absence of sound might not have been a significant liability.

As we move further into the sound era, a subtle but noticeable shift in cinematic technique becomes evident. Such changes can be seen in *The Mummy*. A late 1932 release, the film makes a quantum leap in its sophisticated use of sound. And while its pleasing visuals would do any silent filmmaker proud, the film as a whole represents a point of no return in the horror genre's response to the challenge of talking cinema.

It should come as no surprise that first-time director Karl Freund would appropriate the silent cinema's penchant for memorable, atmospheric visuals. He, after all, manned the camera for many of the silent German Expressionist classics, including *The Golem* (1920), *The Last Laugh* (1924) and *Metropolis* (1927). *The Mummy* unearths a whole sarcopha-

**Boris Karloff and Zita Johann, from *The Mummy*, lurk in the background. Both are excellent in their delivery of the film's polished dialogue.**

gus full of splendid eye-catching moments—the awakening of Imhotep (Boris Karloff), his attempt to resurrect the mummified shell of Anck-es-en-Amon, the flashbacks to ancient Egypt—all bathed in rich black shadows and subdued lighting. Viewing these carefully composed camera compositions, one can almost sense the gods of the ancient world lurking in the background.

What is surprising, however, is *The Mummy*'s effective and inventive use of sound. Karloff and Zita Johann are both excellent in their delivery of the film's polished dialogue, and no horror fan can forget the chilling laugh of Bramwell Fletcher, whose character is driven mad at the sight of Imhotep's "walk." Although minimal, the film's score is an effective opus of moaning cellos and menacing oboes. Just as important, but almost unnoticed, is the ghostly sense of stillness that permeates the film, an eerie quality that is shared by many great shockers of the horror film's Golden Age.

One of the chief complaints voiced about silent cinema is that the form was inherently artificial, leaving the viewer entertained but unconvinced. Such an observation is relevant in our discussion of *The Mummy*. A silent version of this story would by necessity sacrifice a good number of the subtleties that contribute to its status as the one of the most understated films of the early 1930s. Some might argue that this virtue is in actuality a mixed blessing; reviewers have often voiced the opinion that the overtly subtle nature of this film blunts its effectiveness. Critical disagreements aside, it is difficult to image a silent *Mummy* conveying the same power as the version we know today. In all probability, the film would have been reshaped to emphasize the elements of exotic adventure that became a minor aspect of the film's lasting appeal.

From 1933 onward, the horror film continued on its one-way odyssey into the world of sound. Two key releases from that year, *King Kong* and *The*

Karl Freund's cinematography in *The Mummy* (1932) unearths a whole sarcophagus full of splendid eye-catching moments including the flashbacks to ancient Egypt bathed in rich black shadows and subdued lighting.

*Invisible Man*, illustrate how critical cinema's sonic dimension had become. In the former, the sound of Kong's mighty roar, aided by a rousing Max Steiner score, provided a sense of veracity that the film's silent predecessor, 1925's *The Lost World*, could never hope to match. Likewise, James Wales' early sci-fi effort benefited greatly from the voice of Claude Rains, which conveyed madness, megalomania and droll humor in equal measures. Although the visual splendor of the silent era remained an influence, filmmakers were now committed to refining the use of sound as an essential element of the horror film experience.

That progression, in decades to come, would shape genre cinema in ways that go far beyond the novelty of the early talkies. The signature "bus" of Val Lewton's horror series for RKO owes its very existence to the intuitive quality of sound. When the 1950s spawned a generation of creatures from beyond our galaxy, sound helped convince us that the unthinkable had become reality. The Hammer horrors of the 1950s and '60s gained immeasurably from music scores that amplify the terrors onscreen. And in recent decades, zombies, ghosts, psychos and slashers have been taken on additional shading of menace through cues picked up by our ears alone. Today, film audiences routinely have to close their eyes and cover their ears to shield themselves from the terrors of the unknown.

Sound has become so ingrained into the horror film that we now take its very existence for granted. But the manner in which this transition occurred could have easily taken a different path. In such an alternate universe, horror cinema's most important era would have been affected in ways that we can scarcely begin to imagine.

And for some that is a scenario too scary for words.

*The Lost World* (1925) seems archaic compared to the exciting roars of King Kong.

# TERROR FROM 1963 AND BEYOND

## Past 40 Years— Top 50 Films
## by Gary J. Svehla

I wanted to sit down and consider all the horror, fantasy, science fiction movies that truly mattered to me during the four decades of *Gore Creatures/Midnight Marquee*. Bottom line: We have a hodgepodge of personal favorites alongside truly influential and trend-setting productions. But each of these movies ultimately has become important to the genre, movies that I enjoyed then and still enjoy, sometimes much more so, now.

### The Birds (1963)

Revisionist theory is that *The Birds* is mediocre Hitchcock, too dependent upon gimmicky special effects and a mediocre Tippi Hedren performance. However, the master of suspense is working at full capacity. *The Birds* is a pivotal movie detailing nature's revenge, without wasting time by creating a logical motive or reason why... the birds are going crazy and attacking human beings, and that's all that matters. Several sequences are among Hitchcock's best: Hedren's attack by the birds when she enters the little room, and the aerial view of the birds above the service station accompanied by Hedren's frenzied face as the birds attack her in the phone booth.

### The Haunting (1963)

Robert Wise's direction of this atmospheric classic ghost chiller is absolutely perfect... the cinematography's creepiness expands outward from intricate character development. Here Wise maintains the perfect balance between performance and cinematography (and from such visualization mood and atmosphere develops). In the emerging era of color, *The Haunting*'s black-and-white CinemaScope look is classic and holds up well today. Julie Harris' performance remains one of the best in horror film history. One of the few horror classics made for adult intelligence, and for adults, the result is breathtakingly chilling.

**Boris Karloff in *Black Sabbath***

### Black Sabbath (1963)

On DVD the full European version (with the original musical score) has been restored and properly edited, and finally *Black Sabbath/The Three Faces of Fear* can be proclaimed the Mario Bava classic it deserves to be labeled. All three stories work beautifully together, and the replacement of the segments into their proper order now builds taut suspense. The use of color photography, with a masterful score and sound effects, makes this Italian horror classic more satisfying than when it first appeared on American shores in 1963. Some movies improve with age, and the restoration of *Black Sabbath* is a revelation. "The Drop of Water" sequence, with the old woman's grinning corpse becoming one of the most frightening images in horror film history, remains a classic of horror cinema.

### The Girl Who Knew Too Much (1963)

This movie was originally butchered and released on American shores as *The Evil Eye*, but thanks to Image Entertainment, the movie has also been restored to its original Italian director's cut, and once again, the genius of Mario Bava shines through. *Black Sunday*, not to be disparaged in hindsight, is chiefly a mood piece, driven by its atmospheric photography and Gothic horror surroundings, but *The Girl Who Knew Too Much* points the way for future Italian giallo thrillers, a subgenre initiated by Mario Bava and later developed by Dario Argento. Alfred

**Leticia Roman in *The Girl Who Knew Too Much***

**Vincent Price in *Tomb of Ligeia***

Hitchcock's style certainly influenced this movie, the tight plot and wonderful character interaction creating a web of suspense that is both horrifying and nerve-racking. With its dank mood, ominous photography and detective-thriller plotting, *The Girl Who Knew Too Much* is a classic of the suspense genre.

### Tomb of Ligeia (1964)

Forget *Masque of the Red Death* and *Pit and the Pendulum*, Roger Corman's classic Poe adaptations for American International are *House of Usher* and *Tomb of Ligeia*, the two finest entries in the series. *Tomb of Ligeia,* filmed in England with an expansive budget that includes the use of large soundstage sets as well as effective outdoor photography, comes closest to capturing the flavor of Edgar Allan Poe. Vincent Price, with its angular face framed by square sunglasses, is the vision of morbid depression, and the reincarnation theme focusing upon the possession of the innocent by evil, has never been handled better. When it comes to the best performances by Vincent Price, one need not look further than *Tomb of Ligeia*!

### Dracula—Prince of Darkness (1965)

Not a great film (especially when compared to the earlier *Horror of Dracula* and *Brides of Dracula*), but *Dracula—Prince of Darkness* demonstrates one of Hammer's strengths—the sequel and the creation of a series mentality for their Gothic chillers. Here, Christopher Lee demonstrates that Count Dracula as a mute creature of the undead can be just as chilling as the verbal Count from *Horror of Dracula* (and he wasn't exactly a chatterbox there, was he?). While the film's first half is moody yet lethargic, the second half is classic Hammer vampirism, with a marvelous performance by Barbara Shelley as the repressed British housewife who is reborn as a sexual predator. Christopher Lee's physical performance, his red-lined cape used as an essential prop, is mesmerizing and on-screen he seems undead, ungodly and supernatural in a way that Bela Lugosi could never capture.

### Frankenstein Must Be Destroyed (1969)

Ultimately *not* the best entry in Hammer's Baron Frankenstein Peter Cushing series, *Frankenstein Must Be Destroyed* is the classiest looking Hammer production ever made. Once Hammer relocated from tiny Bray Studios to larger soundstages allowing more diverse sets, the budgets appear to have morphed from the B arena to the A. Peter Cushing's performance is almost Shakespearean in dimension and his Baron Frankenstein has never been better. While the monster plot is second-rate and Freddie Jones' sensitive rebirth almost too classy for a horror thriller, still, Terence Fisher's direction is superb and in complete control and Veronica Carlson's

**Diane Clare in *Plague of the Zombies***

performance is multi-dimensional and among the best of any Hammer heroine. Thus, this *Masterpiece Theater*-esque Hammer classic is almost too sophisticated for its own good.

### Plague of the Zombies/The Reptile (1966)

Interestingly, these two beloved Hammer horrors are seen as B offshoots of the traditional Hammer production (which are actually B productions themselves). Most people prefer *Plague of the Zombies*, but I feel *The Reptile* is the best of the duo, demonstrating that veteran director John Gilling was under used by Hammer and perhaps should have been given the productions handed over to Roy Ward Baker and others. Both of these films feature some of Michael Ripper's finest work, and while the movies do not feature Cushing or Lee, they boast interesting scripts with fine casts and suspenseful direction showing that even Hammer's lower- than-B productions had plenty of merit, class and style.

### Quatermass and the Pit/
### 5 Million Years To Earth (1967)

While the first two black-and-white Quatermass movies from Hammer are my favorites, this decade-later release, filmed in color, is almost as good. Andrew Keir does a splendid Quatermass, and Barbara Shelley's inspired performance as the scientist-heroine raises the bar even higher. The special effects were fine for the time, but it is, once

**Andrew Keir (left) from *Quatermass and the Pit***

again, the inspired Nigel Kneale script which uses a science fiction premise to explain mythology and the creation of the concept of Satan, in a marvelously noisy science fiction yarn that makes its audience think as well as leap.

### 2001: A Space Odyssey (1968)

Granted, I consider *2001* to be one of the dullest movies I just happen to respect, and I am constantly perplexed trying to figure out all its imagery, hidden allegory and messages. Perhaps that's the English teacher in me trying to explain all diffused works of literature. Thirty years after the fact, I am still perplexed, but some of the imagery, tied to those classical musical motifs, remains awe-inspiring, and the movie's psychedelic trippy ending culminating with the birth of the star child is still one of cinema's most splendid spiritual moments. I don't particularly like *2001*, but hell, it manages to inspire me to this day. That's still worth something!

### Night of the Living Dead (1968)

George Romero and crew, with a very limited budget, but with massive imagination and vision, concocted one of the pivotal horror classics of the last 40 years. Romero's uses claustrophobic sets to amplify the dread shared by terrified survivors who either barricade themselves in cellars or board up the upstairs to protect themselves from their formerly human neighbors, who are now reanimated living dead zombies compelled to eat human flesh and organs. The film's visualization of cannibalism is still shocking

**A flesh-eating zombie from *Night of the Living Dead***

**Linda Blair as the possessed young girl from *The Exorcist***

to this day, and the violence, even when produced on a budget, still packs a wallop. *Night of the Living Dead* creates goosebumps and demonstrates that visceral horror could be stylish and arty, as well as being disgusting at the same time.

### Vampire Lovers (1970)

Few people realized it at the time, but by 1970 Hammer films were beginning to change radically, as the production company abandoned Bray for larger quarters and began to ignore the artists who created their greatest Gothic chillers during the past 15 years (of course, people like Anthony Hinds abandoned Hammer, and others simply died). Besides retaining Peter Cushing, the look and feel of *The Vampire Lovers* is worlds apart from other recent Hammer Gothic chillers such as *The Gorgon* and *The Devil Rides Out/The Devil's Bride*. However, in this last burst of creativity, Hammer demonstrated that Ingrid Pitt could become a horror film icon, a devilishly sexy one at that, and Hammer wasn't afraid to pull out the stops by dressing the film with nudity and hints of lesbianism, to appeal to the newer, more permissive viewing audience. It was both a beginning and an ending of an era.

### Sisters (1972)

Back in the early to mid-1970s, the premiere of the latest Brian De Palma film was an event, an event in the same sense that the new M. Night Shyamalan film is an event today. *Sisters*, De Palma's first homage to master Alfred Hitchcock, even employing a musical score by Bernard Herrmann, is De Palma taking Hitchcock to the next cutting-edge level. Margot Kidder's dual-role performance as twins, playing against perennial oddball De Palma player William Finley, is brilliantly handled for maximum suspense. The plot is riveting as well as clever, and it keeps the audience guessing until the very, very strange ending. De Palma's mastery of visuals, with kinetic editing by Paul Hirsch and cinematography by Gregory Sandor, makes *Sisters* a nervy, hip and powerful cinematic journey, one that De Palma would continue to make for the next decade.

### The Exorcist (1973)

Over the course of 30 years, *The Exorcist* brought more harm than good to the horror genre. For one, it established the big-budget makeup/special effects mainstream Hollywood horror movie that showed too, too much, depending less on mood and atmosphere (although *The Exorcist*'s cinematography is one of its strengths). *The Exorcist*—big, booming and ultimately *soulless*—is generally considered to have delivered the fatal one-two punch to Hammer and all the other boutique B horror production companies. In one sense *The Exorcist* rejuvenated the sagging horror genre, but in another, it lead horror down the wrong alley, making it mainstream and bright and flashy when it needed to be insular, claustrophobic and left of center. *The Exorcist* made horror movies profitable, but *not* better.

### Black Christmas (1974)

The era of the modern, visceral slasher horror movie is credited to many different movies, but Bob Clark's *Black Christmas* impresses more and more as time passes. Its tricks and gimmicks were sometimes copied by better known movies, but seldom done this well. Clark creates a crafty plot filled with interesting characters and red herrings, and the pay off murders are used more as punctuation points along the plot line rather than ultimate ends in themselves. Whether you view the slasher subgenre as a natural progression of horror cinema or as its bane, *Black Christmas* rises above and becomes, along with John Carpenter's *Halloween* (which followed *Black Christmas* by four years), the slasher genre's most artistic example.

**Keir Dullea from *Black Christmas***

### Texas Chain Saw Massacre (1974)

The anti-*Exorcist* movement can best be described by *The Texas Chain Saw Massacre*, a low- budget Texas produced independent horror project that dared to break boundaries and push the envelope. While debuting director Tobe Hooper never displays ultraviolence on screen, the crafty director knows when to cut from a sequence at the exact second that scene would turn gory, and the unsettling mental image left in the viewers' minds creates the type of grisly horror that only radio drama could evoke in the imaginations of its audience. *Texas Chain Saw*'s image of the anti-family, its suggestion of people getting their skulls crushed in and the unsettling image of sexy hot babes being skewered on meat hooks brought back the suggestion that horror cinema is indeed renegade cinema, anti-establishment in tone and a genre that cuts the mainstream into bloody ribbons for all to admire.

### Young Frankenstein (1974)

The comedic horror romp/satire is one of horror cinema's favorite subgenres, for we need only think of *The Ghost Breakers*, *Ghosts on the Loose*, *Abbott and Costello Meet Frankenstein* (and all the rest) to remember the importance of blending humor and horror. *Young Frankenstein* remains the best example of lovingly blending the spirit of the classic Universal horror thrillers with the wit of Mel Brooks at his most sharpened and hilarious. Today, the film seems to have aged gracefully and remains the best example of the subgenre within the past four decades.

### Deep Red (1975)

During the 1970s when *Deep Red* was originally released in a poorly dubbed and truncated version, this Dario Argento classic still raised eyebrows and gained notice. However, once Anchor Bay released the restored director's cut, the artistry of *Deep Red* becomes even more apparent. Argento, moreso John Carpenter, David Cronenberg, Tobe Hooper, Stuart Gordon, etc. becomes horror's leading visionary director of the past 40 years and consistently produced a new raw energy for the sagging horror genre. Sometimes releasing giallo thrillers (*Deep*

**Gunnar Hansen from *Texas Chain Saw Massacre***

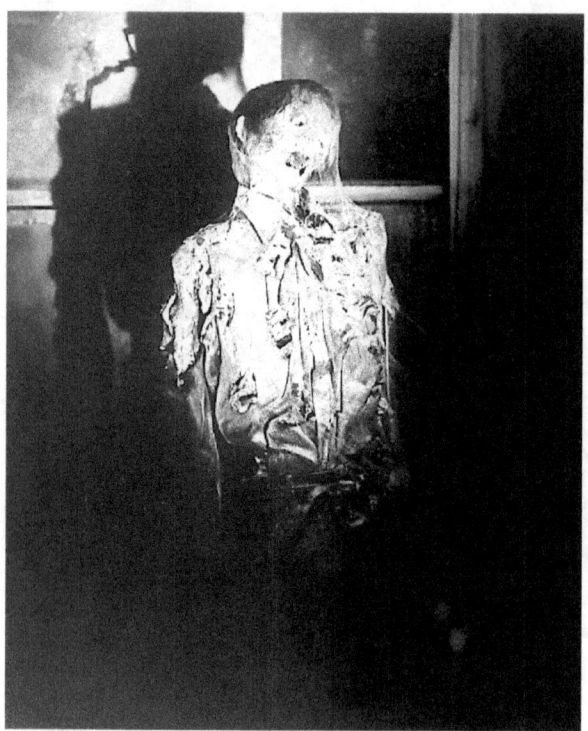

A rotting corpse from *Deep Red*

### Carrie (1976)

Brian De Palma directed some exceptional suspense horror thrillers during the 1970s, evoking the spirit of Hitchcock with his own twisted visual sense of cinema, and while *Blow Out* perhaps remains my favorite De Palma film of the period, I have to give the nod to *Carrie* for being most influential. First, De Palma is less the mimic and more the original here, and his cast (whether we are speaking about the bevy of young, sexy actresses who love to frolic in the nude, Nancy Allen, Amy Irving and P.J. Soles duly noted) more than rises to the occasion in *Carrie*. Sissy Spacek delivers an Academy Award-winning caliber performance showcasing a young girl's maturation into woman, symbolized by her first menstrual period, as metaphor, initiating her psychokinetic powers against all the people who wounded and abused her, especially her religious fanatical mother played by Piper Laurie. And *Carrie* deserves honors (and damnation) for bringing the downbeat ending (yes the movie is over, but there's one final shock left) to the horror genre for decades to follow.

### Suspiria (1976)

Suspiria is to the 1970s what *Bride of Frankenstein* and *The Mummy* were to the 1930s, perhaps the finest examples of (then) current horror cinema. While Dario Argento's plot doesn't always make Red) and other times releasing supernatural chillers (*Suspiria*), Argento's individual style favors quirky characters and pulse-pounding visuals (usually creating a dreamlike state in waking reality), always accented with thumping semi-rock music scores. Argento's style becomes idiosyncratic and deftly controlled in the way James Whale created a unique vision for 1930s horror cinema. Not every Argento film is a classic, but even his failures are always interesting and scary as hell.

### Shivers/They Came From Within (1975)

Too bad David Cronenberg evolved into a pretentious and tedious artist, for *Shivers* may very well remain his classic horror entry, documenting all his quirky flourishes that were developed in latter films. *Shivers* demonstrates horror as an infectious disease, a plague transmitted sexually, with the predatory pathogen taking a decidedly phallic shape and being transmitted mouth-to-mouth via passionate kisses. This world of horror remains claustrophobic and insular, showcasing the occupants of an apartment house as being the breeders of terror, where even your lovely, innocent girlfriend cannot be trusted once she gets that sexual come hither look in her eyes. Cronenberg demonstrates morbid delight in creating an orgy of the undead. At the beginning of the age of HIV/AIDS, Cronenberg's message rings loud and clear: Sex is death!

**Jessica Harper from *Suspiria***

sense (neither do dreams), his perceptive visuals and rhythms/pacing ignite the fear fuse within every one of us making *Suspiria* one of the most frightening viewing experiences ever. When we speak about great movies being a synthesis of sound and vision and great directors using the screen as their canvas for originality, well, Dario Argento and his masterpiece *Suspiria* must be recognized here as being one of the truly frightening and cinematically expansive works that horror cinema has yet produced.

### Star Wars (1977)

With the recent *Lord of the Rings* trilogy coming to the screen, it becomes apparent that *Star Wars* and its reliance on myth and formulaic story telling is more a hodgepodge than an original work. However, George Lucas' sharp vision and enthusiasm for the project transcends its patchwork-quilt creative approach. As every writer realizes, no original stories exist, just variations on the same basic themes, and infusing this love of old-fashioned story telling with the current cinematic technology of the day, *Star Wars* has become more than an iconic science fiction movie, but a movie that became a touchstone for this generation, a techno-*Wizard of Oz* for the end of the 20th and the beginning of the 21st century.

### Halloween (1978)

John Carpenter never made a better film than *Halloween*, only his third feature film. Perhaps responsible for making the "body-count" movie popular and ushering in the teenager-as-slasher-victim, *Halloween* actually rises above that formula becoming one of the best American horror films of the second half of the century. Jamie Lee Curtis, portraying the virginal baby-sitter, survives evil not because she doesn't have sex but simply because she is savvy and aware (most teenagers indulging in sex have their attention elsewhere). Curtis' character is a survivor and her intelligence allows her to survive while her schoolmates fall victim to the evil of The Shape. Employing subjective camera work, moody scoring (by Carpenter himself) and suspenseful cinematography, *Halloween* is a classic of low-budget filmmaking, a true American independent.

### Dawn of the Dead (1978)

George Romero's zombie trilogy must be recognized collectively as the ultimate horror series of the past 40 years (yes, even more so than the *Evil Dead* trilogy), but unfortunately, I consider *Dawn of the Dead* to be the weakest of all three entries. First, *Dawn of the Dead* is much too long and meandering... it would benefit from judicious editing. Secondly, its theme that zombies in death repeat the brain-dead habits from when they were alive, reverting to a mindless consumer mentality, endlessly walking around the local mall, is truly inspired, as is Romero's now full-color special makeup effects. However, too often the unflinching ominous mood that saturated every frame of *Night of the Living Dead* here dissipates as scenes of ultraviolence and tension are exchanged with scenes of dark satire and outright comedy. It is apparent Romero had a larger budget and more creativity to inject a sense of creative *carte-blanche* into the production, and the movie is harmed by that unchecked freedom.

**A living-dead zombie from *Dawn of the Dead***

### Alien (1979)

Is *Alien* horror or science fiction? In space does anyone hear your scream? Is *Alien* too derivative of Golden Age B movies such as *It! The Terror from Beyond Space*? Who cares! Ridley Scott's vision of alien reproduction and the biology of horror features one of the most original movie monsters since Jack Pierce's Frankenstein Monster and becomes a horror classic for the ages, one where interesting characters (Sigourney Weaver, Ian Holm, John Hurt) in a claustrophobic environment clash with each other and with an alien lifeforce almost too terrifying to behold. In the hands of a lesser director, *Alien* could have been mediocre and overblown, but Scott's mounting tension and quick cuts of gnashing, monstrous jaws lit by strobe lighting brings a post-modernist vision to a Golden Age science fiction yarn. Simply one of the scariest movies ever made.

### The Howling (1980)

Thus far, *The Howling* is director Joe Dante's greatest film and perhaps the greatest werewolf film ever conceived (yes, even superior to Universal's lethargic *The Wolf Man*). Working with Rob Bottin's marvelously conceived fairy-tale-gone-bad vision of lycanthropy and using an icon cast of professionals (Dick Miller, Kevin McCarthy, Patrick Macnee, Slim Pickens and John Carradine) with younger actors (Dee Wallace-Stone, Christopher Stone, Belinda Balasky), Joe Dante has created a creepy tribute to werewolf films of old, establishing a colony of werewolves as being akin to a New Age commune. Everyone appears to be having a blast, and when the movie becomes scary, it becomes hide-behind-your-hands-cover-your-face scary. Never has becoming frightened out of your wits been this much fun!

### Basket Case (1981)

Once in a generation an oddity is produced (*Freaks*, *Eraserhead* come to mind) that simply transcends the accepted norms of cinematic good taste. Sometimes such films can be dismissed as interesting failures, but other times, they take hold of the viewer and mesmerize. Such is the effect of Frank Hennenlotter's *Basket Case*, truly one of the trend-setting oddities of the past 40 years. Using grindhouse location photography with quirky performances and less-than-low-budget special effects (which become oddly involving), *Basket Case* attempts to shock and get under the skin by featuring unsettling visual imagery of syringes in the face and bloody operation sequences, yet at heart the film is an emotional film dealing realistically with the shattered relationship between brothers. Hennenlotter weaves *Basket Case* as sibling rivalry at its most horrific.

**Christopher Stone as a werewolf from *The Howling***

### Blade Runner (1981)

Ridley Scott is back, this time merging the ancient world of 1940s film noir with futuristic sci-fi views of the future, and *Blade Runner* becomes a classic for its generation. Harrison Ford, whose cold eyes and non-emotional performance work here to his advantage, interacts with replicants Daryl Hannah and Rutger Hauer and a marvelous supporting cast of eccentrics (including *femme fatale* Sean Young) to produce a science fiction mystery of the highest order, one that focuses on what it means to be human in a technologically unfeeling world. The visuals alone carry the movie, but the interjection of human pathos into this futuristic noir world make *Blade Runner* something extra special.

### The Evil Dead (1982)

Even though most fans prefer the second and third *Evil Dead* entries, nothing will ever surpass this independently-produced released-directly-to-video lo-fi original. Sam Raimi, 20 years from directing the mainstream *Spider-Man* blockbuster, has created a hyperkinetic reanimated living dead zombie film that challenges the Asian hopping vampire movie for ferocity alone. Chisel-jawed Bruce Campbell sets the stage as the properly macho hero. While alone in the isolated rural cabin, he unfortunately reads the Book of the Dead, and suddenly all hell breaks loose, as he fights for his life having to methodically destroy his former friends who return from the grave. Watching this video at home late at night, I literally shivered! *The Evil Dead* is that terrifying! Too bad Raimi's vision changed for the second and third entries.

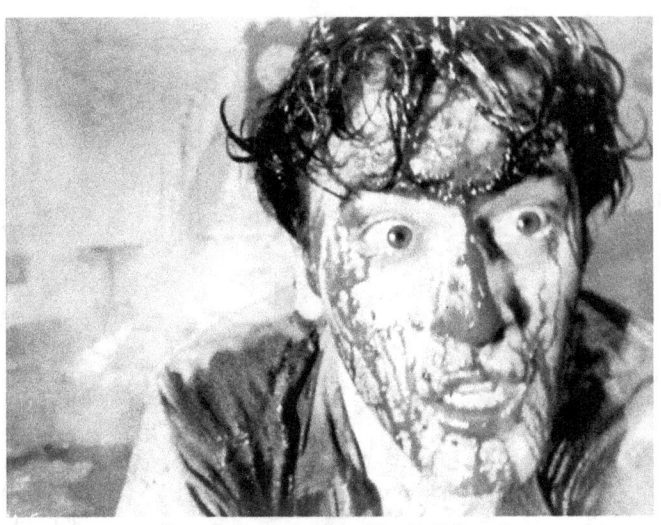

Bruce Campbell in *The Evil Dead*

### The Thing (1982)

Most people argue that director John Carpenter, like Orson Welles, only directed one classic horror movie, *Halloween*. I would argue he directed two, with *The Thing* rivaling the originality and tenseness of *Halloween*. While Carpenter's rethinking of "Who Goes There" by John Campbell comes closer to the literary source than Howard Hawks' 1951 sci-fi classic, Carpenter's rethinking of the original movie has mostly been met with the tag of second-rate, that his remake lacks the wonderful ensemble acting and rapid-fire dialogue of the original. Perhaps this claim is true, but Carpenter's focus is not on man against alien veggie, but man against man, trying to figure out which human is not actually human, as Carpenter's *The Thing* is an alien shape-shifter that can disguise itself as human being. Incorporating state-of-the-art visual effects by Rob Bottin (which still hold up well 20 years later), Carpenter's remake of *The Thing* is involving, intense and bone-chilling, making it another one of the scariest horror movies ever made.

### Poltergeist (1982)

The mainstream ghost film generally works against the intimacy of what most bump-in-the-night movies strive to become; however, this Tobe Hooper/Steven Spielberg production works in spite of itself. True, the special effects carry the movie, rather than the externalization of inner guilt and doubt, the motivation behind most classic ghost stories. Hey, simply for the guilty pleasure of a balls-to-the-wind horror romp, *Poltergeist* is one of the better popcorn horror movies of the era.

Harrison Ford in *Blade Runner*

Jeffrey Combs attends to the head in *Re-Animator*

### Videodrome (1983)

With latter-day films such as *Naked Lunch* and *Crash* and most of his even more recent work, David Cronenberg has become pretentiously boring, but at least with *Videodrome*, Cronenberg was pretentiously insightful. With these early works Cronenberg was a visionary, a director who allowed imagery to tell his story, rather than regular linear plotting, and for 1983, Cronenberg's message of the video age becoming almost an external sensory organ extension of our human bodies was quite cutting edge and inspiring to those of us who played along with the game. Twenty years later, his message is just as powerful.

### A Nightmare on Elm Street (1985)

Forget the franchise, forget the marketing of Freddy Krueger as the next big deal in horrordom; Wes Craven's initial foray into the world of teenagers, mayhem and dream reality was inspiring and visually inventive. Plus, *A Nightmare on Elm Street* was terrifying and disturbing, and the inability to distinguish between waking reality and the dream state was a novel horror film mind game that hadn't been overdone. Forget the sequels, forget the factory mentality... this first entry is simply an inspired B classic and shows Craven at the peak of form.

### Day of the Dead (1985)

Most people consider this third entry in George Romero's zombie trilogy to be the most disposable, but for me, it remains riveting and becomes the most frightening of the series, melding visceral visual effects, makeup, acting and cinematography into a satisfying conclusion. It lacks the initial originality of being the first in a trilogy, but it corrects all the problems with *Dawn of the Dead*—it contains a more taut running time, an ominous and horrifying tone throughout every frame and the overall script is simply more clever and involving. For grisly pulse-pounding shocks, *Day of the Day* cannot be beat.

### Phenomena (1985)

Some critics consider *Phenomena* to be Dario Argento's misstep, another overindulgent exercise in sensory overload, with a ridiculous plot and some mediocre acting. Wrong! Butchered and released in the U.S. as *Creepers*, Anchor Bay, God love them, released the restored director's cut under its original title, and while this is not *Deep Red* or *Suspiria*, it probably comes in third on my list of Argento favorites. Young and sensual Jennifer Connelly plays the lead, a young girl who has the uncanny ability to communicate with insects. She comes under the study of quirky Donald Pleasence, and this nightmarish mystery leads to an intensely horrific conclusion. As is true with Argento's best work, his singular vision heightened by moody cinematography and masterfully designed sets creates an air of intrigue and mystery. Perhaps *Phenomena* is an example of style over substance, but for me, this exercise in dream reality is both inspiring and horrifying.

### Re-Animator (1985)

Just like *Basket Case* before it, *Re-Animator* propels horror cinema into new taboo areas long avoided by horror film directors, mostly concerning the blending of sexuality and horror. Unlike *Basket Case*, *Re-Animator*, filmed on a low budget, has the look of a Hammer film with expansive and imaginatively created sets populated with actors (especially Jeffrey Combs) that give utmost respect to the script and their characterizations. In fact, Combs' performance as Herbert West is delivered as intensely as any Peter Cushing performance, the actor whose technique Combs most resembles. Director Stuart Gordon's background in theater is primarily responsible for taking this world of unbelievability and making it realistic and terrifying. The viewer may shake his head in disbelief, but *Re-Animator* is perhaps the most devilishly outrageous horror movie on this list.

### Blue Velvet (1986)

Not a horror movie in the traditional sense (but neither was *Psycho*), but David Lynch's distorted and horrific vision of the horrors that lie in small town America encapsulates what the horror genre is all about. The world as we know it perhaps is not the same world that others populate in our same sphere of existence. Youthful innocent Kyle MacLachlan explores the underbelly of his idyllic world and discovers a world of sexual depravity, best symbolized by Dennis Hooper's numbingly effective portrayal of nitrous-oxide sniffing Frank Booth. *Blue Velvet* demonstrates that all of us reside on one plain of existence that intercepts other plains, yet we fail to recognize all the other parallel realities surrounding our own insulated world. Visually and intellectually stimulating, *Blue Velvet* is not an easy film to follow and to interpret, but the payoff is tremendous for those of us who make the effort.

### Aliens (1986)

While Ridley Scott's *Alien* is a quintessential claustrophobia horror film that happens to occur in outer space, the direct sequel *Aliens*, directed by James Cameron, becomes the quintessential action-adventure monster romp. Surprisingly, while both films qualify as science fiction, neither film remains primarily science fiction. *Aliens* is once again terrifying, but now the lone alien from the first film is jettisoned for a brand-new colony of alien creatures that manage to intensify the scare quotion. And in the best tradition of Howard Hawks' *The Thing*, the ensemble cast (Sigourney Weaver's kick-ass heroine joined by equally aggressive Jenette Goldstein, countered with comically coward Bill "Game Over" Paxton and almost human android Lance Henriksen) shines making this motley crew quite involving and one the viewers care deeply about. Very rare, but

this sequel is as different from, but remains as effective as, the first entry.

### Near Dark (1987)

Katherine Bigelow, one of the few female directors working in the horror genre, made her classic horror B romp with *Near Dark*, a new south-westernized vision of vampirism as quasi-Confederate "good ol' boys" who blend their vicious streak (Bill Paxton wears spurs to slit the throats of victims) with human compassion. While the vampire cult never becomes heroic, the performances of both Lance Henriksen and Bill Paxton bring an air of dignity to the proceedings. As would be true in the decade to come, the cinematic vampire was being recast in new light (far less Gothic and Euro-based) and *Near Dark* inspires by its reinvention of this ages-old mythology. A stellar script with inspired, committed performances raises this B movie to classic proportions. It's finger-lickin' good!

### Lady in White (1988)

Independent productions often become vanity affairs, but fortunately Frank La Loggia's child molester ghost thriller delivers the goods to a wider audience. The movie is told from the child's point of view, delivered as a 1962 period piece with inspired cliff-side seashore mood and haunted beach-side home. The plot is very involving and cleverly complex, and the family relationships ring true, as does

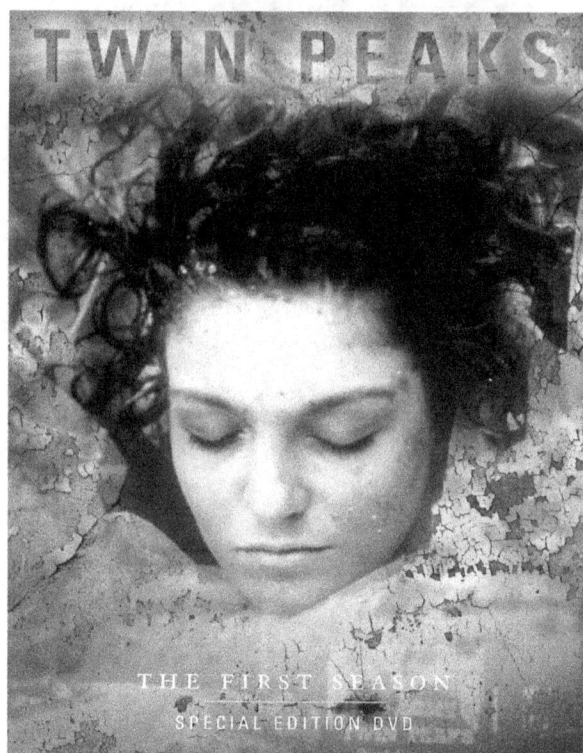

the lead performance by youthful Lukas Haas as the young boy who is accidentally locked in his school cloakroom on Halloween evening. In the darkened closet he encounters the ghastly recreation of the murder of a little girl that occurred years earlier. Focusing upon mood, good cinematography and effective acting, *Lady in White* both entertains and terrifies, leading to a very satisfying ending.

### Twin Peaks (1989)

David Lynch turned to television, with co-producer/writer Mark Frost, to create the most quirky weekly series ever produced, and it even survived into its second season! Somewhat a *Peyton Place* soap opera, somewhat a psycho-mystery, somewhat a Euro-style surreal dream drama, *Twin Peaks*, under the watchful eye of Lynch (who both wrote individual episodes and had a recurring role onscreen), never deviated from its left-of center core, much like *Blue Velvet* before it, creating the sense that suburbia houses a dark underbelly where innocent teenagers and respected parents are not really what they seem. And Frank Silva's portrayal of fiend Bob is perhaps the most haunting villain ever to grace the TV screen. Just as Agent Cooper (marvelously portrayed by Kyle MacLachlan) is oddly effective, everyone in the cast momentarily reveals, at some point, that askew character edge. Television does not get more thought provoking nor visceral than *Twin Peaks*.

### Exorcist III (1990)

*The Exorcist* was shocking on the surface but ultimately failed to resonate; *The Heretic: Exorcist II* contained some major talent and outstanding visuals, but its dreamlike plot ultimately failed the test of logic and of patience. Which leaves the third picture, the almost neglected *Exorcist III*, as the shining light of the trilogy. *Exorcist III*, directed by William Peter Blatty, author and screenplay writer of the original entry, frames his story 15 years after the original, where an old priest (Ed Flanders) and cop come together yearly to remember the late Father Karras. Into the mix comes the original demon who now possesses a demented serial killer known as The Gemini Killer (in a superb performance by Brad Dourif whose monologues steal the show and generate more chills than even the inspired visuals) who murders priests and young children alike. Yes, the exorcist sequence is tacked on and unfortunate, but the movie is chilling in the way that the first two entries could never be.

### Silence of the Lambs (1991)

For better or worse, horror cinema morphed into the slasher/psycho movie of the 1980s, then evolved into the serial killer movie of the 1990s, and this movie, along with *Seven*, is perhaps the finest example of the subgenre. Jonathan Demme

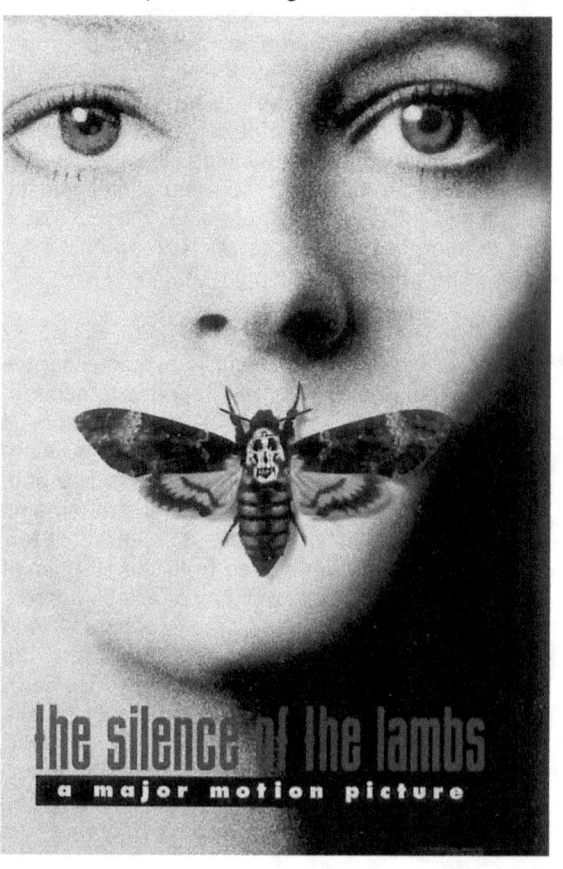

selected a superb cast, headed by Jodie Foster (whose backwoods innocence contrasts well to the sophisticated depravity of the good Dr. Hannibal Lecter, in a performance by Anthony Hopkins that deserves all the kudos awarded). Demme's control of cinematography and tricky editing help to heighten the tension, but it is those quiet scenes where Foster and Hopkins mindprobe each other that truly resonate and linger. Upon my initial viewing of *Silence of the Lambs*, I thought the movie was overrated, but upon the second viewing, its subtle touches and artistry emerged. This is the real deal!

### Ed Wood (1994)

What director other than Tim Burton would have the vision to cast ex-wrestler George "The Animal" Steele as Tor Johnson, himself an ex-wrestler? But the quirky vision of Burton and his inspired casting (of Bill Murray as Bunny Breckinridge, Vincent D'Onofrio as Orson Welles, Jeffrey Jones as Criswell, Johnny Depp as Ed Wood and, most impressively, Martin Landau as Bela Lugosi) make *Ed Wood* a classic of both the Hollywood bio film and of the revisionist history of low-budget horror cinema. Whether Bela Lugosi ever cursed in real life or not, Martin Landau's interpretation is full-blooded and touches the heart, transforming Lugosi into exactly the type of man we always wanted him to be.

### The Frighteners (1996)

Peter Jackson, cutting his eye-teeth on grisly and satiric gore (*Bad Taste* and *Dead Alive*), morphed into a visionary director with *Heavenly Creatures*. But his mainstream chiller, *The Frighteners*, starting off as a light grifter romp, soon evolves into a bone-chilling ghost thriller, realized with just the perfect amount of visual effects to carry off the multidimensionality of the spirit world. Michael J. Fox shines in both a comedic and deadly serious performance, both playing into and against his *Family Ties* persona. But it is Peter Jackson's recreation of ghost cinema into something bombastic and reverberating rather than claustrophobic and quiet that is most remarkable about this emerging talent. The film just gets better with repeated viewings.

### Dark City (1998)

The seemingly unlimited imagination of Alex Proyas has concocted the most visionary movie of the 1990s with *Dark City*, a science fiction movie framed by imagery of American film noir of the 1940s and German Expressionist horror cinema of the 1920s. Here is a sliver of a world, disguised as the planet Earth, where the cityscape changes form almost nightly, as citizens are drugged and made unaware of their changing identity. Perfect performer Rufus Sewell is our titular hero, a man unsure of his past, distrusting of his own memory, who is on a mysterious journey to discover who these *Nosferatu*-esque citizens are. The movie is well-scripted, well acted and well photographed—and the audience is intellectually engaged throughout every minute.

### The Sixth Sense (1999)

What Brian De Palma meant to movie fanatics a generation ago, a M. Night Shyamalan production means today... a cutting edge director, focused on one specific genre (De Palma with his Hitchcock fixation and Shyamalan with his supernatural/horror overtones), whose every project seems to be a hotly anticipated event. While not his first film, *The Sixth Sense* is Shyamalan's first breakout film to really get noticed, as its midsummer quiet release proved to have legs when the movie continued filling theaters for the next six months. A devilishly twisted plot (both gimmicky yet satisfyingly inspired) combined with sensitive acting (a subdued Bruce Willis and an expressive child star Haley Joel Osment) and smothering mood punctuated with visceral shocks produced perhaps the horror classic of the 1990s.

### From Hell (2001)
Dripping with mood and a bombastic soundtrack, *From Hell*, this graphic-novel updating of the Jack the Ripper mythos, is not only the best Ripper movie ever made, it is perhaps one of the most outstanding horror movies of the past 20 years. Albert and Allen Hughes' vision is always of the ghetto, the bleak underbelly of urban hell, and instead of working within their *Menace II Society* modern American ghetto, the Hughes brothers turned their attention to the British ghetto of Victorian times. Combining the kinetic energy and staccato editing of low-budget movies such as *The Evil Dead* and *Re-Animator* with the mainstream look of big-budget Hollywood and Hammer-esque mood (with dripping fog everywhere), *From Hell* makes mainstream Hollywood look dangerous once again!

### The Others (2001)
Alejandro Amenabar, the director of the original Spanish version of *Open Your Eyes* (to be reborn as *Vanilla Sky*, with Cameron Crowe's Americanized version), reinvented the ghost genre for a new generation of fans who never saw *The Haunting* or even *Legend of Hell House* in the theaters. Boasting the star power of Nicole Kidman in a sensitive performance, acting alongside two children (shades of *The Innocents*), Amenabar manages to imbue the insular world of *The Others* with nuance making every image count. The film occurs either within the home or directly outside, so the chill quotient grows and grows as the hauntings, very subtle at first, become more thumpy-and-bumpy in the night. What is most outstanding about *The Others* is its vision of our plain of existence being only one of multiple plains, where individuals throughout time still occupy the space where they once lived and breathed and thrived, and even after death, they are not aware of their own mortality and fail to recognize that they themselves are the ghosts of the dearly departed. *The Others* displays psychological denial to the most extreme degree. Marvelously chilling. Atmospheric horror is once again on the rebound.

### The Lord of the Rings: Fellowship of the Rings (2001); The Two Towers (2002)
Isn't it amazing that quirky New Zealand moviemaker Peter Jackson, the same director who created the blood feast *Dead Alive*, was given *carte-blanche* to create his vision of J.R.R. Tolkien's *The Lord of the Rings* (the first two segments already in release). And surprisingly, the mythic intensity of these movies has created a trilogy very much this generation's answer to George Lucas' landmark original *Star Wars* trilogy (1977-1982), but Jackson's movies cut even deeper and contain even more substance. In fact, as Sue shared with me, it becomes clearer and clearer as time goes on that Lucas himself was inspired by Tolkien's literature that emphasizes epic battles between good and evil demonstrating how ultimate power always corrupts, even the most innocent among us. Whether we note the first real CGI character (Gollum) ever created worthy of Academy Award consideration or the evolution of CGI special effects to the next level—much as *King Kong* did for stop-motion 70 years ago—it is refreshing to note that Jackson's visual style never overpowers either plot or character, as his balance remains impeccable.

# The Spider

## Weaving a Web of Suspense

### by Michael H. Price

*Nobody is to leave this theatre!*
—A command issued early on in
*The Spider* (Fox; 1931)

"Barnum was right—Herrmann was wrong," declared Edmund Lowe, cryptically stating a case for his new starring picture. The year was 1931, and *The Spider* was strategically well positioned to become a significant broadside in the launching of a genre complete unto itself, the wired-for-sound horror film.

Lowe was speaking not of P.T. Barnum's famous line about "a sucker born every minute"—although that might apply, too—but rather of a lesser-known philosophy of entertainment from the pioneering impresario.

"I mean," Lowe explained, "that Barnum was right when he said that slow, natural motion [in the performance of magic] deceives the spectator, and that Herrmann's theory of the hand being quicker than the eye is incorrect.

"I refer, of course, to Herrmann the Great, the magician, not Babe Herman, the outfielder," Lowe added.

The occasion was an interview contrived by the publicity department of Fox Film Corp., and so Lowe, who was as much in charge of the Q&A process as his character—a magician embroiled in amnesia, murder and the violent Haves vs. Have-Nots conflicts of the Great Depression—would prove himself in charge of the weirdness at large in *The Spider*. The actor proceeded to mystify the anonymous interviewer with a vanishing-card trick at a leisurely pace, then: "You see, Barnum was right."

"I must inform the public at once!" the interviewer quoted himself, facetiously. "Where is my portable typewriter?"

"Where you left it," replied Lowe, pretending to retrieve the machine from under the writer's coat. "And here's your watch. And your wallet. Careless, aren't you?"

Here was an unusual promotional stance, and particularly so by comparison with campaigns for kindred films of the day as a bandwagon began to gather momentum.

In its promotion of *Dracula*, the watershed film of this talkie-terror movement, Universal Pictures had promised forbidden romance and underscored that intention audaciously with a Valentine's Day opening in 1931. For its later-in-1931 follow-through *Frankenstein*, Universal had taken a similar tack—but only

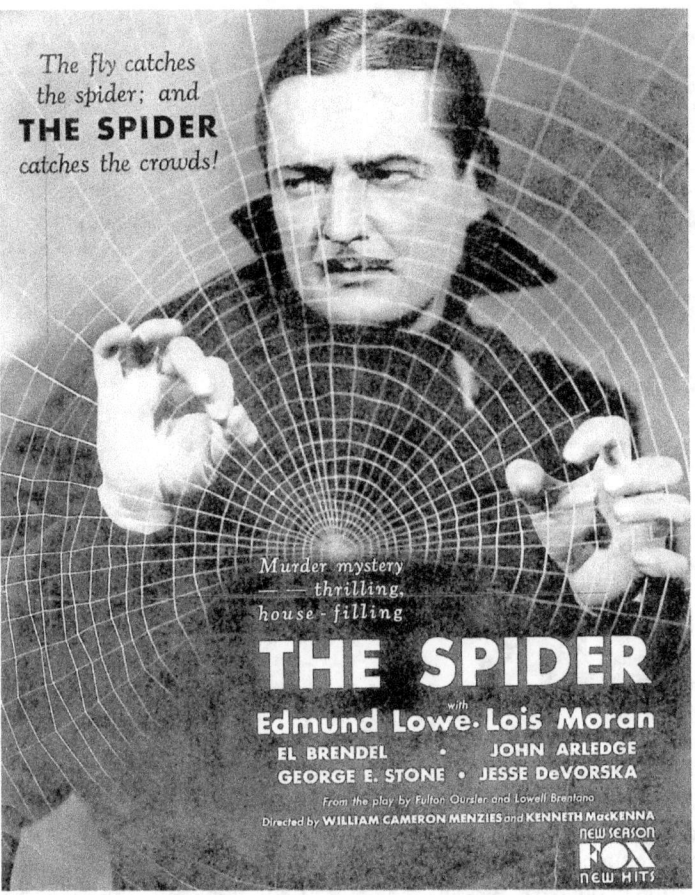

for so long as Bela Lugosi, the exotic leading man of *Dracula*, had been attached to *Frankenstein*'s pivotal role of a humanlike creation of renegade science. Upon Lugosi's rejection of the part and Boris Karloff's ascent to the career-cinching assignment, Universal let the publicity campaign find its own level of terrified anticipation. Universal's *East of Borneo*, from the autumn of 1931, bears regard as a horror picture but was marketed more as a hard-bitten adventurous entry, and perceived accordingly by the public.

Paramount, with its 1931 opening of *Murder by the Clock*, touted the novelty of sound, in the form of a horrendous mechanical wail that issues from a mausoleum with a nerve-wracking unpredictability. For its 1931-32 opening of *Dr. Jekyll and Mr. Hyde*, Paramount took a sensationalistic, star-driven approach to selling the horrific appeal of the material.

Warner Bros. brought to the table *Svengali*, a haunting tale of mesmerism in the service of evil, but marketed this film more in terms of the snob appeal of star player John Barrymore and the innocent beauty of Barrymore's chosen leading lady, Marian Marsh. Warners allowed a prompt follow-up from the same unit, *The Mad Genius*, to glide by on the coattails of *Svengali*. For that matter, *The Mad Genius* might not exist without *Svengali* as its springboard.

In the case of *The Spider*, which gives a procedural detective yarn a generous garnish of eerie menace and the illusion of audience participation, Fox couched its fall-of-1931 pitch to the public in terms of antic wit, a whiff of the supernatural and an ambiguity as to whether Edmund Lowe might turn out to be a threatening character. The comic-relief shenanigans of El Brendel, a popular Swedish-dialect goof, provided a key selling point. There is a residue of the silent-era mystery-farce, and indeed *The Spider* had its own Broadway origins, however distinctive. But this quality is merely a touchstone to the familiar, helpfully placed alongside the film's bolder use of depth-of-field and sound itself in an attempt to involve the audience beyond absorbed observation.

Where the audience attending a conventional mystery-farce could witness at a comfortable distance the mayhem threatening the inmates of some confining mansion, the audiences for *The Spider* were themselves situated in theaters not unlike the venue shown on screen, the physical reality of an auditorium becoming a telescopic extension of the picture at the appropriate moments. This was a calculated strategy on the part of co-director William Cameron Menzies, a championship set designer and art director who fancied a fuller involvement of the audience to be a logical next phase in the evolution of filmmaking. He was quite ahead of his time, as usual: In this respect, *The Spider* proves itself a foreshadowing of Menzies' more striking experiments in depth design of a generation later, including *The Maze* (shot in a three-dimensional process) and *Invaders from Mars* (which could scarcely have seemed more three-dimensional if it had been shot in 3-D).

This array of films from 1931, though patently the new foundation of a genre, constituted not so much the beginning of a trend—for staged terrors, even though not quite designated a genre as such or as yet, had been crucial to the cinema since its early outcroppings—as it marked a turning point geared to the emerging technology of synchronized sound.

The second all-talking feature film had been Warners' *The Terror*, from 1928, a farcical maniac-at-large piece that did scarcely more than carry on the Broadway-derived traditions of such Jazz Age silent-movie hits as *The Cat and the Canary*, *The Bat* and *The Gorilla*, all reprised sooner or later as talking pictures. The surviving soundtrack elements of *The Terror*—the film itself can be presumed lost beyond recovery—play out almost like a self-contained radio melodrama, as if underscoring but not necessarily adding anything to the images that graced the screen.

But 1931 would become the year of the big detour, serving emphatic, crowd-pleasing proof in a

**Lois Moran and Howard Phillips meet Edmund Lowe (Chatrand)**

handful of pictures from only four major studios that a uniquely cinematic genre, beholden to no style handed down from the silent screen, was ripe for development and exploitation. Of this formidable lot, The Spider has suffered the most damnable long-term obscurity. If the larger history of cinema were a top-40 oldies radio station, then *Dracula* and *Frankenstein* would be Motown and The Beach Boys and *The Spider* would be some seldom-played deep-cuts act like The Thirteenth Floor Elevators or The Vejtables. Even Rouben Mamoulian's 1932 *Dr. Jekyll and Mr. Hyde*, acquired outright by MGM as the basis for a more pretentious but ultimately lesser 1941 remake, finally returned to prominence after years of dog-in-the-manger suppression by MGM.

The prevailing school of thought holds that obscurity is usually deserved—that the cream rises and the inferior content settles unnoticed. A truer understanding, however, lies in the realization that the popular culture procreates so prolifically that most of its progeny, whether brilliant or tarnished, hasn't a chance of getting recognized without exhaustive promotion and over-merchandising. Mass man must be served by mass means, as the satirist Roger Price once averred, hammering this chillingly self-evident truth about the culture: "If everybody doesn't want it, then nobody gets it." For everybody to want it, then, it becomes necessary that everybody be told (by the advertising and marketing industries) that they must have it.

Outbreaks of mass marketing over the long haul have kept *Frankenstein* and *Dracula* as familiar now as they were when unspooled fresh. The 1932 *Dr. Jekyll and Mr. Hyde* was kept forcibly obscure for generations, lest anyone get wise to its superiority in comparison with the remake. But when MGM mounted a big-screen reissue during the early 1970s, the big studio set aside its own version and released its long-hidden acquisition from Paramount, with a bombastic publicity campaign. *Svengali* is better known today as folklore than by its literary and cinematic outcroppings; a lapsed copyright has made the Warners version a perennial among the off-brand video labels. That curious companion-film, *The Mad Genius*, has become a forgotten picture despite the boon of copyright maintenance for television syndication.

Fox's *The Spider*, on the other hand, enjoyed its day in the glare of the carbon-arc projector beam. It made back its investment, and then some. It helped to bolster Edmund Lowe in an extended career of playing suave, often mysterious chaps—including, a year later, the title role in Fox's *Chandu the Magician*, with Menzies and Marcel Varnel co-directing.

Whereupon *The Spider* found itself retired to the vaults. Its resurrection for early-day television came without fanfare, and when seldom the film resurfaces

today it is heralded by the finest of fine print in the night-owl TV listings. To the viewer willing to regard it as more than an antique or a curiosity, *The Spider* rewards the most eager attention. It should go without saying that the title is figurative, although the image of a spider proves significant. Herewith, the story:

A magician known as Chatrand the Great (Lowe) announces via a radio broadcast that he seeks to find the true identity of a victim of amnesia—his assistant, who answers for now to the name of Alexander. Alexander (Howard Phillips) was found, wounded and unconscious, two years ago in Washington. He has become a mind reader in Chatrand's routine, but Alexander cannot read his own mind sufficiently to dredge up any memories of his previous self.

Listening intently to the announcement is Beverly Lane (Lois Moran), whose brother Paul Lane has been missing for two years. Beverly's uncle, big-shot businessman John Carrington (Earle Fox),

Chatrand the Great (Edmund Lowe) and his assistant perform for the enthralled audience.

dismisses Chatrand's announcement as a publicity hoax. Beverly insists upon attending Chatrand's next performance, and Carrington goes along with her.

Surveying the audience from behind the curtains, Chatrand recognizes Beverly from a photograph in a locket that Alexander carries. As the performance progresses, Chatrand blindfolds Alexander and calls upon the youth to describe objects carried by various patrons. When Alexander is asked to describe Beverly's locket, identical to his own, Carrington objects and resorts to violence to halt the routine.

Chatrand's second assistant (Manya Roberti) cuts the lights. A hand, wearing a ring bearing the likeness of a spider, fires a gun. Carrington drops. The police arrive to corral the audience and staff while one showgoer, Dr. Blackstone (George E. Stone), attends to Carrington.

Inspector Riley (Purnell Pratt) finds a gun behind Alexander, who is unconscious. Beverly embraces Alexander and identifies him as her brother. Snapped out of his trance, Alexander, recognizing his sister, declares: "He tried to kill me! I had to do it!"

Riley orders Alexander and Beverly sequestered in an office. Chatrand steals away through a trap door. Alexander recalls the circumstances that brought on his amnesia: Carrington had tried to take control of the siblings' fortune, and Alexander suffered a head injury while dodging an attack from Carrington.

Chatrand learns that Carrington has been under threat from a disgruntled investor. Carrington is pronounced dead, and Alexander is arrested for murder. Chatrand persuades the law to allow him to conduct a séance, the better to smoke out the true killer. As a ghostly voice appears to speak through Chatrand, another shot is fired. Chatrand takes this development as a hopeful sign and orders Alexander, in mind reader mode, to track down the killer. After several false starts involving various embarrassing secrets among the audience, Alexander mentions the spider-ring and prepares to reveal the killer. Again comes gunfire, followed by Dr. Blackstone's unveiling as the killer. The physician declares that Carrington deserved to die for his financial racketeering, which had betrayed the trust of Blackstone and many other investors.

Chatrand, wounded in the last outburst, is comforted by Beverly. She seems to have become infatuated with the magician.

When it débuted on Broadway in March 1927, *The Spider* impressed the theatergoing public as a galvanic novelty: Playwrights Fulton Oursler and Lowell Brentano, breaking severely with stage tradition, shattered the footlights' barrier between the performance and its customers to make the entire auditorium the setting of the play. An extended run was the play's reward.

For the movie version, directors Menzies and Kenneth MacKenna determined that they must retain both the witty dialogue and the tornadic intimacy of the play. Their success not only overcame the talk-over-action imperative that generally afflicted the early talking pictures, but they brought to the project some purely cinematic inventions, especially in the smooth editing and great variety of camera angles, that were beyond the capabilities of the stage. Shrunken today to fill the video screen, *The Spider* loses much of this gripping presence—but the imaginative viewer can summon the atmosphere of an early-'30s movie palace and thus embrace the film on a level nearer its original presentation.

Much of the film's charm still fares nicely in a living-room situation, where the interest might be compounded by the chance discovery of a low-profile telecast. James Wong Howe's photography is a marvel of confining vastness, conveying at once the high-ceilinged spaciousness of the locale and the sense of enthralled imprisonment. Howe's cameras range unimprisoned—conveying the excitement of a festive theatrical event, establishing the immensity of the setting and the occasion, and darting about more freely than most pictures of the age were accustomed to doing. The lighting is often of portrait quality, the better to emphasize the anxieties of leading lady Lois

**Chatrand and Alexander (Howard Phillips) read audience minds, but Alexander cannot read his own mind.**

Moran and the dashing urgency of Lowe's maverick investigation.

Menzies' involvement is more that of a supervising art director, granted additional control of the (melo)dramatic thrust of the piece. MacKenna, an actor-turned-director, concentrates upon the more conventional functions of directing, the pacing of dialogue and motion and the relative placements of the players. Gordon Wiles, formally credited as art director on *The Spider*, said he drew inspiration from Menzies' conception of the aisles of an auditorium as strands of some gigantic spider web.

Lois Moran, a stage-trained player, told the press that one of her greater annoyances was a recurring question as to what differences she found between acting for the screen and acting in person before an audience.

"There is a difference, of course," said Miss Moran, "and it affects theatrical people who have played in both mediums in different ways. In my own case, it is the audience. In the theatre, one feels the response of the spectator to one's work. It is personal. In the studio, this contact is gone. One's work becomes abstract." (It is significant that Miss Moran quit the screen altogether after 1931 to concentrate on stage work, then formally retired in 1935 after marrying well.)

"However," she added, "when we were making *The Spider*... I felt all the glamour of the theatre again. For the whole [soundstage] had been turned into a theatre for the production.

"I was seated [among the audience] for my part, in which I am the ward of a designing uncle, Earle Foxe, who is keeping me from my brother... Suddenly, I recognize my brother on the stage... When Edmund Lowe brings him down to me, and Mr. Foxe interferes and there is a struggle, I could feel the thrill of the audience's response, even though they were my fellow players. Then, when the lights go out and a flash and a gunshot pierce the pitch-blackness, you could feel that whole crowd throb with excitement."

That same crowd had ample reason to throb with laughter, as well, thanks to the broad-stroke buffoonery of El Brendel, who plays a talkative, put-upon member of the audience. The comedian fairly steals the show during its opening moments, using a self-effacing brand of humor that would be amusing even without the broad Vaudeville Scanda-hoovian

Edmund Lowe, in his Chatrand the Great guise, sells Lucky Strikes!

think it is the seventh or eighth time Edmund Lowe and myself have been pictured as bitter enemies."

Lowe said his rehearsals for the picture involved as much magical stagecraft as dramatic exercise.

"The mind-reading and spiritualistic séances are easy for me," Lowe told the press, "because they only call for acting and the reading of lines… But the sleight-of-hand and other tricks requiring dexterity, those are something else. For one thing, I've mastered the tricks called for in this picture. I certainly should be an expert at parlor games…" The film's choicest example of magic is a presentation of the classic Hindu Decapitation Illusion, with Manya Roberti as Lowe's beheaded helper.

Fox Film Corp. took especial pains to show *The Spider* to an invited audience of magicians. This was presumably an acid test, although the resulting endorsements suggest something more along the lines of a publicity ploy. The artists involved included Howard Thurston, whose name by 1931 had become synonymous with magic; Mme. Adelaide Herrmann, widow of Herrmann the Great; and such well-established prestidigitators as Nate Leipzig, John Mulholland, Louis Zingone, Elmer P. Ransome, Ernest Davids and Julian J. Proskauer. All pronounced the magical pivot of the film well done—according to Fox's publicity department, at any rate.

Fox—or its forced-merger descendant, 20th Century-Fox—returned to the 1927 play in 1945 for another film called *The Spider*, which is not so much a remake as it is a reworking of the idea along the lines of B-unit film noir. Gone is the dominant theatrical setting, and the magician character is now known as the Great Garonne (played by Kurt Krueger), who finds himself under suspicion in a series of murders dating back several years. The heroic presence belongs to Richard Conte, as a private eye. The busy African-American comedian, Mantan Moreland, plays a valet who has a quip for every desperate occasion.

And while we're about it: Two serials from Columbia Pictures, *The Spider's Web* (1938) and *The Spider Returns* (1941), have no bearing here—being derivatives from the pulp-magazine exploits of a masked crimestomper known as The Spider.

dialect. This genial lowbrow element is compounded by Kendall McComas, a smart-mouthed kid player who provokes some of Brendel's more ticklish moments.

George E. Stone, a dignified but emotional character man, conveys well the tensions driving the doctor-in-the-house who proves to be a vengeful killer. He appears nervous but game at first, and then makes a show of refusing to let Edmund Lowe's Chatrand put him on the spot for the sake of a stage routine. Stone seems almost too eager to rush to the aid of the fallen big shot, but then manages to redirect suspicion onto various other characters. The revelation of the murderer notwithstanding, the truer villainous presence belongs to Earle Foxe, as the grasping Wall Street wolf who precipitates the immediate crimes by presenting himself as a ready victim. By Foxe's reckoning, The Spider marked "my 43rd death in films, I believe." He added: "I also

**The imaginative viewer can summon the atmosphere of an 1930s movie palace as Chatrand joins the audience.**

**CREDITS:** Associate Producer: William Sistrom; Directors: William Cameron Menzies and Kenneth MacKenna; Assistant Director: R.L. Selander; Based upon: *The Spider*, a 1927 Broadway Play by Charles Fulton Oursler and Lowell Brentano, and "The Man with the Miracle Mind," a Story by Samri Finkelle [Pseudonym of Fulton Oursler]; Continuity and Dialogue: Barry Conners and Philip Klein; Contributing Screenwriters: Albert Lewis and Leon Gordon; Photographed by: James Wong Howe; Art Director: Gordon Wiles; Western Electric Sound Engineered by: Albert Protzman; Sound Recording: Alfred Bruzlin; Editor: Alfred De Gaetano; Costumer: Dolly Tree; Musical Score: Carli Elinor; Running Time: 65 Minutes; Released: Following New York Opening on September 4, 1931

**CAST:** Edmund Lowe (Chatrand the Great); Lois Moran (Beverly Lane); El Brendel (Ole); John Arledge (Tommy); George E. Stone (Dr. Blackstone); Earle Fox (John Carrington); Manya Roberti (Sonya); Howard Phillips (Alexander); Purnell Pratt (Inspector Riley); Jesse De Vorska (Goldberg); Kendall McComas (Kid); Ruth Donnelly (Mrs. Wimbleton); William Pawley (Butch); Warren Hymer (Schmidt); Ward Bond, C.A. Bachman and Anders von Haden (Cops); Raymonda Brown, Marguerite Caverly, Doris Morton and Lee Kinney (Usherettes); Pat Haley (Electrician); John Lester Johnson (Nubian); Robert Kerr (Stagehand); Charles Wheelock, Anita Wilson, Doris Campbell, Bond Davis, Irene Dale, June De Vaney, Eleanor Frances, Mel S. Forrester, Baldy Belmont, Violet Bird, Marie Stapleton, Morris Selvage, Jerry Storm, Margaret Mayo, Dorothy McLaughlin, James McPherson, Ruth Magden, George Milo, Walter Lawrence, Helen Long, Helen Lambert, Richard French, Rupert Franklin, Peggy Graham, Jimmy Gray, Jenny Gray, Beauregard Bonifacio, Frank Henry, Charles Hammond, Samuel E. Hines, Caryl Lincoln and Charline Burt (Audience Members)

**Theater display for *The Spider***

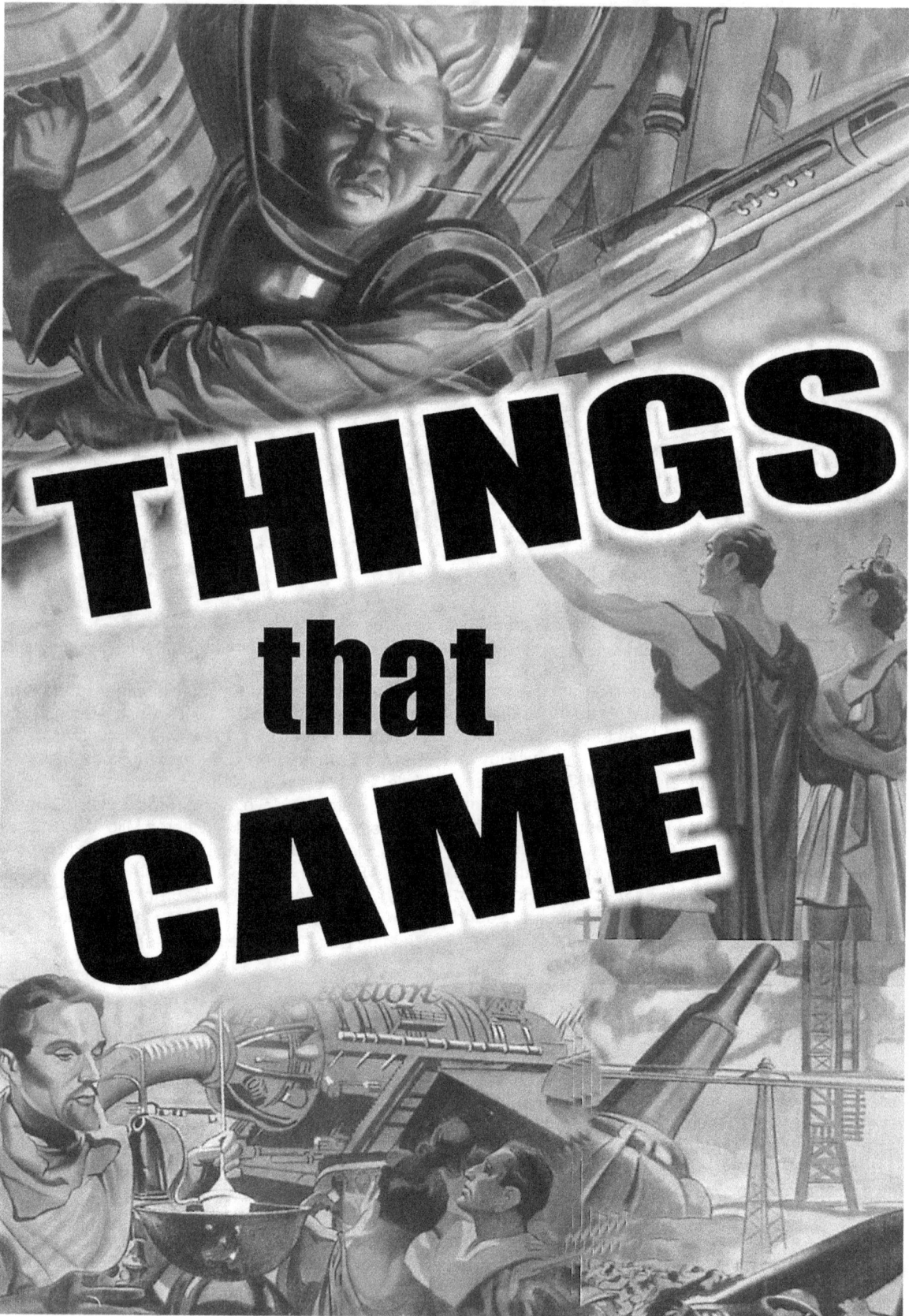

To help celebrate our 40th year of publication (1963-2003), *Midnight Marquee* put out requests to all fans of classic horror/science fiction cinema to name the five most influential trends that affected the horror, science fiction or fantasy film genre during the past 40 years. Interested parties could simply submit lists or include explanations and defenses for such lists. Neither set format nor length was factored into the equation. What we received is a very insightful and varied smorgasbord; even people who overlapped and included the same or similar trends often times had diverse reasoning for naming the trends selected. So, without further delay, let us dig into the pile and see what today's horror/sci-fi movie fan considers to be the most important trends of the past 40 years. Comments are always appreciated.

Videotape was invented in 1956; the first tape machine debuted at a National Association of Broadcasters conference late in the year, around November, and the networks started using them late the following year once manufacturing started.

The best event/invention would be home video, which made so many films easily available. I don't have the exact year this begun, but I had a VCR in 1978 and our neighborhood Fotomat kiosk stocked some film titles.
—Lawrence Dunkel

1. *Famous Monsters of Filmland* magazine: This magazine almost single-handedly revived the entire classic monster era.
2. The release of *The Exorcist*: This film terrified the country (if not the world) and changed the face of horror film history, sadly tolling the death bell for the classic-style horror being released in the theaters.
3. The Life and Death of Hammer Films: This period saw some of the best and worst times for the beloved Hammer, which forever left their mark on horror film history and helped spawn similar endeavors by Amicus and Tyburn films.
4. The release of the *Evil Dead* trilogy of films: perhaps modern (1980 and after) horror's most influential films.
5. *The Rocky Horror Picture Show* phenomenon: the original horror cult film
—Dave Hagan

My list for Most Important Horror/Science Fiction Film Events of the Last 40 Years will be as follows:

*Star Trek* (TV series, 1966-69)
Videotape
Stephen King
*Star Wars*
*Lord of the Rings: Fellowship of the Ring* (2001)
—Dennis Fischer

1. The rise and fall of Hammer Films
2. *2001: A Space Odyssey*
3. *Star Wars*
4. Invention of home video and DVD
5. Computer special effects for films
—Gary Heilman

1. Ray Harryhausen's Gordon E. Sawyer Lifetime Award Oscar
2. *Silence of the Lambs* sweeps the Oscars.
3. Rick Baker's Oscar winning makeup and SPFX
4. Willis O'Brien becomes rediscovered
5. George Pal
—Kevin Clement

In chronological order:
1. Syndication of *Star Trek*
2. *Star Wars*
3. Steven Spielberg
4. Home Video/DVD
5. Home PC/The Internet
   Keep in mind, I don't think the things I listed are necessarily good things, just important things.
—John Clymer

1. *The Rocky Horror Picture Show* (1975) for its ability to acquire and retain the large audience despite its underground, "bizarre and immoral" content.
2. *Night of the Living Dead* (1968) for introducing the world to George A. Romero's talent, and (re)

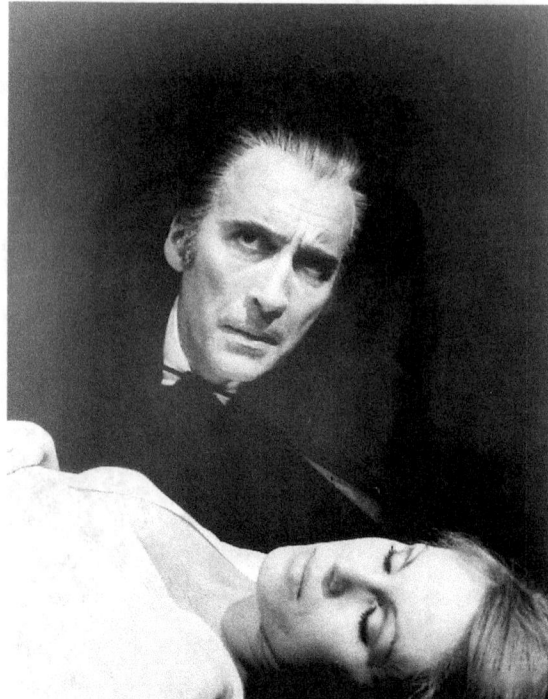

*Satanic Rites of Dracula*: Christopher Lee is still going strong in 2003.

1. Hitchcock directs *The Birds*
2. Corman directs *Masque of the Red Death*
3. Polanski emerges with *Repulsion* and *Rosemary's Baby*
4. *The Exorcist* and *Jaws* make big-budget horror attractive to studios
5. *Silence of the Lambs* is the first horror film to win a Best Picture Oscar
–Steve Haberman

1. The Assertion of Populist Genre scholarship—This development was bound to have come about, with or without the emergence of consumer video technology, computerized publishing devices and the Internet. But of course, such watershed conveniences have only made it easier for everybody to pitch in beyond the range of fanzines and fanboy conventions. The shirtsleeves-scholarship phenomenon is a mixed blessing, of course, with the clear-cut disadvantage of allowing a voice to many people who have absolutely nothing to declare but who go ahead and declare it anyhow. A more positive effect is the increased accountability thus demanded of the accredited and published authorities—merely by enabling civilian enthusiasts to compare notes and impressions more directly with those who have attained, and sometimes even earned, a mass-media forum.
2. George A. Romero—The low-key arrival and gradual popular acceptance of *Night of the Living Dead* in 1968—a derivative and raggedly collaborative off-Hollywood production, rendered distinctive

inventing the contemporary gory horror picture on a low budget.
3. *Star Wars* (1977) for proving that science fiction isn't such a silly genre after all!
4. *The Empire Strikes Back* (1980) for reinforcing the above statement.
5. *The Exorcist* (1973) for being the scariest film of all time and bringing horror to the Oscars once again.
—Paul Meyd

1. The creation of the title creature in *Alien*. H.R. Giger gave us one of the most frightening monsters in genre history.
2. *The Exorcist*—The first mainstream in your face shocker (blasphemous in some circles). It even made the cover of *Time* (*Newsweek*?) magazine.
3. CGI—In terms of EFX it can "go where no man has gone before."
4. Hannibal Lecter—right up there with Norman Bates.
5. Christopher Lee—He's still going strong (81 years old this year); the last living horror icon. They just don't make 'em like they used to

Thank you for asking my opinions. Gary—you and I were born the same year; I too have been a fan since the debut of *Shock Theater* (in my small town it was known as *Spooktacular*).
—Gary Billings

**Alfred Hitchcock's *The Birds***

and truthful by director and co-writer George Romero's bleak expectations of a human species under pressure—signaled a Sea Change within the genre. Blatantly inferior imitators accounted for the downside, naturally, but otherwise, Romero's breakthrough enabled comparable viability for such re-inventors of a genre as David Cronenberg, John Carpenter, Tobe Hooper and Wes Craven. The jury is out as to Romero's staying power in a treacherous industry, but even so he has delivered some formidable work within the big-studio mainstream.

3. The New Freedom in Hollywood—The slackening of institutionalized censorship during 1968-69 was no overnight development, even though it conveyed all the impact of abruptness. This can hardly be reckoned a Good Thing, inasmuch as it essentially freed mainstream Hollywood to begin pillaging the storehouses of sensationalism that had given the off-Hollywood exploitation studios an edge of forbidden allure since the Depression years. The near-simultaneous development of a ratings system by the Motion Picture Association has proved less meaningful than outright censorship, although there once was a time when an R-as-in-Restricted seal signified thoughtful maturity and provocative intelligence in a film thus labeled. The long-term effect has been an inflationary devaluation of the coinage of caustically resonant language, dramatically valid erotica and/or violence, which are more effective when subjected to the power of suggestion. A PG-rated picture today can get away with raunchy business that would have demanded an R rating as recently 1985—and since when does a kid-audience movie require a PG, anyhow? Not to mention that filmmakers as a class were a great deal smarter when obliged to contrive ways of getting around Hollywood's repressive Legion of Decency without being too blunt about it.

4. The Kidult Movie—Vincent Canby coined the term "kidult" in *The New York Times* in a sarcastic effort to account for the massed appeal of John McTiernan's *Die Hard* (1988). The word betokens a sad acceptance of the fact that many moviegoers' tastes and values have been welded into place by age seven-or-thereabouts—fixed beyond any hope of growth, save for their inexorable coarsening and cheapening, like scar tissue, over the course of a customer's life. Hence the kidult: An adult by legal and chronological standards, but with all the attentiveness of some thrill-starved kid. This is the presumed audience for whom most horror/fantasy/SF movies are made (to say nothing of comedies and general-purpose adventures), and any subject matter more challenging need not apply.

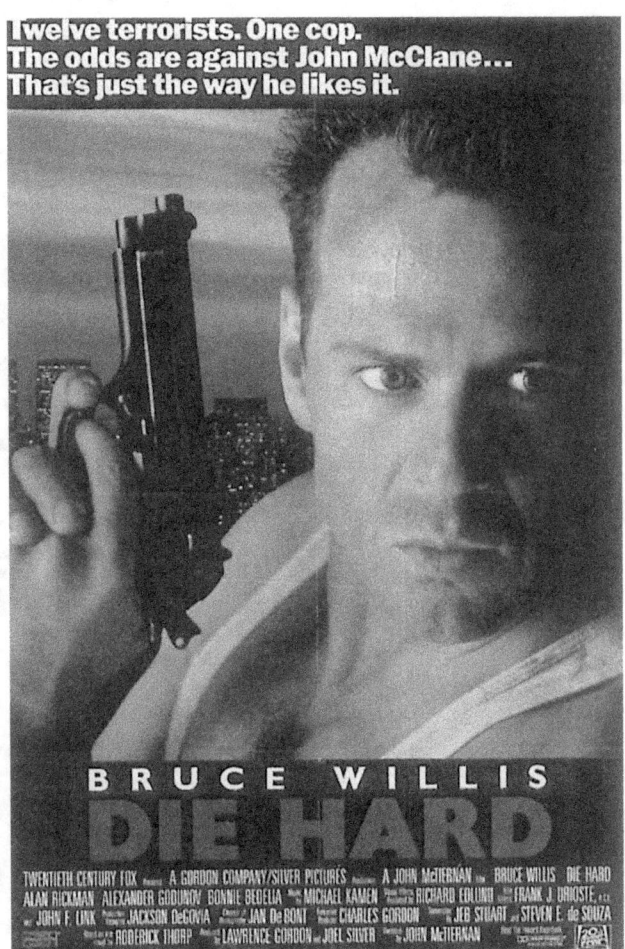

*Die Hard* and the emergence of the kidult movie

Such abuse of a fundamentally intelligent genre has become epidemic since the 1980s. Its most repugnant example may lie in 20th Century-Fox's plagiarism-with-impunity of an disturbingly intelligent low-budgeter of 1980, Greydon Clark's *Without Warning*, for the sake of equipping Arnold Schwarzenegger with a lunkheaded starring picture, John McTiernan's (him, again) *Predator* (1987). One can only wonder whether the kidult is really all that powerful a social force—or whether the movie industry merely assumes a proliferation of kidults in its campaign to demean the narrative medium.

5. Steven Spielberg—His breakthrough (as a director on the 1969 tele-pilot for Rod Serling's *Night Gallery*) is hardly as auspicious a beginning as that of George A. Romero (above). But Steven Spielberg has vindicated himself time and again as the guy who has kept Hollywood safe for science fiction—and the kidult mentality (also above) be damned. No accounting for taste, of course, and many enthusiasts will find a crippling niceness in Spielberg's SF pictures. But his fidelity to Philip K. Dick in a 2002 filming of *Minority Report* validates Spielberg's credential

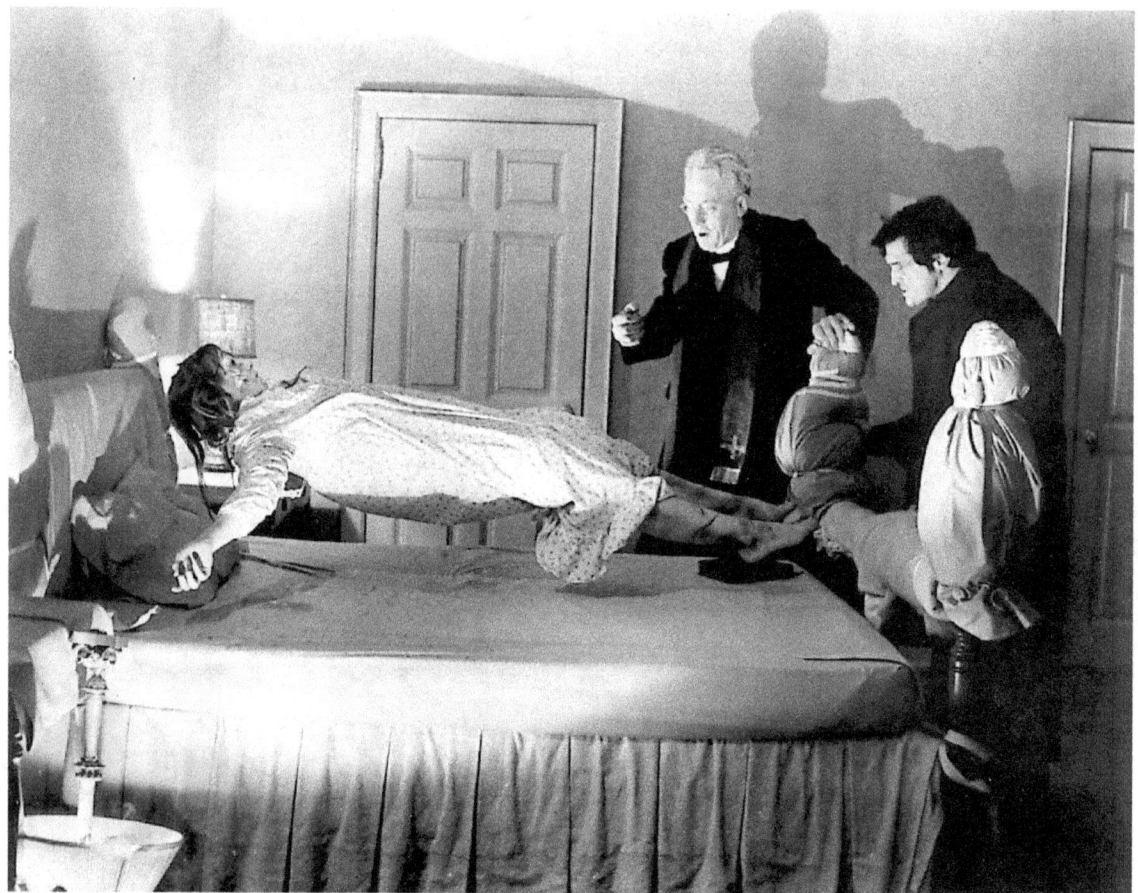

*The Exorcist*: William Friedkin directs a horror flick that makes over one hundred million dollars.

across the board as both a devotee and a practitioner of thought-provoking speculative fiction.
—Michael H. Price

In my opinion, it would have to be the DVD format. This format has really opened up the world of more obscure horror (particularly Euro-horror) to people who had no previous exposure.
—T. Hardin

1. *The Exorcist* (novel and film)—William Peter Blatty writes a horror bestseller and then William Friedkin does the unthinkable: directs a horror flick that makes over 100 million dollars! Horror movies for the Joe on the street.
2. Brian De Palma's *Carrie*—Brian De Palma single-handedly creates an industry: Stephen King. Because of De Palma's masterpiece, King becomes a household name. Stop 10 people on the street; ask them who wrote *Rosemary's Baby*, who wrote *The Exorcist*, who wrote *The Others*? Nine out of 10 *Fangoria* convention goers couldn't answer that question, let alone the guy on the street. Now ask that same guy the name of the author who wrote *Salem's Lot*, *The Shining*, *Cujo* or *Carrie*? Chances are he'll know. Thanks to De Palma, Stephen King became not just a top-selling horror writer but also the top-selling author of all time.
3. The 1974 *Famous Monsters* Convention in New York. Though I couldn't attend (I was a 13-year-old West Coast monster geek), I read all about it in *FM*. The first real horror con, it gathered thousands of monster fans, gave them a sense of community, and paved the way for today's Fangoria, Monster Bash and FANEX cons.
4. The Internet. For better or worse, suddenly you can find out who starred in *I Spit on Your Grave*, who directed *Shriek of the Mutilated* and who actually liked *Attack of the Mushroom People*. All at the click of your mouse. No more hunting through old back issues of *Photon* and *Midnight Marquee*. It's just too easy. On the down side, there are a lot of "critics" in cyberspace who have way too much time on their hands.
5. *Halloween*—Though I acknowledge that John Carpenter's *Halloween* is a classic, it heralded a lot of bad stuff. The end of the 1970s (a decade of horror I am particularly fond of) and the beginning of a wave of ultraviolence that pervades all of entertainment to this day. Carpenter's not to blame though. *Halloween*

*Young Frankenstein* brought attention to the classic Frankenstein films with updated humor.

is a subtle chiller. No gouged eyes, no entrails, no dismemberments. Unfortunately, when *Halloween* became the highest-grossing independent film of its time, the talentless hacks hanging around Hollywood took notice, but not notes. So we were subjected to *April Fool's Day, Maniac, Friday the 13th*, and, yep, *Halloween 2, 3, 4*, etc. Blood and intestines substitute for mood and menace.
—Peter Enfantino

Man Lands on the Moon
The Internet
Home Computers
*2001*
*Star Wars*
—Kevin Shinnick

As for a top-event pick between 1963 and 2003, I'd say film colorization, because the controversy about it brought so much attention to classic films.

As a second thing, I'd say the film *Young Frankenstein*, again because it brought attention to the classic Frankenstein films, but it also added updated humor to maintain our interest.
—Marian Clatterbaugh

The 40 years between 1963 and 2003 have been rich for fantasy films—these have been both years of triumph and loss. Do we pinpoint those turning points that have had a deleterious effect? Or is it best to err on the positive?

Because life is both good and bad, I would suggest that the five keys events are:
1. The good: the release, in 1968, of *2001: A Space Odyssey* and *Planet of the Apes*. The science fiction comes of age.
2. The bad: the release, in 1977, of *Star Wars*. Science fiction (and film in general) takes a quantum leap backwards. *Star Wars*, more than anything else, helped kill the science fiction film of ideas, and created the "blockbuster" culture. Sob.
3. The (very!) bad: the release, in 1982, of *Blade Runner*. For 20 years, the science fiction film is mired in bad attitude, black leather and cheap nihilism. With the success of the equally dreary *The Matrix*, there is no relief in sight.
4. The good: the ascendancy of Tim Burton. For every lump of coal (*Mars Attacks!*), there is a diamond of great price (*Edward Scissorhands, Ed Wood*).
5. Finally, the good. Somewhere—around 1992 or so—Monster Kids suddenly had a nostalgic

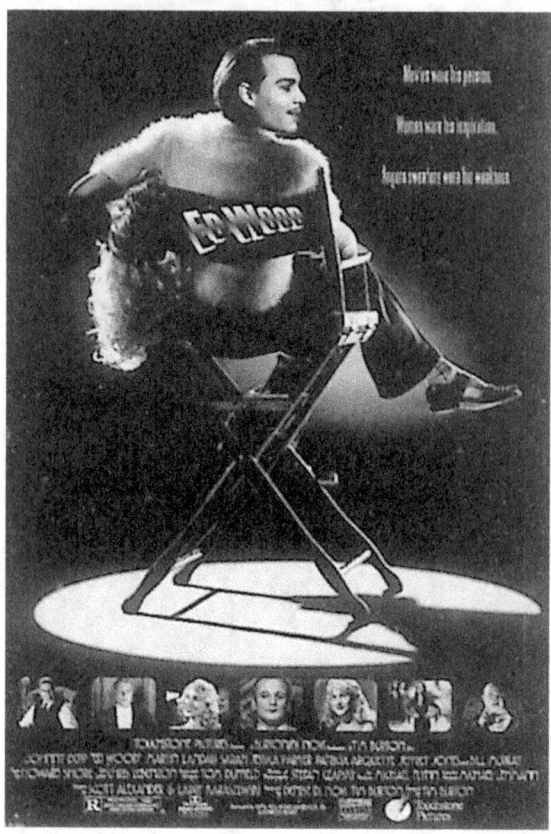

epiphany. Because of that, classic monsters and the scholarship of classic films are vital once again. Thanks to all the scholars and fans who made it possible.
—Bob Madison

1. **Emergence of Steven Spielberg:** Give credit where credit is due. Just pick three of his films—*Jaws*, *Close Encounters* and *ET*—and they are extremely successful and influential films over all three categories of horror, sci-fi and fantasy films. He has made these three genres big box office more than anyone else. He got so successful that he formed his own studio—Dreamworks—which is basically like another arm of Universal. They have even grown so huge that they deemed to take on Disney, which had a stronghold in the animated genre. With Spielberg's production of *Shrek* came a fantasy cartoon for adults, one that their kids could enjoy equally. His name—Spielberg—evokes images of power in the entertainment industry, and that says it all. And this isn't about me being his No. 1 fan, either, because that's not necessarily the case. It's all about giving credit where credit is due.

2. **Emergence of Stephen King:** Stephen King's novels during the 1970s and 1980s have been turned into countless classic horror films. Just go down the line—*Carrie*, *Christine*, *The Shining*, *The Dead Zone*, *Pet Cemetery*, etc. He brought horror to a nationwide television audience when several of his novels were made into well-executed miniseries such as *The Stand*, *It* and *The Langoliers*. He has also done something equally important for the horror-film industry, encouraging many youngsters to read, which is certainly a fine thing. He has even appeared on both the big and little screen in several well-noted cameos, such as the character he portrayed in a segment of the film *Creepshow* or his featured role in the television mini-series *The Stand*. He has no doubt done wonders for the horror genre. In fact, as I write, he is still making contributions with his books providing the material for recent fantasy films such as *The Green Mile* and *Dreamcatcher*.

3. Emergence of Vincent Price: Along with producer/director Roger Corman, he created the Gothic horror genre in the late 1950s and early 1960s, and rode that through countless excellent horror films in the 1960s. In the early 1970s, he gave us that chilling character of Dr. Phibes, and also hosted *The Horror Hall of Fame* special on ABC.

Then, in the 1980s, just when you thought it was safe to turn on the radio or TV, he brought horror to the mainstream audience through pop music and his appearance in both the Michael Jackson *Thriller* video and his narration in the song of the same name. He also lent his voice as the narrator of the Haunted Mansion in EuroDisney. Many followers of NFL Films often refer to longtime NFL Films narrator

**The emergence of Stephen King is seen in movies such as *Cujo*.**

John Facenda as "the voice of God." Perhaps Vincent Price should be known as "the voice of horror."

4. *Famous Monsters of Filmland*: Our good friend Steven Thornton stole my thunder with the inception of video, but that's okay since I could only narrow my list down to six. Now, instead, I get to include an equally great invention, the Jim Warren publication, *Famous Monsters of Filmland*, which for most of the '60s, '70s and '80s, helped give new-life to older horror and science fiction movies such as the Universal Creature Features, not to mention early science fiction silents such as *Metropolis*. Yes sir, Forrest J Ackerman's excellently-edited, and well-written publication spawned an army of fans for the horror/sci-fi genre; people who would go on to became influential members of that genre—two of which top my list—and who learned their craft by reading Uncle Forry's fine-feathered scribblings. This magazine educated youngsters—and more importantly, got them interested—in the work of older and, in some cases, deceased actors; People such as Bela Lugosi, Lon Chaney, Lon Chaney, Jr. and Boris Karloff, just to name a few. And while it was huge in the horror genre, it was pretty darn big where sci-fi was concerned, as well. In fact, it was Dr. Acula himself, who coined the phrase "sci-fi." And, that's just another reason why his fine publication belongs on this list.

5. DVD: An even better format than video, these films have been given even more new life with this invention. And, with all the extra features, people have taken to collecting DVDs as if they were books, at a much-more rapid pace than videos. That's something many in the movie industry did not expect. While videotape may never completely die, DVD has improved the home video format much like CDs have improved the sound beyond cassette tapes in music. And just try to find a store that still sells records. Well, DVD has already done that and more. Movies such as *Metropolis* are already a favorite in many a genre fan's DVD rack. And just consult eBay to see what the old Universal Monster DVDs are now going for. And what better films than horror, sci-fi or fantasy movies to enjoy on such a visually pleasing format as DVD. Yes sir, with this new-and-improved format, it seems the best is yet to come... or at least be re-released on DVD!
—Sam Borowski

*Night of the Living Dead* showed fans and filmmakers alike that it was time for horror to get nasty.

5. M. Night Shyamalan
4. Wes Craven
3. Steven Spielberg
2. John Carpenter
1. Alfred Hitchcock
—Robert Harari

1. Videotape was a brilliant pick! Everything was changed, radically, once it became affordable and recordable to consumers.
2. Let's not forget the importance of fanzines, which opened a lot of doors for me with regards to locating some of the more obscure Eurotrash I enjoy.
3. E-mail has been a boon, internationally *especially*.
4. Let me toss out Dario Argento's *Bird with the Crystal Plumage* as an important directorial debut... perhaps *the* most important, in my book.
5. And speaking of books, I would cite the publication of Michael Weldon's *Psychotronic Encyclopedia of Film* as an important breakthrough that was very influential (it helped reactive *this* fans interest in genre movies).
—Bob Sargent

1. October 1, 1968: *Night of the Living Dead*, whose immense success and subsequent notoriety brought a whole new visceral take on terror (and spawned an entire subgenre of films), hits the screens. *NOTLD* showed fans and filmmakers alike that it was time for horror to get *nasty*.
2. December 26, 1973: The phenomenon that was *The Exorcist* brings big-studio respectability to the

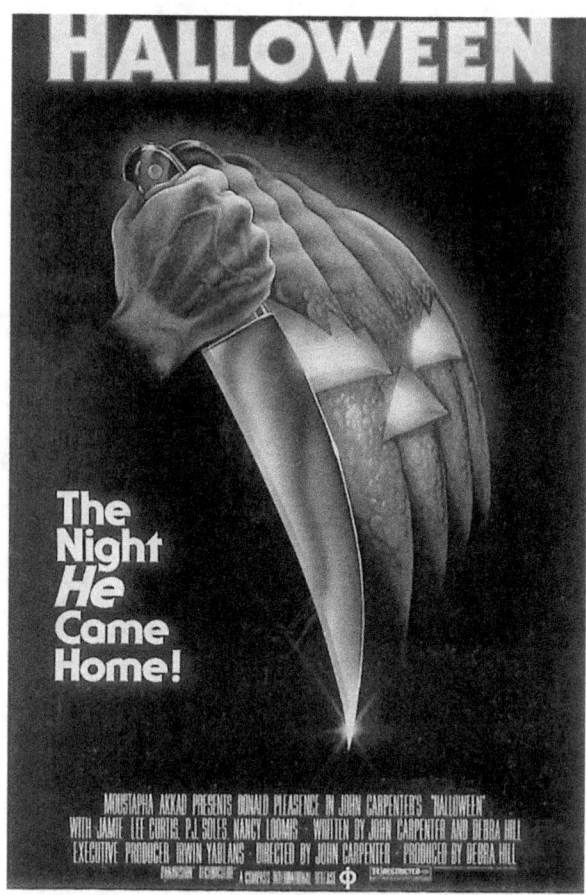

horror genre (and spawned its own little Satan-possessed subgenre), earning a head-spinning number of Academy Awards and nominations. From then on, horror was no longer a dirty word, and big-budget bogeys became part of the Hollywood vernacular.

3. June 13, 1980: Though *Halloween* preceded it by two years, it took the poorly-made, poorly-acted (future-star-to-be Kevin Bacon shows none of the thespian talent here that would later propel him to the heights of Hollywood), ultra-successful *Friday the 13th* to open the floodgates and let the sea of slasher cinema spray out. Blame the countless slice-and-dice, stalk-and-slash, slay-and-spray teen-kill pics that every producer in the 1980s, without an original idea in his or her head, suddenly rushed into production on the coattails of this mean-spirited, unpretentious popcorn-muncher. Whether you love it or loathe it, there is no denying the importance of this film in genre history. The sheer number of imitations and variations that followed, made solely to jump on the slasher bandwagon, ensures this and its far superior predecessor, *Halloween*, a place in cinema history.

4. Early 1980s: The VCR revolution takes root. When those initial top-loading, two-head, mono VCRs abruptly dropped their outrageous $1,000-plus price tags down to the still outrageous but more affordable $400 region, and the $25 tapes eased into the $5 category, viewing habits changed forever, and genre aficionados receive the priceless gift of accessibility. Affordable sell-through movies were still a few years off, but rental stores were multiplying like the oversized rabbits in *Night of the Lepus*; and now we could scour our *TV Guide* for upcoming broadcasts of our favorite horrors to tape. Suddenly, innumerable genre films—the classics, the dross, and the in-betweens—were readily available. It was an exciting time of taping, trading and building, allowing fans, researchers and writers access to things undreamed of in the pre-VCR philosophy. Fuzzy third-generation dupes, cut television prints, grainy film-chained 16mm copies—we didn't care, as we finally were able to see such elusive then-rarities as *Murders in the Zoo*, Karloff's *The Ghoul* and even *Invasion of the Saucer-Men*. I know I could never have written the books I have without the extensive film library I compiled during that oh-so-wondrous time. *Viva la Revolucione!*

5. June 11, 1993: The amazingly life-like dinosaurs of *Jurassic Park* make a thunder lizard-sized leap in special effects technology. For better or worse, the success of *Jurassic Park* brought computer generated imaging (CGI) to the forefront of horror/sci-fi (and mainstream) effects. After this, *anything* was possible, from the overdone wall-to-wall CGI silliness of *Attack of the Clones* to the more judicious (and more effective) CGI thrills of *Lake Placid*, *Reign of Fire* and *Eight Legged Freaks*. Technology had finally caught up with imagination. (And let's hope the latter sees as much use as the former).

—Bryan Senn

This one is tough one, so many things to choose from. I chose not to include any movies because there have been so many influential films made from 1963 to the present. So here we go…

1. The fanzines and magazines that came out after *Famous Monsters of Filmland* were very important to fans. Everything from cinema secrets, interviews with genre personalities and film reviews could be found within their pages. More to choose from meant more variety and more to read, something for everyone in other words. Even though *Gore Creatures* and a bit of *MidMar*'s run was before my time, I consider it very important to fandom; I buy very few magazines of late but *MidMar* is always one of them, without question one of the most intelligent magazines in the market.

2. Stephen King has to figure in here for this fan in particular and I am sure many would agree. Almost all of his books are highly engrossing and a wonderful way to spend quiet time. They have sold in the hundreds of millions and countless movies have

been made from them, so something went right for King and fandom.

3. The invention of the VCR. Now fans didn't have to wait for TV stations or theaters to rerun their favorite movies, they were available at many video rental shops.

4. The inventions of laserdisc and DVD. Most of our favorite genre films from the silent era right to the present are available with terrific supplements and they have never looked so darn good.

5. The day the Internet became accessible to anyone and everyone. This might be fandom's biggest event. Now you could meet and chat with people across the world about your favorite movies, comics, magazines, toys, conventions etc. You could buy, sell and trade genre items with the click of a few keys, and lots of information on just about any horror/sci-fi/fantasy film ever made can be found on the Internet.
—Ed Luskey

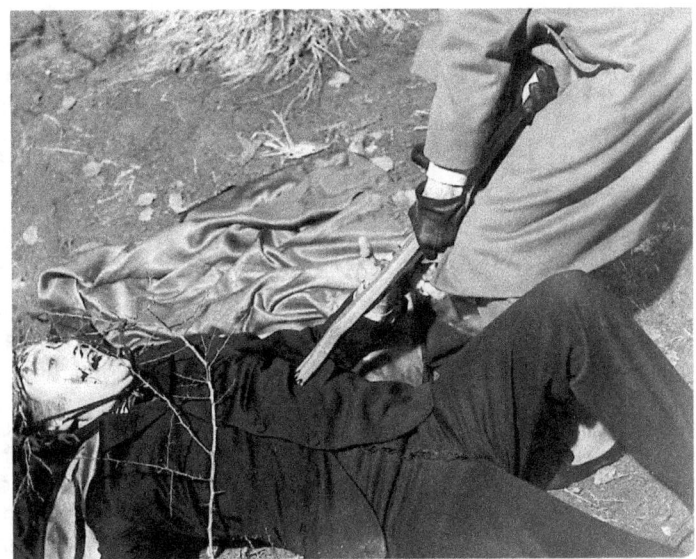

*The Satanic Rites of Dracula*: **A particularly somber note of finality occurs in the destruction of Count Dracula.**

1. 1968—The downbeat ending of *Night of the Living Dead*. Had there ever been such a solemn, horrific ending to a fantasy film before? The fact that the menace is still running amok and all the film's protagonists are dead seems very much a reflection of the cultural crisis in America at the time; it also predicted the rise of the downbeat ending in horror films to come, a marvelous fission-inducing device until it became as overused as the pat "happy ending" of traditional fright films.

2. 1973—The final shot of Peter Cushing as Dr. Van Helsing in *The Satanic Rites of Dracula*. There has always been a particularly somber note of finality in the destruction of Count Dracula (Christopher Lee) in this film; something in the grim expression on Cushing's face suggests to me that even he realized this moment commemorated the passing of an era in fantasy cinema—the end of the Hammer House of Horror. Yes, the company did release a few more films after *Satanic Rites*—and the ending of Cushing's final outing as Baron Frankenstein, *Frankenstein and the Monster from Hell*, certainly allows the possibility of yet another entry in that series—but for me the end of the Dracula series represents the end of Hammer.

3. 1977—Virtually every moment in *Star Wars* is iconic, but the massive, screen-filling sight of the Imperial Star Destroyer overtaking the tiny Rebel ship really blew me away back in 1977. Even now that gigantic space ship symbolizes to me the new order of fantasy films—superior special effects and other technical elements, albeit often at the expense of good storytelling and top-notch acting.

4. 1989—The Batplane's shadow on the moon in *Batman*. This brief visual reference to the famous Bat-Signal acknowledges not only the merchandise-fueled Batmania of the late 1980s/early 1990s, but also the established iconic power of the Caped Crusader.

5. 2002—The light saber duel between Count Dooku (Christopher Lee) and

The downbeat ending of *Night of the Living Dead*: **Had there ever seen such a solemn, horrific ending to a fantasy film before?**

**MIDNIGHT MARQUEE #69/70**     55

Yoda in *Star Wars 2: Attack of the Clones*. [How cool is it for Christopher Lee to have this fight scene win the MTV Movie Award in June 2003 as Best Fight Sequence!] There are many, many problems with the latest entry in the *Star Wars* series, but this climactic duel makes up for all of them. For the first time Yoda becomes a useful character, and the fact that Christopher Lee is fighting the duel—50 years after he broke into movies crossing swords with the likes of Errol Flynn—is an acknowledgment not only of fantasy cinema's last great star, as well as a reference to the many kinds of action-adventure films that inspired George Lucas to create the *Star Wars* mythos in the first place.
—Jonathan Lampley

1. The first major turning point that everyone can point to would be the explosion of graphic violence, which reared its ugly head in 1963 with *Blood Feast*. From there the floodgates were opened and more directors followed suit. I think the roots go back even a few years earlier with *Psycho*, which to me is the number one influence on the modern horror film. I believe that nearly every film that featured a knife- (or pick your favorite implement of violence) wielding maniac owes its debt to *Psycho*, and this covers a lot of territory, from *Texas Chain Saw Massacre* to *Halloween* to *Friday the 13th* to *Scream*, etc. Not to mention the Italian giallos, erotic thrillers that peaked in the 1990s with films like *Basic Instinct* to the derivative homage from Brian De Palma or to the outright remake by Gus Van Sant. The list goes on and on. The real shift from the old Gothic horrors of yesteryear to the graphic terror films of today can be placed squarely on the doorstep of the Bates Motel.

2. Aside from *Psycho*, the second major development of the last 40 years has been Hollywood's slow adaptation of the low-budget exploitation (or B) film into its own blockbuster status. Once films like *The Exorcist* and *The Omen* began making millions of dollars, not to mention *Star Wars* and *Close Encounters* from the sci-fi genre, you could see the slow, gradual erosion of the independent film. Sure there were still notable exceptions like *Halloween* and *The Blair Witch Project* to name a few, but the little guys often get the short end of the stick, and more and more big budget "mainstream" films seemed content to push the limits of bad taste even further, which was almost unheard of before the 1960s.

On the other hand there are directors that can overcome the obstacles of either a low budget, or lack of major studio push to succeed in making movies on their own terms. I point to the films of Quentin Tarantino, David Lynch and David Cronenberg, to name only a few. It is due to original, daring film-

*My Bloody Valentine*: **The slasher floodgates were open.**

makers like them that have kept the pulse of fantastic filmmaking alive all of these years.

3. The third point is the onslaught of CGI dulling the special effects arena so much over the last 10 years, diluting the talent responsible for the breakthrough of the SFX masters getting proper credit from the late 1970s onward. The simple craft of creating something that is real instead of computer-generated has taken some of the steam away from effects-orientated pictures, making the final set piece of The Mummy Returns, for example, resemble something more akin to a video game than an actual motion picture. But again on the flipside there are directors like Steven Spielberg (Jurassic Park) and Peter Jackson (Lord of the Rings trilogy) who seem to know how to handle this technology properly, and in Peter Jackson's case crafts the most human CGI character ever viewed on the big screen, Gollum, from The Two Towers.

4. My forth point would be that once video took over the industry, the sheer amount of great horror films that played in your local theater has dropped significantly since 1985, while the sci-fi and action genres seem to still flourish, but with varying results of course.

5. The fifth point, and greatest advancement or breakthrough for fantastic movies over the last 40 years; however, has to be the creation and development of DVD. No single home media gadget has swept the nation faster than DVD. Now that we can go to our local video store and find pristine, letterboxed and uncut prints of our favorite films from any era is a major revelation. It is almost to the point where we as consumers are being spoiled by all of this product trickling forth every week. The days of videotape and laserdisc are a thing of the past, as DVD has brought film into the 21st century with a bang, and that is the best thing fans could have hoped for over the last 40 years. I should mention that having Midnight Marquee along for the ride doesn't hurt either!

—Dave Kosanke

French poster for The Whip and the Body: sadomasochistic love, death, revenge

While many defining moments of horror, science fiction and fantasy had taken place before 1963, we've certainly seen a few since.

Alfred Hitchcock's The Birds took flight in the spring of 1963, and to this day we can't look at a flock of our feathered friends without wondering "what if?" and being at least a little afraid.

By 1963, director Mario Bava's Black Sunday (1960/61) had already bridged the gap between old-style atmosphere and new-style graphic horror, the latter of which had already been established by Hammer Films. But, like Hammer, Bava was just getting warmed up. 1963 alone saw the release in Europe, and Stateside shortly after, of three more of his efforts that would doubtless influence other filmmakers. Black Sabbath blended Bava's gift for sustaining terror with the presence of another master of the game. Boris Karloff hosted this eerie anthology while appearing in one segment as a vampire (the only time Karloff portrayed one). That same year saw Bava's The Whip and the Body, a tale of sadomasochistic love, death and ghostly (?) revenge. Rounding out the year was The Girl Who Knew Too Much, known in its edited and dubbed American version as The Evil Eye and considered by many to be the first giallo film. Bava himself improved upon this the following year with Blood and Black Lace and a plot that served merely to propel a faceless killer's rampage through an assortment of beautiful women. A repellent premise made compelling and terrifying in the hands of a maestro. Bava then set his sights toward science fiction, but with a Gothic slant. Planet of the Vampires (1965) may well have been the partial inspiration for Ridley Scott's Alien (1979) among others. 1971's stylish body-count thriller, A Bay of Blood, must surely have inspired Sean Cunningham's vastly inferior Friday the 13th

(1980). But it was Mario Bava who defined and redefined screen horror in a way that many have attempted to imitate to this day.

From a defining career to a defining *year*...1968. With America in the throes of social revolution, rioting, assassination, war and madness, there were equally disturbing events on screen to reflect much of what was going on around that time. First was director Roman Polanski's *Rosemary's Baby* with Mia Farrow as a young bride whose efforts to protect her unborn child come to naught as said child is made the property of his unholy father, the Devil himself. The defining moment where Evil wins was a stunner, but would become commonplace and overused in the years ahead.

Madness and mass murder were on display that year in director Peter Bogdanovich's *Targets,* where a deceptively clean-cut young man (Tim O'Kelly) goes on a shooting spree, indiscriminately picking off motorists on the freeway and later at a drive-in movie. In attendance, an elderly horror film star played by Boris Karloff (near the end of his own life) meets this new-age terror. *Targets* marked a defining moment of sorts, as the king of classic horror passed the torch to a new generation, part of an era of real-life horror that was sadly passing him by, just as it did with his character in the film.

Death itself would not halt *The Night of the Living Dead*, director George Romero's gripping, low-budget blend of social comment and flesh-eating zombies. A young black man takes charge of a group of people trapped inside a house besieged by cannibalistic corpses, only to be shot dead for his efforts by a band of vigilantes who presume he's an undead enemy.

Mankind had blown it and finally blown it *up*. The future looked bleak indeed on the *Planet of the Apes* where intelligent talking simians were the dominant life form while non-speaking humans were slaves.

For all the doom and gloom represented by 1968's other key offerings, there was a ray of hope for the future with Stanley Kubrick's *2001: A Space Odyssey*. Amid the wonders was technology run amok in the form of the HAL9000 computer. The film's eye-catching visuals would set standards for sci-fi blockbusters to come.

Horror, science fiction and fantasy are ever evolving, and the trends established by Bava and his predecessors, and later by the handful of trailblazers in 1968, merged in ways that would seem fresh while retaining the familiar.

The nature-in-revolt theme of *The Birds* would mingle with ecology-minded issues of the 1970s to give birth to a menagerie of monstrosities, from frogs and smog monsters to giant rabbits and other creatures great and small.

**The future looks bleak indeed on *The Planet of the Apes*.**

Combine the supernatural elements and "Evil wins" approach of *Rosemary's Baby* with a serial killer plot and you have *The Omen* (1976). By then, another defining period in horror history transpired… that of the horror blockbuster. *The Exorcist* (1973) made a hell of a lot of money and, in turn, led to a number of devilish imitations, mostly misfires. It also heralded the demise of what some consider the Silver Age of Horror. Roger Corman had long since gone on to other projects. The prince of horror, Vincent Price, more or less called it quits by the mid-1970s. Hammer Films went out of business. Christopher Lee moved on to mainstream productions. Peter Cushing went strong until the demand for his talent simply subsided midway through the decade.

Along with Universal's prime time TV ad campaign, Steven Spielberg kicked the blockbuster into high gear with a killer shark in *Jaws* (1975). He followed that up with friendly aliens in *Close Encounters of the Third Kind* (1977), cliffhanger and supernatural thrills in *Raiders of the Lost Ark* (1981), another friendly (and more marketable) alien with *E.T., The Extra-Terrestrial* (1982) and the computer-generated (and marketable) dinosaurs of the *Jurassic Park* movies of the '90s. The same year as *Close Encounters* (and since), George Lucas' *Star Wars* and its sequels and prequels have captured the imaginations of science fantasy fans (and toy collectors) of all ages.

*The Hills Have Eyes Part II* continues the story of the deranged desert-dwelling clan.

Running parallel to the blockbusters of the 1970s were some smaller films that drew from the decade previous to unleash some scary hybrids. Blend a bit of Bava violence with Romero's cannibals and Bogdanovich's serial killer and you almost have Tobe Hooper's *Texas Chain Saw Massacre* (1974). A new age of American Gothics and new horror directors was underway. Wes Craven's *Last House on the Left* (1972) was an unsettling account of brutality, murder, outrage and shattered lives, while his *The Hills Have Eyes* (1977) pitted a vacationing average family against a deranged desert-dwelling clan. John Carpenter's *Halloween* (1978) brought the horror back home, while those damned *Friday the 13th* movies took it to summer camp. Through sequels, the young and more impressionable filmgoers were being conditioned to root for the killer! Even our dreams weren't safe in Craven's *A Nightmare on Elm Street* (1984), and the director has since carried on and reinvented his own trend with his 1990s *Scream* pictures, which by this time cleverly reworked the exhausted slasher genre. Since the 1970s and across the sea, Italy's Dario Argento has more closely followed and expanded upon the Bava-style of horror. The age of talented genre directors continues to this day with Peter Jackson, M. Night Shyamalan and others.

While escalating budgets continue to dominate the horror scene, appre-

**Mia Farrow in *Rosemary's Baby*, which demonstrates how evil wins.**

ciation and rediscovery of the classics remain active through another defining moment... the advent of home video and DVD.

As enjoyable as the 1999 version of The Mummy is, take away the expensive trappings and you have the 1931 version, itself still a model of understated terror. Special effects extravaganzas such as the Lord of the Rings epics continue to entertain and make money, as do a wave of films that take an intimately frightening approach to the unseen, including The Sixth Sense (1999), The Others (2001) and Signs (2002). Much of what is old is new, and much of what is new is old. Prior to the past 40 years and ever since, the defining lives and moments have left their mark... through artists who inspire others... through years of turmoil and hope... through decades of transition... with an ongoing appetite for more.
—Joe Winters

1. Boris Karloff and Peter Lorre touring with The Raven at selected theaters.
2. Christopher Lee in two top films of the year, Lord of the Rings: The Two Towers and Star Wars: Attack of the Clones
3. Christopher Lee autographing his book in NYC, as part of his Midnight Marquee Press-sponsored book-signing tour.
4. The Forrest J Ackerman auction in NYC
5. The Famous Monsters Convention in Virginia with many stars in attendance
—Lou46bud

So much has happened in the last 40 years; pretty much all the sci-fi fiction novels of the 1920s and 1930s we've seen come dramatically to life. So, it's difficult to narrow it down to five major events in genre film history, but I'll give it a shot.

1. Videotape and DVD have been named by numerous contributors to this piece, so I'm going to go a little further into the future and name Home Theaters as a major film occurrence. Gary and his friends still trot over to George Stover's musty basement once a week to see rare television shows and the few features not available on DVD on noisy 16mm. However, I much prefer to stay home and watch high quality DVDs in our home theater. Two years ago we decided to make our house a dream home, so with the help of a home equity loan and a home theater company, we now have a state-of-the-art movie theater right in our own home. The screen is 8'x6' and I think there are 9 speakers in the room along with a DLP Dwin projector. This is really Gary's toy, I can only turn it on, but when I saw Annie Get Your Gun, Singin' in the Rain and White Christmas for the first time on the big screen, I hate to admit it, but I actually cried each time. Home Theaters are no longer a dream of the idle rich, but in the reach of most homeowners. Many new home contractors are even offering a home theater

**A state-of-the-art home theater (this one is *not* ours) in every home?**

Ian McKellen as Gandalf from *The Lord of the Rings*

package. Now, all we need is for studios to realize how much more money they can make by beaming first run features into the homes of people like us, commercial theater haters, and we'll really be set.

2. CGI and computer animation. I know it's difficult to replace Ray Harryhausen, who was a god to most Baby Boomer genre fans, but the quality of CGI in films such as *The Two Towers* is simply outstanding. Also, animated films such as *Shrek* were witty eye candy appealing to both children and adults. I can't wait to see *The Chronicles of Narnia* done with a big budget and state-of-the-art CGI.

3. A decidedly negative occurrence has been the newly popular fandom theory that interviews with genre stars are the only worthwhile film writing for film/fanzine articles and books. Another negative trend is the prevalence of books of lists and film encyclopedias that sell for outrageous prices and contain credits, a few photos and a paragraph of plot synopsis. I hate to think genre fans have grown so lazy they will not take the time to read and think about insightful and thought-provoking analysis of films (literary criticism has been a respected genre for hundreds of years, and in our pages, it continues), but instead more people prefer easily done interviews with has-been stars talking about people long dead, people who can't defend themselves, or the creation of boring and easily compiled lists that call themselves research/books. We know *MidMar* readers don't fall into the category, but you are definitely in the minority.

4. The reappearance of Christopher Lee as a major film personality. I'm sure Gary never believed his favorite Dracula would be appearing in *Lord of the Rings* and *Star Wars*, on cereal boxes, collectibles and MTV. If only the other stars such as Bela, Boris, Vincent, Chaney, Jr. and Peter Cushing had lived to see the day when a new batch of influential directors would honor their contribution to horror films with juicy roles in big-budget A films.

5. I would like to think classic horror film conventions, of which FANEX was really the first, other than the two *Famous Monster* Conventions held in New York, made their mark during these past 40 years, but while we began the conventions as a way to meet fellow fans to discuss films and to honor rarely noticed genre actors and directors, I think we let loose a 600-pound gorilla as we have had to watch a noble idea degenerate into a depressing exposition. There are now so many "conventions" held you could actually attend one once a month, most only existing to make a quick buck. Stars have discovered their signature is worth money and have turned into convention vendors, selling their signature and even charging extra for a picture taken with them (how some of the stars literally scream at shows when an eager fan snaps an innocent snapshot). There are still classy stars who truly appreciate meeting their fans such as Jane Adams and Elena Verdugo, but they are few and far between. Intellectual panels and talks have disappeared to be replaced by rock bands, scream queens who have never appeared in a film and dealers rooms composed of toys, wrestling, pornography and serial killer memorabilia. I think the day I saw a baby T-shirt with images of body parts and a tribute to the current killer of the moment, well, I knew the death knell was sounding for FANEX. It was a noble attempt and I hope we brought some pleasure and information to true film fans, but like the poor dinosaurs, our time has seemingly passed and the dark side of the Force has won.

—Susan Svehla

*Star Wars, The Exorcist* and the Emergence of the Genre Blockbuster—Not so long ago, the cinema of the fantastic resided in a lonely and somewhat disreputable corner of the film world. First came *The Exorcist*, a mainstream, big-budgeted horror filled with unsubtle shocks, name performers, graphically realistic makeup and dialogue. Then along came *Star Wars* a few years later, a film that combined the "gee whiz" quality of science fiction with the slam bang action of video games. Oh sure, there were other successful sci-fi films released during the 1970s (*Alien* remains my favorite), but this was the "must see" movie that sent space operas soaring to unprecedented levels of popularity—the mythic element of adventure cinema had returned. Hol-

lywood soon realized there was gold in them thar blockbusters and the world of genre films hasn't been the same since.

The Birth, Death and Resurrection of Atmospheric Horror—In 1963 *The Haunting* was released and it remains one of the most frightening horror movies ever produced, all its bone-numbing chills generated on suggestion, atmosphere and mood (featuring a literal script intended for adult consumption). Then the era of enhanced special visual and makeup effects proliferated the horror cinema, leading to the era of the graphic, ultra-gore, slice and dice mutilation epics where horror no longer was suggested but graphically depicted with all its visceral mayhem painted over the cinematic landscape. Horror film scriptwriting had slipped to appeal solely to adolescents, as the adult mentality was left behind in the emerging *nouveau* horror film market. However, as of late, the atmospheric adult horror movie seems to be making a comeback, just in the nick of time (the 1990s almost killed off the genre, much like the even worse faring Western genre). Movies such as *The Sixth Sense, The Others, The Ring, Session Nine* and *The Devil's Backbone* have elevated the subtlety of cinematography and writing to new highs in modern horror and seem to be encouraging a resurgence of atmospheric horror in the genre once again. This can only be considered a good thing.

The Home Video Revolution—It's a movie lover's dream come true. The latest releases, vintage classics and the quirkiest oddities are yours for the asking thanks to the phenomenal popularity of DVD home video. Hard core horror buffs can now seek out shockers that haven't been viewed since their original release, a trend that has significantly raised the bar in the field of contemporary film criticism. But the most essential aspect of this home video revolution has been the rediscovery of Euro-horror in its subtitled, original length, uncensored formats. Now fans can forget the butchery of Mario Bava's *The Evil Eye* and enjoy *The Girl Who Wasn't There*. We can forget the American International reediting, rescoring of Bava's *Black Sabbath* and enjoy *The Three Faces of Fear* as it deserves to be seen, with stories in the proper order, uncut, featuring the original musical score. We can forget the truncated, poorly dubbed and censored versions of Dario Argento's best work and now see *Suspiria,*

European horror classics such as *Blood and Black Lace* are now available on DVD in uncut versions.

*Halloween*, one of the first and best slasher movies, actually elevates the subgenre.

*Deep Red, Opera, Phenomena*, etc. as they were meant to be seen and heard (in pristine widescreen prints). I formerly disliked Euro-horror for all these reasons, but with archival DVD releases through Image, VCI and Anchor Bay, I am rediscovering the artistry in these modern Italian horror movies that I never was allowed to see before. For me, this has been the biggest eye-opening trend of the past 40 years.

*Friday the 13th* and the Slasher/Body Count Film—The traditional Gothic horror film was on its last legs in the 1970s (Hammer and the innocent drive-in monster romps were being replaced with exploitation and *really* bad cinema) when the slasher film came along and almost killed it off for good. As typified by product such as *Friday the 13th*, the slasher became the thriller for a more jaded era, one that reinvented yesterday's indestructible monsters in the guise of the modern serial killer. Although the heyday of these slice-and-dice epics is now past, their repetitive plots and gore-soaked excesses continue to influence horror cinema today. Please note, films such as *Halloween* and *Black Christmas* and the best of Bava and Argento elevate this subgenre, yet such quality remains the exception as the hacks in the majority sank to the lowest common denominator artistically.

The Emergence of the World Wide Web—As a young film writer, I can remember researching credits in the hefty pages of the Don Wllis, Harris Lentz and Claros Clarens film research/reference guides, encyclopedic masterworks which were the most reliable sources for accurate and complete cast and credits lists (as well as important film facts). However, today, no matter how flawed, infinite research possibilities exist on the World Wide Web, with websites including the Internet Movie Database, the equally impressive Cinebooks movie database on TVGuide.com and other sources of online research which mushroom monthly. True, every database has flaws, and so did the hardprint volumes referenced above. But credits for even regionally released independent productions are a point and click away. For all of us who write or simply research film history, the Internet is a tool unfathomed 40 years ago and one that has become indispensable today. The Internet has extended the influence of film fandom, before confined to small press magazines and the printed page, but now the venom and egos from the letters column spill over to message boards, chat rooms and other websites and online e-zines. So the emergence of the WWW has not been entirely a good thing, unfortunately.
—Gary J. Svehla

# THE WICKER MAN

## FORUM/AGAINST 'EM

In a fit of hyperbole, *Cinefantastique* magazine once called *The Wicker Man* (1973) "the *Citizen Kane* of horror films" (*CFQ*, volume 6, no. 3, 1997, p. 5)—an odd epithet, considering its narrative structure is in no way as complex as Orson Welles' 1941 masterpiece. But *CFQ* was arguing by analogy: *Wicker Man* is to horror films as *Kane* is to cinema. David Bartholomew, the writer of the magazine-length article, was responding to a unique film created by *Sleuth* author Anthony Shaffer and director Robin Hardy—a film shabbily treated by its distributor which never got a proper release, and, at the time, seemed to exist only in truncated form.

Now, in these days of DVD, when formerly obscure films can be re-evaluated and lost footage is frequently restored, *The Wicker Man* can be seen in all of its glory—depending on the disc you buy. Anchor Bay sells the 88-minute theatrical rendition but also offers a limited edition DVD that contains this version and the extended 99-minute edit. Anchor Bay will make available an even longer "Director's Cut" as a separate release later in 2003.

Even in its most abbreviated length, the movie has garnered a fine reputation among many horror-film aficionados—although there are some who question its status as a classic or even a very good genre picture. In this informal FANEX panel, Mark Clark takes on all comers to suggest that *Wicker* is a *Man* of straw…

Contenders, in order of appearance:
Bob Tinnell, filmmaker, *auteur* of *Frankenstein and Me* (1996) and *Believe* (2000), among others.
Mark Clark, critic, author of the forthcoming *Smirk, Sneer, and Scream: Great Acting in Horror Cinema* (McFarland).
Cindy Collins Smith, doyenne of Jack-the-Ripper film criticism and owner of the Hollywood Ripper website (www.hollywoodripper.com).
Jonathan Malcolm Lampley, author of *The Amazing Colossal Book of Horror Trivia* (Nashville, TN: Cumberland House, 1999).
Brian Smith, author of "Selling the House: The Campaign to Hype *House of Frankenstein*" (*Monsters from the Vault*, no. 7, Fall 1998) and "Burning Down the House: *House of Dracula* and the Death of Universal Pictures" (*Monsters from the Vault*, no. 11, Winter/Spring 2001).
Bryan Senn, author of *Golden Horrors* (Jefferson, NC: McFarland & Co., Inc., 1996), among others.

### The First Salvo

Bob Tinnell (dropping an innocent remark): I think *The Wicker Man* is simply a wonderful film. Works for me on every level.

Mark Clark: We're both Pittsburgh Steelers fans, Bob, so let me use a football analogy. To me, *The Wicker Man* is like this: It's the fourth quarter. The Steelers are down by six; they have the ball at the 50, and there are five seconds left on the clock. Tommy Maddox drops back, scrambles to buy time, and then lofts a beautiful 60-yard Hail Mary into the end zone. Plaxico Burress is waiting. He leaps in the air, stretching over the heads of the defenders; the ball hits him on the hands... and he drops it.

No, now that I think about it, it's more like this: Plaxico reaches for the ball, and, suddenly, he's hit in the face with a cream pie! He drops the ball; the Steelers lose, and a Mack Sennett pie fight erupts.

*The Wicker Man* contains a lot of good ideas and one of Christopher Lee's best performances, but the film shoots itself in the foot with some major lapses. First of all, the pagan rites look like something out of bad Andrew Lloyd Webber—I mean, they're just hysterically funny. I can never watch Britt Ekland's "seduction dance" without convulsing with laughter. These absurd moments badly undercut the film's lofty aspirations. They also, for me, make the film not scary in the least. I have some other quibbles, but

"But I started to sympathize with him when it became obvious there was going to be a human sacrifice." Officer Howie confronts the Wicker Man.

my three biggest issues deal with the film's ending:
1. What is the film's ethic? One of my best friends loves *The Wicker Man*. He reads the film as a statement against intolerance. Sergeant Howie (Edward Woodward), who's so secure in his Christian superiority, turns out to be the Fool and pays with his life. Okay, except that the film seems to send just the opposite message: if the islanders are all scheming to commit ritual murder, doesn't that mean Howie was *right*? The film suggests that people from other cultures, or those who do not share your values, are not to be trusted. At the end, I always picture Howie jumping up and down in his wicker prison and screaming, "I told you so!"
2. Then there's the Wicker Man itself. Every time I see this film, I think, "Geez, no wonder they don't have any crops. The whole island's been working for months to build that big, idiotic-looking structure."
3. Also, I resent the way that Howie is dispatched. Not only is the whole burning-Wicker-giant thing just silly, but also the way the action is cut is very cheeky. We never actually have to watch Howie shrieking in agony as his still-living body is consumed in flames. (Compare this to Oliver Reed's awful, fiery demise in *The Devils* [1971].) I guess we're supposed to titter at Howie's naïveté, even though he's going to suffer a gruesome fate for nothing worse than doing his job and trying to save a little girl he thought was in danger. I would rather see Lord Summerisle (Christopher Lee) take a knife at the end of the film and carve Howie's still-beating heart out of his chest (the way the Incas performed their sacrifices). At least that would have been an honest depiction of the kind of brutal act our "heroes" perpetrate at the end.

Cindy Collins Smith: How you respond to Howie has a lot to do with how you "read" the film. I didn't like his smugness. But I started to sympathize with him when it became obvious there was going to be a human sacrifice. (I figured that out pretty early on in the film; I just didn't know that the sacrifice was going to be Howie.)

Mark: I think he's a closed-minded schmuck, but he doesn't deserve to die.

Cindy: No, of course he doesn't deserve to die. You said something earlier about the pagans' silly

"No wonder the pagan customs are silly! It's kind of like a New Age reconstruction of paganism." Christopher Lee as Lord Summerisle

"Sgt. Howie dies for his relgious beliefs, just like a true martyr; Howie never questons his faith."

customs. Well, the depiction of the pagans and their silly customs is part of the point. These aren't people with an ancient, unbroken pagan past. These are people living a 100-year-old paganism made up out of books. It's kind of like a New Age reconstruction of paganism, except that it dates back to the 19th century. No wonder the pagan customs are silly!

And as for the plot to murder... *precisely*! It *is* a murder plot. The Summerislanders don't have the courage of their convictions to kill the king. They don't have the courage of their convictions to choose a *willing* sacrifice... which was part of the criteria for sacrifice in most of the pagan cultures from which these people drew their paganism. So they seduce an *un*willing sacrifice who doesn't even share their faith. According to most pagan beliefs, the sacrifice will *not* work, and they will either have to sacrifice Lord Summerisle next year, continue to seduce ineffectual, unwilling sacrifices from the mainland or give up their "paganism."

Jonathan Malcolm Lampley: I don't see it as a betrayal of their faith. They specifically say they need to find someone who meets all the requirements mentioned (as Howie does). Nothing in the film suggests to me that the pagans are betraying their beliefs by using an unwilling victim—although the point that next year no less a sacrifice than Lord Summerisle himself will do seems added to the film's finale to underscore the filmmakers' ultimate lack of sympathy with the extremist views of the pagans.

Some people "read" *The Wicker Man* as anti-Christian because it seems to take the side of the pagans, who, as Cindy correctly points out, actually practice a relatively recent reinvention of paganism. But Jeff Thompson and his parents, who saw the film for the first time on video a few years ago, thought the film was pro-Christian! As Jeff points out, Sgt. Howie dies for his religious beliefs, just like a true martyr; Howie never abandons or questions his faith, and he follows his beliefs, right or wrong, until the end. Not many people can say that these days!

Mark: Apparently the film can be read either way. It's difficult for me to tell what the intent truly was, because I don't particularly like or identify with any of the people in this film.

Jonathan: I believe that *The Wicker Man* is anti-fanaticism, not pro- or anti-Christianity (or paganism). Howie is supposed to be a jerk, and he is—he has *no* respect for the beliefs of others, and his zeal to solve the mystery comes from a very ambivalent motivation: Yes, as a Christian and as a cop, Howie feels it's his duty to "save" Rowan Morrison (Geraldine

Cow-per), but he's also planning to bring the forces of British law and order down on the island and "force" the pagans to accept the "normal" way of life. Several times he warns the islanders of his intentions to report their activities to the highest authorities; it is implied that these authorities will make things "right," including correcting the "unreasonable" beliefs of the islanders.

Mark: Believe it or not, I have never even thought about *The Wicker Man* in terms of it being pro- or anti-Christian. I've always thought of it as pro- or anti-tolerance. My friend Ken Hardin reads the film as a statement against intolerance. As I said, I don't think that holds up. The film actually seems pro-*in*tolerance! I didn't really think of it as pro-Christian because I never equate intolerance with Christianity, or with any specific belief system. (It may or may not apply to any religion.)

I suppose, if the film's saying, both of these points of view are wrong, that would explain the ambivalence of the story's resolution, and also the utter lack of likeable characters in the story. I'll keep that in mind, the next time I see the movie. Although

"As a Christian and as a cop, Howie feels it's his duty to 'save' Rowan Morrison." Geraldine Cowper plays Rowan Morrison, the film's missing girl.

making a movie where audiences wind up having sympathy for nobody seems a little counter-intuitive.

Jonathan: When we consider that *The Wicker Man* was released during the early '70s, a time when '60s' anti-establishmentism was still quite fresh in everybody's mind, it is reasonable to assume the producers want us to dislike Howie and even vicariously share in his humiliation, ridicule, and, ultimately, his destruction. Yet, when we figure out that these goofy, "New Age" pagans really intend to sacrifice Howie, we experience a reversal of sympathies, which is a neat and difficult trick for filmmakers to pull off, but which I really enjoy when I see it happening (as it does in *The Others* [2002] and *The Usual Suspects* [1995], two fine and tricky films whose "twist" endings and sympathy shifts took me totally by surprise—but I never see the endings coming of good movies). Initially, just because of their beliefs, the Summerisle residents—all of whom are nice folks, specifi-

"We suddenly see Summerisle and his gang for what they are: psychotics, religious fanatics..." Christopher Lee as Lord Summerisle participates in a pagan rite.

"The Britt Ekland dance sequence is pretty hilarious—but it is necessary to show Howie's 'last temptation'."

cally cast and directed to seem like normal rural Scots—are treated shabbily by Howie, the symbol of British authority (and thus a symbol of oppression, as all *Braveheart* [1995] fans doubtless note). Yet, at the end, we suddenly see Summerisle and his gang for what they are: psychotics, religious fanatics every bit as determined as Howie to fulfill the requirements of their extremist religion, no matter who gets in the way. The film shows us that extremist belief systems, especially religions, are bad.

So, in the end, I buy the bizarre plot, and I love the cast, especially Lee and Woodward, but Ekland does a good job, too. I really dig the music—this film is really a horror/mystery/musical with suggestions of the old miracle plays thrown in for good measure. I agree that the Ekland dance sequence is pretty hilarious—but it is necessary to show Howie's "last temptation."

### The Extended Version: Better, or Just Longer?

Mark: After numerous *Wicker Man* fans told me, "If you haven't seen the extended version, you haven't seen the film," I finally saw the restored 99-minute version of *The Wicker Man*. Here's my verdict:

The cut version is superior to this restoration in every respect. In fact, now that I've seen the longer version, I think the short version is one of the most judicious and effective editing jobs I've ever seen. Surprisingly, the longer version doesn't seem much longer than the short version. Although the extended version is 11 minutes longer, it doesn't feel much longer; its tempo remains good. So the trims didn't have a dramatic impact on the movie's pacing. However, the edited version makes a number of more profound improvements on the movie's dramatic structure.

Jonathan: Wow. We so totally disagree on this point. I think the short version is *very* inferior to the longer cut.

### The Pre-Credit Sequence

Mark: About half of the additional footage is concentrated on a pre-credit sequence that shows Howie puttering around on the mainland, before his trip to Summerisle. In this version, we learn immediately that the inspector is a self-righteous prig. In the short version, we know nothing about Howie when he steps out of his seaplane. As a result, in the short version, we learn about Howie while Howie learns about the villagers. This is a much more interesting narrative structure.

Brian Smith: There are two crucial things that we need to know about Howie: He is a devout Christian, and he is a virgin. Without the prologue

"The other major scene... is the one where Lord Summerisle brings a young boy for Willow to deflower."

on the mainland, we wouldn't really know the depth of his religious belief. Just seeing his reaction to the paganism on Summerisle doesn't really tell you whether Howie himself is a very religious person. And it would be difficult to deal with the virginity issue in a way that wasn't awkward or forced.

Mark: I really didn't have any problem gleaning Howie's religious fervor. The mere fact that he doesn't join in the first orgy he stumbles across (most men would climb aboard) speaks volumes in and of itself. I understand the issue with Howie's virginity, but I'm willing to make that small leap of faith here in order to avoid having one scene after another basically wallop me over the head with something I already learned during the first four minutes of the film.

Plus, since the longer version spoon-feeds us everything we need to know about Howie up front, many of the later sequences become repetitive and pointless. Either the opening sequence or some of the scenes with the villagers needed to go, and I think it made much more sense to cut the pre-credit sequence.

Bryan Senn: As Brian points out, it is essential that we know Howie is a virgin, and, in the prologue, his sniggering colleagues imply this via a dialogue exchange. So there *is* purpose to it.

Mark: Yes, but on balance it hurts the piece, and the function it serves isn't absolutely essential to our understanding of the character or the story. I don't think it's absolutely critical that someone tells us Howie is a virgin. He avoids sex, acts like a prig, and we're told at the end that he's a virgin. I'm willing to accept that he is, based on the behavior he's demonstrated throughout the course of the film. I'm willing to make that leap of faith.

Besides, I don't really think we must have everything handed to us, or know all the answers. For instance, even with the inclusion of the cut scenes, we're still left wondering about a whole slew of other issues. The biggest of these is how did the islanders know Howie so well and select him as the target for this little charade? That, to me, is a much bigger leap of faith than accepting that Howie is a virgin without having someone flat-out say so. Everything points to Howie's virginity. But nothing supports the idea that residents of this incredibly insular community are traveling off-island to gather intelligence on potential victims or have some sort of network of informants to spot potential sacrifices for them.

We have to take some things at face value and/or suspend disbelief. I don't think anything is gained by the opening sequence that the viewer doesn't learn later, with a little acceptance and suspension of disbelief.

Jonathan: I think the pre-credit sequence is absolutely necessary. The nice bit where Howie wipes "Jesus saves" off the wall shows that Howie is a by-the-book cop whose dedication to the job surpasses even his dedication to God. Later on, we will see this attitude subtly reversed when Howie starts breaking and entering and taking every opportunity to emphasize his religious beliefs to the islanders.

Mark: You read a great deal into Howie's single line about "a time and a place for everything." All I learn about Howie from the pre-credit sequence is that he's a devout Christian and an uptight dweeb, all of which comes across perfectly well later in the film. And even if there is some sort of shift in his priorities, I don't agree that that's essential to our understanding of the character or his motivation. Clearly, the villagers and their customs, not to mention their lack of cooperation, increasingly frustrate him and this ultimately causes him to proceed rashly. I really don't think it makes a difference whether or not that additional element is present because the final effect is the same.

### The Defloration Scene

Mark: The other major scene that's added back in is the one where Lord Summerisle brings a young boy for Willow (Britt Ekland) to deflower. (Lucky kid.) In the short version, characters talk about Lord Summerisle frequently, but he doesn't actually appear until fairly late in the film. In order to see Summerisle, Woodward has to travel to Summerisle's castle, across his estate, through his door, down his hallway, etc. All this buildup makes Summerisle seem even more imposing. (It's the Harry Lime effect—the power of the delayed entrance.) The long version sacrifices this quite effective device, and for what? Summerisle, after sending the boy up to Willow, stands around in the garden, reading a soliloquy to no one in particular while watching a couple of copulating snails. One of the worst scenes included in either version of the film! Only Ekland's side-splittingly hilarious "seduction dance" is worse.

Brian: Am I the only one who likes Ekland's nude dance?

Mark: Well, I like that she's nude...

Bryan: I find it quite—ahem!—intriguing, too (and it fits in well with the paganistic, *outré* tone, I think).

Jonathan: In the short version, Britt's seduction dance—which doesn't really work for me, either, by the way—is moved up to the film's beginning, which totally destroys the "last-temptation-of-Howie" effect for which Hardy was striving and makes the film seem far more exploitive. I don't remember if the short version keeps Lee's soliloquy—

Mark: It doesn't.

Jonathan: But I love that bit. It's kind of funny, sure, but it's also a very interesting insight into Summerisle's mindset—and, since we don't actually get a good look at Lee at this point, the sequence builds up suspense regarding his eventual appearance.

Mark: Don't get a good look? He's got a series of close-ups, intercut with those shots of the hormonal snails.

Jonathan: Okay, Lee has some close-ups, but, in most of those scenes, he's always partially obscured by shadow.

Brian: I don't think that showing Summerisle briefly here detracts from the build-up to his later meeting with Howie. And this scene with the boy and Ekland is important—it's a fertility ritual that foreshadows the fertility ritual at the film's end.

Mark: We know some sort of scary, secret rite is in the works. I don't think we need to know more. Matter of fact, I *like* that we don't know more. Sometimes it's more interesting when you're left to wonder and worry.

"Harrowing, absorbing, eerie and erotic...A must-see!"
~ Leonard Maltin

a chicken that had no bone..." And Bluto comes over, grabs the guy's guitar and smashes it? Well, that's my reaction to the hippy-dippy music in *Wicker Man*. I find it insipid and annoying. I could probably stand it if it were confined to the soundtrack itself, but I simply can't keep from convulsing with laughter during the scenes where the whole cast bursts into song. I *like* musicals, but I don't think you can make a musical *scary*. At least, I've never seen one that was scary, and this one certainly isn't.

Brian: I agree that it would be difficult to like the movie if you don't like, or can't at least tolerate, the music. The music is integral to the movie. But I don't think the music has an impact one way or another on how scary the film is. *The Wicker Man* isn't trying to be scary. It has a few shocking moments, but essentially it's a puzzle, a mystery with a twist ending. If you took all of the music out, the film still wouldn't be very scary.

Mark: I'm not so sure about that. There are sequences—especially toward the end—that seem calculated to frighten. Some of them nearly work—like the sight of the villagers, in their festival masks, popping up over the horizon and watching Howie in his seaplane when he tries to leave. That's a very evocative shot. I actually think, if they had eliminated the singing and dancing and made some other revisions to lend the picture a different tone, this might have been a very scary film. Envision a version by Terry Fisher, or maybe George Romero. Or at least in that style! *That* would be scary.

Brian: The soliloquy to the snails, now that you point it out, does seem a little silly.

Jonathan: I *like* the copulating snails. It is a very strange, bizarre, and funny sequence—and that is part of the charm of *The Wicker Man*. Its eccentric use of imagery and its thematic versatility are what make the picture so endlessly fascinating.

### The Musical Numbers

Mark: In the extended version, the film's ludicrous musical numbers drone on even longer, particularly the ones in the bar.

Jonathan: What can I say? I really like the music in *The Wicker Man*.

Brian: I like the musical numbers—but that's just a matter of taste.

Mark: I think liking the musical numbers is absolutely essential to liking the film. The music is a major drawback for me. Remember *Animal House* (1978)? The scene where the little folkie geek on the steps is serenading his girlfriend: "I gave my love

Brian: As for the scenes when the cast burst into song—remember, Summerisle is a place that has deliberately separated itself from modern society. There's no radio or TV. The Summerislanders provide their own entertainment. In a pre-mass-media culture, it would be a very common thing for people to gather at a pub and sing bawdy songs together. We're conditioned to think that sort of spontaneous group singing is ridiculous and phony, something that only happens in musicals. But if you think of Summerisle as a society that, in many ways, is still in the 19th century, you may be able to watch those scenes without bursting into laughter. You'll probably still feel they're insipid and annoying, but at least you won't think they're unintentionally funny.

Mark: There's absolutely no way I can listen to drivel like "Gently Johnny" and that Maypole song without laughing, no matter what century the Summerisleans are stuck in. I know I sound like I'm totally down on this movie, but, actually, there are many things in it I like. For me, though, there's simply no getting around the fact that big chunks of this film seem just goofy as hell. I think it's very uneven.

**The Scene with the Physician**

Mark: Take, for example, the scene with the physician: The doctor has a funny line, but, as he points out, the Inspector knows full well that the death certificates would be kept at the records office. Therefore, it makes no sense that Howie comes to him looking for these documents—unless the function of this scene is to inform us that Howie is an idiot. But, despite his other faults, I don't think we're supposed to think that he's a complete numbskull.

Jonathan: I grant you that Howie knows he needs to go look at the records—I write this scene off as the director thinking that perhaps ordinary moviegoers would not know this. (Such expository scenes are often necessary, but they do tend to be annoying.)

Brian: The scene with the physician is probably unnecessary—although the vipers in the medical bag are a great image.

Mark: Oh, yeah. I really like everything about that scene, actually, but it doesn't advance the plot at all and really makes no narrative sense. But the doctor is funny, and all the little touches are great.

**The Bottom Line**

Mark: There isn't a single scene added back into the extended version that strengthens the film in any way. As I see it, *The Wicker Man* in its short version is a two- to two-and-a-half- star movie (on a four-star scale) and probably a one-and-a-half to two-star movie in its extended form.

Jonathan: The longer version of *The Wicker Man* is a five-star film—a classic of cinema. The short version I saw is bastardization unworthy of ranking, but I could give it two stars since so much of what I love about *Wicker Man* survives the cutting process.

Mark: I wouldn't grant any version of *The Wicker Man* five stars (or four stars, depending on your scale). I wouldn't call the shorter version a "bastardization." I think it's far superior. Moreover, nothing essential is removed in it, and some of the changes actually improve the dramatic structure of the piece. The shorter is better than the longer, but neither one is anything worth writing home about.

Jonathan: *The Wicker Man* has depths that one could write *dissertations* about.

Mark: And if you write 'em, Jonathan, I'm sure they would be fun to read. But I'll definitely leave those to you.

**And the Last Word Falls to the Man Whose Innocent Remark Started It All…**

Bob: I know that some folks are down on the film these days for its dated appearance, occasional schizophrenic storytelling, and, of course, the musical numbers. But I must say that, after all this time, I find it a fresh and thoughtful film that still packs a punch even after you know the twist.

*The Wicker Man* is interesting to me for a variety of reasons. In the early 1980s, when I finally got to see it, I thought the Edward Woodward character was a loser and a fool. Now that I've made my way back to God and church, I see him as a noble martyr. The film didn't change, of course. Guess my different reading of the film has changed how I respond to Howie, like Cindy says.

The film's attention to detail is quite impressive. The pagan-influenced cakes on display, the way the islanders' "religion" seems to be a part of every aspect of their lives, the well-thought-out and logical rules that govern their worship and sacrifice—all of these things make the whole of the experience seem almost documentary in execution. Now think about *The Blair Witch Project* (1999): similar goals and, at times, similar attempts at execution—but always only *attempts*.

The film's imagery is often inspired. The hare in the coffin, the nude woman weeping on the tombstone, the Maypole sequence (yes, you chuckle at first, but it gains power as it goes along), the cask floating in the ocean, the woman suckling the babe in the ruins of the church. And of course, the Wicker Man himself. Quite stunning.

Now I'm not claiming the film is a masterpiece or anywhere near perfect. It stumbles—often. The Britt Ekland dance, which *Playboy* once lauded for its eroticism, is, in fact, pretty laughable and embarrassing. At times this picture *is* a musical. But it has much to offer on many levels and very interesting performances, to boot—particularly those of Woodward and Christopher Lee.

Final thoughts: My wife, Shannon, absolutely hated the picture. Just ragged on it the whole way through. Then she proceeded to talk about it the rest of the evening and several times the next day as we were driving around running errands. Her final analysis? "I guess it must be a good film because I can't stop thinking about it, and it in turn makes me think of other things that relate to it."

I don't know if that's a good definition of a good film, but it'll do for an interesting one.

# RETURN OF THE APE MAN

## Revisiting the Wartime Savage from a Post-Modern Perspective— Wink, Wink, Nudge, Nudge...

by Erich Kuersten

Most film scholars shamefully overlook the recurring themes of wartime dehumanization and post-modernism in the *oeuvre* of infamous "quickie" producer Sam Katzman. They prefer to waste their time analyzing the more obvious explorations by the likes of Kubrick, Godard and Welles. Unjustly so! I have just seen the neglected 1944 cheapie *The Return of the Ape Man*, and at first glance, yes, it's pretty damn bad, but under the same examination usually reserved for acknowledged masterpieces, *Return of the Ape Man* yields a complex and fascinating study of the masculine psyche worthy of exploration.

Like most thawed caveman movies, there is a feeling of stifling sadness to the future to which the titular ape man "returns." The "present" (or the ape man's future) is here viewed entirely within obvious film sets, uniformly undernourished and unrealistic. Perhaps this is due to the no-frills budgetary approach generally associated with this sort of gorilla-filmmaking, but even for a low-budget thriller, this movie's sets are awfully bare. Our titular caveman has awakened into a world that remains entirely and obviously within the confines of a soundstage, a world with all the drab flatness of a bad dream. And like a dream, all the characters are merely aspects of one dreamer, archetypes of a masculine unconsciousness trying to transcend its prison.

Not a sequel to Monogram's *The Ape Man,* the "return" in the title may as well refer to the vanquishing and inevitable re-appearance of the savage. Made in 1944 (during W.W.II), a time when the ape man archetype returned in not just this B-movie, but in Europe, where men have reverted to killers, becoming in themselves as post-modern as the architecture they were toppling around them. In this film, primitive, civilized and infantile aspects of the self stand next to each other in a dream basement, like the many stages of astronaut Bowman interacting at the conclusion of Kubrick's widely praised *2001: A Space Odyssey.* The ape man is the past unleashed into the present, needing to be successfully integrated into a prosperous future, a necessary new ingredient for adaptation to a changing world. The return of the ape man completes a cyclic form, opening the stairwell to a new "floor" of evolution, a floor where man's veneer of culture caves in on itself, and savagery emerges from its unconscious prison.

The movie's title cards depict a gorilla behind bars; the beast is locked away in all of us. We get excited at the credits, since we are promised the ac-

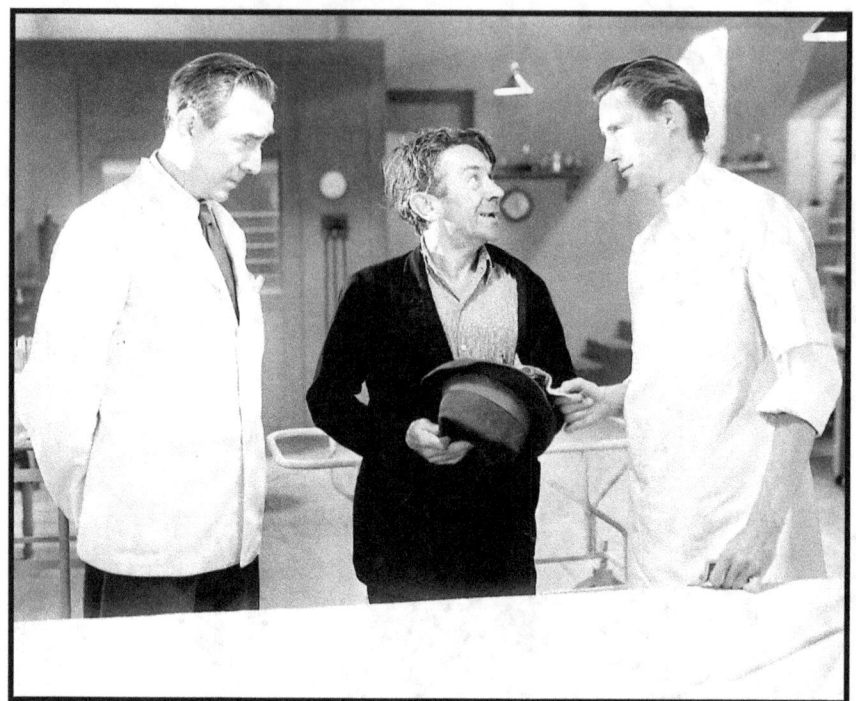

How can a man with no address be truly "missing?" Bela Lugosi, John Carradine and Ernie Adams

tor George Zucco as one aspect of the ape man (he will in fact never appear). We fade into a shot of the local paper: It reads that a local vagrant is missing and the "residents of his park bench are beginning to worry." Right off, the world of this movie is established as fragmented, and surreal. When has any newspaper ever written about a missing vagrant? How can a man with no address be truly "missing?" It doesn't make sense. The effect of this nonsensical opener is to paralyze the conscious mind of the viewer, accessing the unconscious dream-self. Everyone in the movie is "missing" something, since they are all archetypal aspects of one consciousness. Our next image is of a round white clock or thermometer, with its black arm pointed due south, splitting the round symbol in half. Like a Zen "ying/yang," this sets the stage for the parade of split/opposites we will later encounter.

Next we see Bela Lugosi as Dr. Dexter and John Carradine as his friend/colleague Dr. Gilmore, working down in the basement in the lab. Dexter and Gilmore are thawing out the missing transient after a four-month test freezes. Excited about their success in reviving the frozen hobo, they talk about what it would mean to revive someone frozen for a hundred years or more. Realizing they can't wait that long to find out, they set out to the Arctic to find a pre-frozen caveman.

We cut to a rear-projected indoor Arctic. Surrounded by stock footage, Dexter and Gilmore argue over their progress. It has been 10 months and they have found nothing. A look at their two assistants in the background, gently waving their pickaxes at the floor, and we understand why they have had so little success. A dream-like feeling of futility and unreality pervades. Dr. Gilmore, beginning to show his adult "difference" from Dexter, says he wants to go home; he misses his wife. Dr. Gilmore is an "adult" with sexual urges whereas Dexter is the boy interested only in finding his monkey man. "I am married to science," Dexter says. Dexter is on the "path" to self-discovery via science. The sterilized and harnessed Gilmore only wants to give up and go sulking back to his wife.

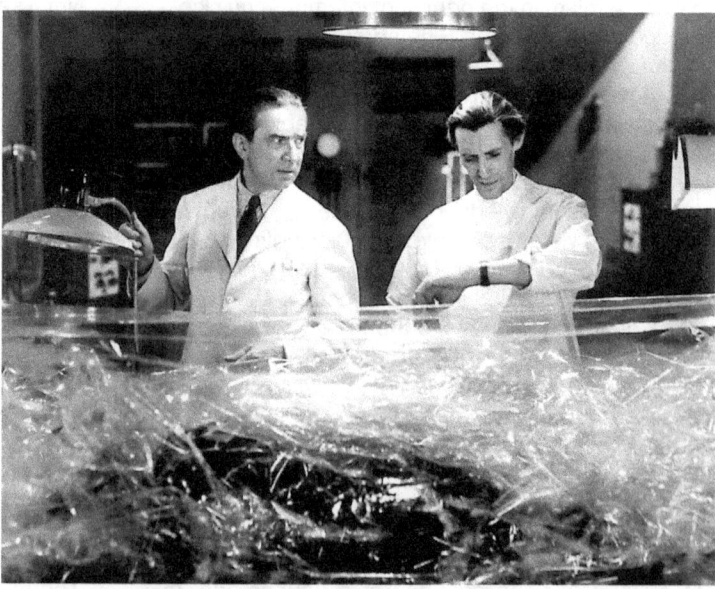

Dexter wants the ape man all to himself, to harness and incorporate it, society and personal safety be damned.

Before these two can be separated, an ape man is found. Back home in the basement, Dexter melts the ice block encasing it with a blowtorch, eager to open his new toy. Gilmore seems more interested in getting it over to the Museum of Natural History. He is civilized man at his weakest, anxious to turn away from discovery and its inherent danger. Dexter, on the other hand, is contemptuous of this attitude. He wants the ape man all to himself, to harness it and incorporate it, society and personal safety be damned.

The ape man comes alive as soon as he is thawed, and attacks them. Accessing the wild-man archetype is one thing, controlling it another. Dexter backs it into a cage ("returning" or repressing this newly released power) with a blowtorch. Fire is ice's opposite and the symbol of man's evolution and progress as well as destruction. Dexter has the idea of transplanting a part of someone else's brain into the ape man's skull. This is a unique variant from the plot of most of these gorilla brain transplant films, for he only wants to use *some* of the new brain. This unusual approach further cements our theory, as his aim is to unify disparate elements of the psyche into a timeless, post-modern man.

By now these two boys are late for a dinner party. We leave them in the basement and zip up the street to Gilmore's house where we meet his wife Hilda, his niece Ann and Ann's fiancé, Steve Rogers. The party looks like it will be exceedingly dull. Cutting back to the two scientists in the lab, it is made obvious that neither one of them really wants to leave their project and tread upstairs for the mother's call of "dinner-time." But Dexter has promised Gilmore, who is duty-bound to his matriarchal ruler, Hilda. She is the pillar of culture and civilization, his master in the way Dexter is trying to be the master of the ape man. Appropriately, Hilda sees Bela's Dr. Dexter as a threat to her position of dominance, a "bad influence" with whom she doesn't want her "son" associating.

Bela's character of Dr. Dexter is, of course, the very definition of a bad-influence friend. He

Bela Lugosi as Dr. Dexter and John Carradine as his friend/colleague Dr. Gilmore

certainly has no sense of empathy. However his lack of respect for human life in the context of the film is understandable. All the other characters are mono-dimensional automatons. One look at Dexter impatiently smoking a fat cigar after dinner and his psychopathology becomes apparent. It is as if he realizes he is in a dream and no longer feels compassion for those around him. "Some people's brains would never be missed," he comments in the movie's one legitimately funny moment. He is like a boy anxious for dinner to be over so he can resume working on his model down in the basement. He sees the other guests purely as transplantable brains on stilts.

At this point, Aunt Hilda, the organ grinder, urges her trained monkey Gilmore to the piano. While Gilmore dutifully bangs away at the "Autumn Sonata," Dexter seizes his opportunity. He slyly asks Steven to drive him home, and then invites him in for a drink, which he drugs, thus knocking him out. A lot of very slow screen time then unravels as Dexter carries Steve to the basement, lays him on the table and changes out of his dinner jacket into his white lab coat. Some will dismiss this lengthy stretch as mere padding, but the careful critic knows there are always deeper meanings, even in the randomness of cheap cinema. The black/white coat switching being in this instance an insight into Dexter's dual nature, the savage and the civilized being as interchangeable as a

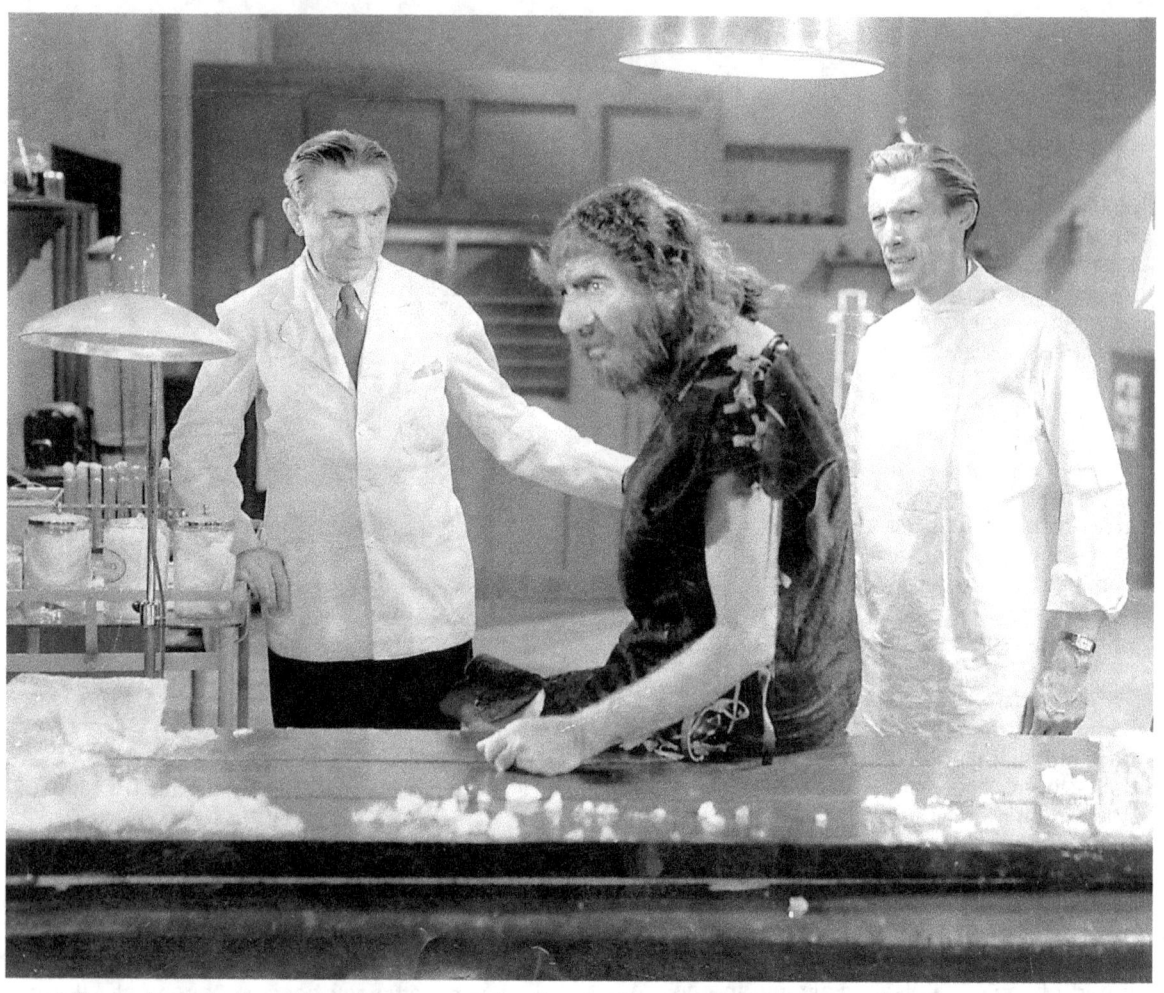

**Dexter is on the "path" to self-discovery via science. The sterilized Gilmore only wants to give up.**

coat, foreshadowing the impending operation itself. However, no sooner does he have his white coat on, than Gilmore sneaks up behind him with a gun.

**Gilmore**: That was the most contemptible thing a man could ever do to his friend.
**Dexter**: My dear Gilmore…
**Gilmore**: You deliberately tried to murder someone dear to me!
**Dexter**: He might not have died.
**Gilmore**: That's a comforting thought to you. Do you see what it might mean to that boy? If he lived the operation would leave him an idiot!
**Dexter**: And what about science?

We get our first glimpse of Dexter's childlike "but it's all for science" rationalization and also Gilmore's lack of a suitable response to a situation outside society's norm. The brave thing for Gilmore to do would be to call the police right then, but that would require a masculine decisiveness that civilization has eroded in him. Instead he saunters off, advising Dexter to kill the ape man, and thus symbolically neuter himself the way Gilmore has. Dexter replies in a typically adolescent manner. "When I need advice from you I will ask for it," then when Gilmore leaves, Dexter mutters like an angry child: "You'll pay for this!"

Gilmore returns to the safety of his home while Dexter plots a trap with electricity (he is an adept of both fire and ice). The ape man is used as guinea pig in the trap planned for Gilmore, and then, his bars bendable as rubber (in Dexter's "house," the unconscious is not well repressed), escapes through the basement window. However, he soon finds that in this "civilized" world, there no longer is any outdoors in which to escape. The exteriors are so clearly and obviously sets, barely decorated and almost completely deserted. The ape man finds a woman to menace, however, and an idiotic cop on the beat, who hilariously can't decipher which of them is the threat. "Break it up you two" he yells, pushing the woman away. The ape man kills the cop with one of the phoniest looking punches in all of cinema. Dexter has now come out into the street and we see him

"So my self-righteous friend was going to tell the police, eh? You trusting, stupid fool."

calmly strolling along with his blowtorch. He finds the ape man hunched over the form of the cop. He puts his arm consolingly around the ape man to lead him back home. "You brainless fool, get out! Get home!" he says. Suddenly, when he remembers he should be brandishing the blowtorch, he waves it menacingly, and the ape man snaps out of his stupor to resume his pose of harried, fearful savage. The ape man is now revealed to be bonded in some way to Dexter, his sadistic "father." Dexter's home is the ape man's prison. He is both safe and trapped, the same fate as his mirror opposite, Gilmore, suffers at his house up the street.

Note that we have already heard much use of the words "idiot" and "fool," reflecting the pre-adolescent mindset of many of the characters. Name-calling is a childhood weapon, a means of establishing dominance. Coupled with the amateurish, child-like play "fighting" that passes for action in the movie, we feel that in this dream, every male character is a child and this is all dream/play or regressive drama therapy.

Fade to morning of the next day as Gilmore cracks open his morning paper to read the headlines: "Evidence of Brute Force in Slaying of Policeman!" He puts down his paper to answer the phone. A delighted Dexter is on the line, voice laden with false pathos over the incident; "it's terrible."

"I was just about to finish my breakfast and go to the police," Gilmore replies, passionlessly. You would think the fact that a prehistoric man he helped thaw out has recently murdered a policeman might inspire him to phone the cops before continuing with his breakfast, even cause him to raise his voice, but *not* our Gilmore. A very long pause in the film begins as Gilmore seemingly listens to something Dexter is saying, but the blankness on Carradine's face is astonishing. More than ever, in these long seconds of dead air, his conception of Gilmore as a civilized automaton is affirmed. Eventually he agrees to come right over and help Dexter dispose of the ape man.

On the way out his wife reminds him, "Don't forget the concert this afternoon." The matriarchal overseer is cracking her whip in a gentle reminder

The "bonds" of Gilmore are easily escapable but Gilmore does not test his bonds, to escape.

that, though ape men may run rampant at the Dexter house, Gilmore is one monkey who is most definitely on a leash.

Down in the basement Gilmore refuses to shake hands with Dexter. "I wouldn't have come for any other reason than the killing of the ape," he says. The civilized adult will not "return" for any reason except to destroy forever the reminder of his savage past. He has agreed to reverse his forward evolution and re-enter the basement of pre-adolescent experimentation only if it will mean permanently silencing the jailed savage within. Of course, this is a trap that civilized man has been falling into time and time again. And on cue, Dexter paralyzes him. "So my self-righteous friend was going to tell the police, eh? You trusting, stupid fool." Gilmore is now the fool, and will become the "idiot," a fate he saved his future son-in-law from the night before.

Dexter begins to bind the paralyzed Gilmore in one of the most unconvincing tie-up jobs in screen history. "The ape man, after I've finished with him, will no longer have the primitive instinct to kill," Dexter explains. "He'll be a righteous citizen, just like you are… you know why? Because part of your brain— the righteous part, will be in him." The ape man with Gilmore's brain will be similar in many ways to Dexter himself, an incorporation of civilized and savage elements. Dexter predicts sarcastically that he will be even better, since he will have "morals." Though he is hardly tied up at all, Gilmore cannot resist Dexter's commands, displaying only tired resignation. "I'm glad it's me," he confesses. "I feel partly responsible for this whole mess." The complete repression of his natural instincts has caused a rift in the masculine psyche of which all the male characters in the film are somehow part. In allowing himself to become isolated at the top of the civilization ladder, he has let himself grow stagnant as a man.

"Spoken like a true scientist," says Dexter. Though he has betrayed his true nature by becoming a trained "monkey-suit" wearing robot, Gilmore still can, by submitting to this operation, aid masculine "science." Dexter's sewing a piece of Gilmore's brain into the wild man will not just tame the wild-man, but untame Gilmore.

Dexter helps him onto the table to begin his operation. As we cut back and forth to reaction shots from the ape man, the scene takes on decidedly pre-sexual S/M proportions. The "bonds" of Gilmore are easily escapable, and the bars of the ape man's prison are just as easily removable. The fact that neither tests his/its bonds to escape shows an agreed upon sense of imagination among the three. They play like children acting out a horror movie they've just seen on TV.

Back at the Gilmore house, the civilized family waits for Dad to come home so they can go to the concert. Without their father figure, the family automata cannot move forward. The head of the household is essentially neutered, but still the head. They wonder what to do, agree they should do something but do nothing. They are just as paralyzed as Gilmore himself. Back to Dexter's basement: The partial brain transplant is already over and Dexter is trying to communicate with his now semi-cultured ape man. This Gilmore/savage construct cannot seem to remember much of either identity, however.

"These things take a little time," Dexter assures him in a comforting, fatherly tone. But when he suggests another operation, the ape man runs off, shrieking. Once again it is "out" in the "street," but of course it can only go back to the Gilmore house (the closeness of the two houses once again has a childish parallel, like two neighbor children who are always visiting each other.).

The cops arrive and are shown to be inept, ineffectual enforcers of society.

Ann suggests calling the police because she is worried about her uncle, but Aunt Hilda forbids it, saying, "That would only cause a scandal." We are reminded of H.G. Wells' Eloi in *The Time Machine*, for whom the most rudimentary survival skills have been lost through over-civilization. Meanwhile upstairs, the ape man crawls into the house, sees the piano and begins playing. Hilda comes into the room; the ape strangles her. He runs off, chased by Mark. The cops come. In an interesting blooper Ann mispronounces the word fiancée. She says to the police, "My fiancé (*fee-ance*) chased him across the garden." With this mispronunciation, Ann reveals her difference from the other female, the devouring mother Hilda. Like the men in the film, she is "playing" and doesn't know how to pronounce words of adulthood.

The cops arrive and are shown to be inept, ineffectual enforcers of society. They look at the body of Aunt Hilda and try to figure out the motive or cause of the death. "Just plain murder by the looks of it," one deduces.

Then in the garden. "Hey Sarge, a footprint"

"Nah, it looks too big to be real," says the Sergeant. Like the Gilmore family, they have lost the

Policemen are all living in denial of that which doesn't conform.

**MIDNIGHT MARQUEE #69/70**     **81**

*Dexter's home is the ape man's prison. The ape man is both safe and trapped.*

ability to think outside the parameters of their stagnant culture. Because the footprint is big, it can't be real. They are all living in denial of that which doesn't conform.

The ape man/Gilmore now returns to Dexter's basement. Dexter admonishes him like a weary, harried husband, like Ricky Ricardo might chastise an errant Lucille Ball

**Dexter**: Where have you been?
**Ape Man**: (grumbles)… my home.
**Dexter**: Did you… kill somebody again?
**Ape Man**: I killed Hilda.
**Dexter**: Mrs. Gilmore? Why did you kill her?
**Ape Man**: (pause) …didn't mean to.

But of course he did… the wild ape rebelling against his zookeeper, "returned" ape man reclaiming the phallus his civilized double surrendered to the devouring "mother."

Steve and the cops converge on Dexter's place. Steve is beginning to forge, under the pressure of this situation, his character as a man. Dexter answers the door: "Monster? I don't know what you're talking about?" He has locked the ape man behind a sliding wall in the basement, and when the cops come down to search it, Dexter's confidence gradually crumbles, as the ape man pounds his way out of the wall. Dexter comes up with the excuse that "it must be from next door," and the cops, ever the sheep, are ready to run and look. But by now Steve has developed a free will of his own, and he stops them. In the movie's one exciting piece of action, the ape man bursts through the wall and kills Dexter who is unable to get his blowtorch started in time. The cops shower the ape man in a hail of gunfire, or rather, gunfire noises. Obviously no bullets are actually fired since the ape man doesn't even wince. Instead, he mortally wounds Dexter by rubbing his neck gently with his naked arm. Then he scares the cops into total paralysis by waving his arms and roaring, like a child pretending to be a gorilla. Before he dies, Dexter whispers to Steven the truth, that fire is the only way to kill the ape man. An alchemical change has now occurred that parallels the union of the ape man and Gilmore. Dexter's last words—how to kill the ape man—instill in young Steven the ability to vanquish this threat. Though Dexter could not man-

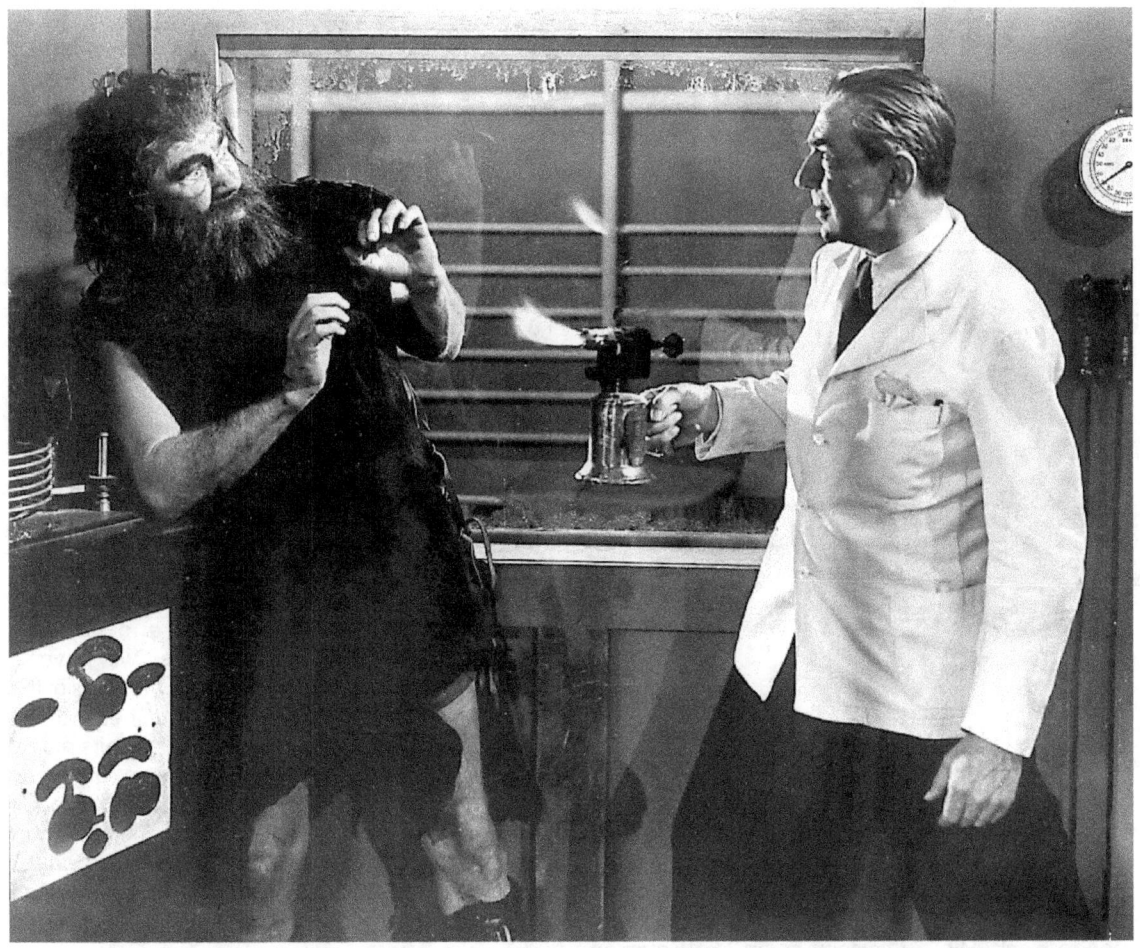

**Dexter brandishes the blowtorch, waving it menacingly, and the ape man snaps out of his stupor.**

age to successfully "father" the Gilmore/ape man, he does succeed in fathering Steven, passing along his alchemical knowledge to the boy/man with his dying breath. Steven is thus transformed from potentially neutered automaton into "real" man. Into his hands now falls the task of continuing the evolution and change begun by Dexter.

Meanwhile the ape man runs back to the Gilmore house and abducts Ann. One is reminded of Dr. Morphius' Id monster in *Forbidden Planet*, killing everyone who stands in the way of his repressed desire for his own daughter. He carries her over the rooftops and in a post-modern "fourth-wall" moment, even carries her off the sets of the film and into the parameters of the soundstage. But he is clearly lost and intimidated outside the close confines of Dexter's basement, so that is where he returns.

"They will not find you now," he assures her back in Dexter's laboratory. Like a restless child he is forever running away from and back to "home." No sooner has he said this, however, the police come through the door. Struggling to utilize his vague memories of science, the Gilmore/ape man attempts to freeze Ann, to "preserve" her in ice, or subjugate her to his own unconscious. But when the freezer doesn't work he ends up pulling out the electric cables and starting a fire. The savage instincts are not the part of man that perseveres; they only destroy thereby creating change. The ape man has come up against the brick wall that is his stage's evolutionary limit. Steve meanwhile gets the door open, and tries to run down the steps into the smoke and rescue Ann. The police try to stop him

"Don't be a fool, you can't make it!" they say to Steve. Again the word fool is used, but this time Steve is ready to ignore the negativity of their "rational" minds, thus permanently transcending from civilized automaton afraid of "scandal" to a hero who has incorporated the strength of the Wild Man. He becomes the archetypal hero of myth who rescues the girl from the "dragon" of the fire. The policeman cower in fear, like the ape man, but Steve has mastered the mystery of flame.

The final shot, unforgettably bleak, shows the ape man dying in the back of the frame. In the foreground are rows of beakers and test tubes, and all

The archetypal hero of myth (Steve) must rescue the girl from the "dragon" of the fire (the ape man).

around the super-imposed fire. We fade to black, the end, and the gorilla image in the cage repeated from the opening credits. The cycle is complete. We are allowed no epilogue shot of the happy couple enjoying some civilized honeymoon, just a quick, nihilistic fade-to-black. While this may seem like Katzman economics, it goes much deeper. The final shot, with its chemistry equipment and wild man's symbolic sacrifice, is an alchemical equation for the future. The ape man has done his job; he has wrought the necessary havoc to jump-start the stale society that revived him. However his own limitations doom his physical survival just as Gilmore's limitations did him. Shrinking back into the shadows, hunted by the cleansing flames of evolution, the ape man is destroyed until his inevitable future "return." Ann and Steve are escorted out of the burning house and into the unknown. Their honeymoon exists outside the parameters of this movie. It's as if the final shot of the film is in itself some sort of a deep freeze.

One wants to walk away from this movie depressed and angry that an hour or so of their lives have been wasted, but the scholar will exit with profound insight in- to the evolutionary masculine psyche. If we bear in mind that this film was shot in 1944 and therefore those involved in the production were not serving "over there," this indictment of the "cultured" male becomes doubly significant. Everyone involved in the cast is trying to atone for their non-participation in the far-off bloodshed.

Today the Wild Man remains in a deep freeze. Few of today's comparatively sheltered males have the courage to thaw the ape man out and start the necessary havoc that prefigures real human change. If our collective masculine psyche is to recapture that primitive energy, if the ape man is going to, in fact, truly "return" to us, we need to pull the cables from the wall and not be afraid of rushing headfirst into the flames of our burning basements. If contemporary men are ever to successfully merge their primitive and cultured minds, they will have to ignore the warnings of the police, and head down those smoky stairs alone. When they do, only then will there be the epilogue of two young lovers, shrugging off the "Monster Slain" headline with a vacant chuckle on the way to their endless honeymoon beyond the credits, where George Zucco finally appears.

CREDITS: Producer: Sam Katzman and Jack Dietz; Director: Phillip Rosen; Screenplay: Robert Charles; Cinematographer: Marcel Le Picard; Editor: Carl Pierson

CAST: Bela Lugosi (Dr. Dexter); John Carradine (Dr. Gilmore); Fred Moran (Ape Man); George Zucco (?); Mary Currier (Hilda); Michael Ames (Steve Rogers); Judith Gibson (Ann)

# Midnight Marquee Back Issues

 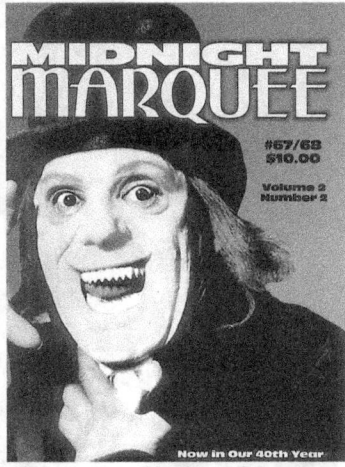 

Midnight Marquee 65/66, 128 pages, 7x10, $10
Midnight Marquee 67/68, 128 pages, 7x10 $10
Mad About Movies #3, 128 pages, 7x10 $10
Subscribe to *Midnight Marquee* and *Mad About Movies*
for One Year for $30 for both Mags!

## Coming
### October 30-Nov. 1, 2003

All films must be in the horror, fantasy or science fiction genres. Awards will be presented in the following categories:
Best Film; Best Short Film; Best Documentary; Best Documentary Short Subject; Young Filmmakers (ages 5-10); Young Filmmakers (ages 11-13); Young Filmmakers (ages 14-17); Best Actor; Best Actress; Best Director; Best Screenplay; Best Special Effects; Best Film Poster

   The Award will the the prestigious Laemmle Award designed by famed sculptor Henry Alvarez
   Visit the following websites for further information, events and participating hotels: www.chesapeakearts.org or www.midmar.com or call Susan Svehla at 410-665-1198.
   The Chesapeake Arts Center is a non-profit multi-purpose facility dedicated to the literary, visual and performing arts and is located south of Baltimore city.

**The Maryland Fantastique Film Fest is Looking for Horror, Science Fiction or Fantasy Films and Documentaries**

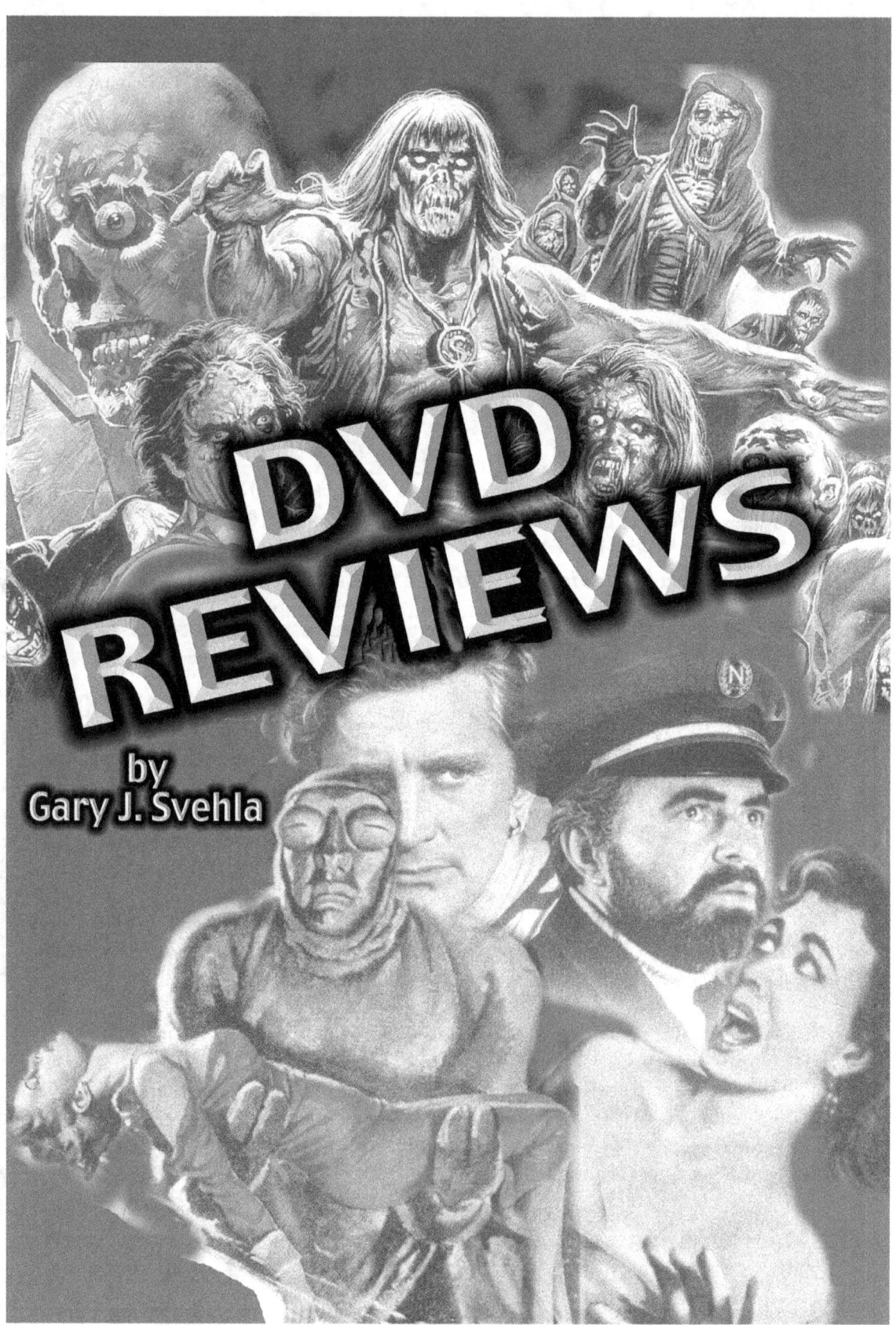

Ratings: 4: Excellent; 3: Good; 2: Fair; 1: Poor

## CITY OF THE DEAD
**Movie: 3.5; Disc 3.5**
**[VCI Entertainment]**

In the wake of elaborately set-decorated Hammer film productions, oozing in Technicolor and gore, and in the wake of elaborately photographed widescreen Gothic Poe excursions created by American International, comes this British anomaly *City of the Dead* [aka as *Horror Hotel* in America], which, like *Burn, Witch, Burn* released three years later, seems a throwback to earlier times with its stark black-and-white photography, low-budget sets and dripping mood. Christopher Lee becomes the center of attention in the production with his modern-day suit and ties and academic demeanor. Yet *City of the Dead* remains one of the better horror movies of the 1960s, resembling more frequently Mario Bava's *Black Sunday* with its dominant theme of a witch who was burned at the stake and inflicts revenge on the heirs of the very people who burned her. And while the reanimated witch (Patricia Jessel as Elizabeth Selwyn) is never as sensual as Barbara Steele, both productions are immersed in dank photography, underground crypt design and sets drenched in fog and smoke.

The lovely Venetia Stevenson, portraying the doomed college researcher Nan, creates the right tone of vulnerability, shock and screaming terror as she investigates the supposed reanimation of witchcraft in the quaint hamlet of Whitewood, a New England village appearing to have remained in the timeless image of the era of the Salem witch trials (thus allowing the production to be modern with its mod academic image in half the scenes and period Gothic with its fog-shrouded timelessness during the other half). And Christopher Lee, whose performances were played more for his physicality with not much dialogue up until this point, becomes a regular orator with his expertise in the witch burnings and history of Whitewood. By the conclusion, his other identity comes as somewhat of a surprise although Lee's countenance is easily identified even when he wears the sacrificial robes and hood.

*City of the Dead* shines by virtue of its simple yet involving script, its fleshed-out and truly human characters, its moody cinematography and its taunt direction by John Moxey. Christopher Lee becomes the icing on the cake, and his performance as the sinister professor who just might be trying to hide his alter ego is quite engaging.

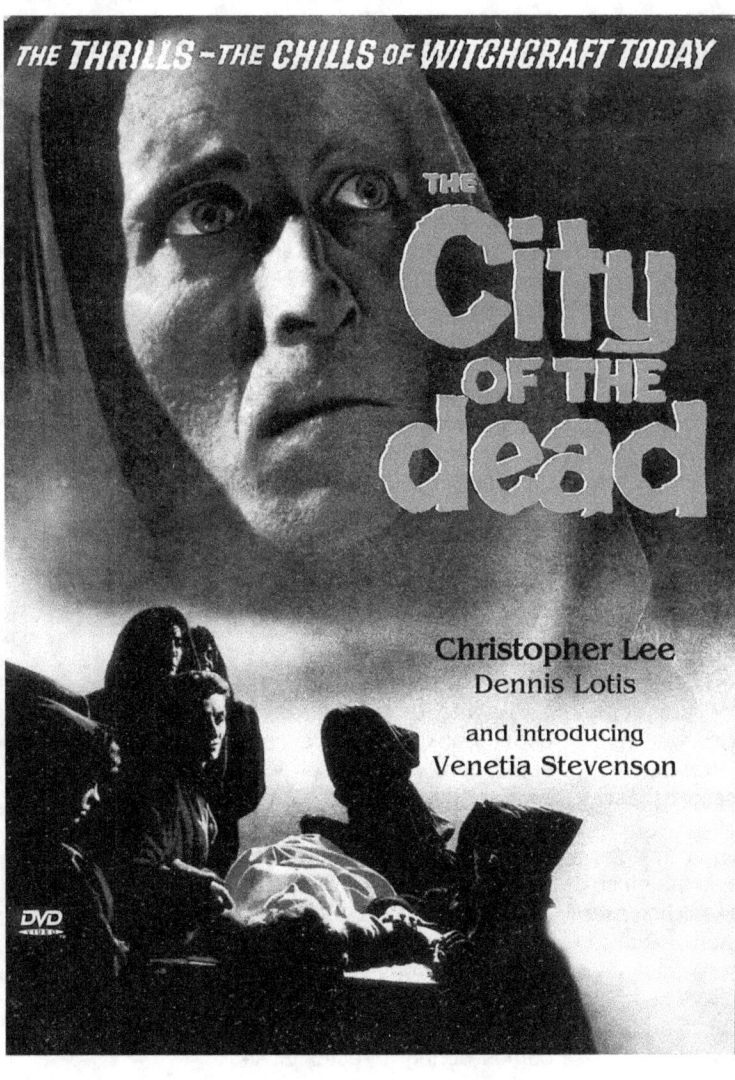

VCI made this DVD release quite an event by including a British print which is two minutes longer than the American version. The print offered here, letterboxed and enhanced for 16:9 monitors, is stunning, crisp with dark density. Extras include audio commentary with Christopher Lee, and an onscreen 45-minute interview as well. Also star Venetia Stevenson and director John Moxey are interviewed onscreen. Also included are trailers, photo gallery and bios of the cast and crew. All in all, VCI offers a deluxe package here that serves well a horror classic too often neglected.

### E.T. THE EXTRA-TERRESTRIAL 2-DISC LIMITED COLLECTOR'S EDITION
Movie: 3.0; Disc: 4.0
[Universal DVD]

Surprisingly, many of Steven Spielberg's earlier movies do not age as well as expected (*Duel* seems almost anal retentive in its singular vision; *Jaws* is not as horrifying as it once was and *Close Encounters* inspires just as many yawns as awes), and *E.T.* was one movie that I dreaded returning to 20 odd years later. However, for some reason, *E.T.* really held up well, even the new CGI-embellished version that seemed to only finalize the initial vision, rather than become an unnecessary add-on. The print used is simply marvelous, showcasing those foggy backyard sequences where Henry Thomas first encounters E.T. The John Williams score seems fresh and swells with emotion, and the interactions between this typically dysfunctional family seem real.

Surprisingly, when the government men arrive, in their insulated suits, the movie still holds up well. What I feared here, with E.T. becoming sick and ultimately dying (only momentarily, of course), was that the manipulative efforts of Spielberg might swell into overload, but the film maintains the proper balance of humor, awe and pathos, without allowing Williams' score to oversaturate the viewer's emotions in too much sugary-sweet sentimentality.

Besides offering a nice print of the original release version, as well as a gorgeous print of the newly restored and CGI spruced up version, the package carries tons of extras including a special intro by Spielberg, coverage of the live performance of John Williams conducting his score at the 2002 premiere, a making of *E.T.* featurette, a reunion and discussion by the cast in 2002, production designs, drawings and original advertising.

The Amblin logo, a still freeze-frame of Elliott riding his bike through space, crossing the shadow of the giant moon, with E.T. resting on his handlebars, was of course a pivotal image from *E.T.*, and in this newly struck version, that sequence creates deeply emotional resonance and that sense of wonder that is only rivaled, perhaps, by the climax of *Close Encounters*. No wonder Spielberg selected that one split-second magical moment as the visual image of what his production company represents. *E.T.* seems to improve with age and one viewing of this exceptional DVD package makes clear why.

### BLADE II
Movie: 3.0; Disc: 4.0
[New Line Platinum DVD Series]

*Blade II* is my type of comic book movie, the anti-super hero who himself was born half-vampire but still hates and fights to eliminate the devil's brood. The series is a comic book, a bloody one at that, come to life, extremely visual, resting upon mesmerizing set-pieces and almost non-stop action. But while hyper-drive action usually becomes boring, director Guillermo Del Toro (who also directed *Devil's Backbone*, *Cronos* and *Mimic*) manages to create interesting characterizations and allows enough screen time for Blade to confront his personal demons and demonstrate the human struggle inside.

*Blade II* is a visual trip, the plot detailing the rise of a mutated group of super vampires who threaten the original vampire race with annihilation. Interestingly, Blade's main enemies, the vampires, approach Blade to join forces, to form a Bloodpack, to together wipe out the threatening new vampire race. The vampires warn that, first this mutated species will destroy the race of vampires, then they will come for the human race. Of course Blade reluctantly joins this unholy alliance, and his interaction with his fellow Bloodpackers, with dramatic tension flaring almost in every sequence, only leads to expertly choreographed battle sequences, all enhanced with digital effects and wonderful shots of disintegrating undead warriors who splatter with every prick of the sword. The plot turns more complex when the audience learns that Blade must trust creatures who will ultimately betray him, and the final resolution

is always fast-paced and violent, but well staged and photographed. The team of Blade and Whistler (Kris Kristofferson) is reunited, even though the Kristofferson character died in the first film, but his return appears logical and it is good having the team back, with the addition of a third party, Norman Reedus, who causes tension with Whistler because the wily veteran simply does not trust the young assistant.

Again, this is not Shakespeare, but if you enjoy rumbling the walls and vibrating the floors, watching nonstop action with a very violent bent, then *Blade II* is your cup of blood. The two-disc DVD set is packaged containing both a Dolby Digital EX 5.1 and DTS ES 6.1 soundtrack. Extras include the usual music video, deleted/extended sequences with insightful commentary by Del Toro, a series of documentaries, a director's notebook, art gallery, trailers and video game survival guide. But the quality of the DVD print, boasting superlative looking original source material and state-of-the-art audio surround sound, is what *Blade II* is all about. For what it is, *Blade II* is powerful entertainment that will showcase your home theater's potential.

### SPY KIDS 2: THE ISLAND OF LOST DREAMS
Movie: 3.0; Disc: 3.5
[Dimension Home Video]

Even though *Spy Kids 2* may not equal the sheer energy and imagination of the first entry, most importantly this film demonstrates how an expensive-looking film may be produced for far less money than it appears. This film shows how one individual can be the creative core behind every aspect of production.

Most people did not realize that Robert Rodriguez, besides producing and directing *Spy Kids 2: The Island of Lost Dreams*, also wrote the script, was co-musical scorer, was the cinematographer, editor and production designer. In more ways than one, in this modern era of so many chefs sticking his or her fingers into the cinematic pot, Robert Rodriguez shows that the director can still be king, if the production looks like $50 million and costs only a fraction of that actual amount.

One of the Special Features on this DVD is a short, hosted by Rodriguez, called *Ten-Minute Film School* where he shares how almost all of the film was filmed in his native Texas with one day of shooting exotic locations in Costa Rica to be intercut into the final production. Clever means showing how Rodriguez gets his shot but does it on the cheap. Young filmmakers would be wise to visit and learn from this documentary.

This time out, the story features maturing "kids" Alexa Vega (Carmen) and Daryl Sabara (Juni) being threatened by the new spy kids on the block, the son and daughter of new chief Mike Judge (after Antonio Banderas is passed over for the prized position). The movie is filled with action and gadgets and fights and double-crosses and surprises. But most impressively is the obvious tribute to the special effects created by Ray Harryhausen in the movie's second half, once the children arrive on the so-called island of lost dreams, helmed by the deliriously zany Steve Buscemi as monster-creator Romero. Using all the imagination allowed by digital animation, Rodriguez stages a skeleton fight that almost rivals a similar classic sequence from Harryhausen's *Jason and the Argonauts*. We must admit that the creaky old stop-motion animation created by Ray Harryhausen still possesses a heart and soul missing from the CGI monster playground created by Rodriguez, but what *Spy Kids 2* presents is solid entertainment and a loving tribute to the master.

By movie's end Banderas is in and Mike Judge is out, as are his children, and even with interference from grandparents Ricardo Montalban and Holland Taylor, the Cortez family triumphs and Juni and Carmen manage to save the day, once again. Robert Rodriguez manages to create a film geared toward adolescents that holds the interest of adults as well, and his vision and execution in helming all the important areas of filmmaking show just how much control one director can still possess in an A production filmed on a B production budget (perhaps a very high B budget). Here is a wonderful example of insidious filmmaking at its most entertaining.

### RINGU
Movie: 3.0; Disc: 3.5 [Dreamworks Home Entertainment]

Japanese cinema has held my interest of late, recently discovering both this little gem from 1998 and *Audition*, two of the most riveting horror thrillers released during the last decade.

Of course, most people know the American remake called *The Ring* that took audiences by storm during the last year. The American *The Ring*, directed by Gore Verbinski (who also directed the comedic shennigans of *Mouse Trap* a few years ago), steals quite blatantly from the Japanese original, perhaps even upping the ante by including a wonderful horse suicide sequence aboard a ship (the digital death sequence, where the horse literally jumps to its death by going overboard, is

haunting), which the Japanese version lacked. But every icon from the Japanese original (the two teens who joyfully open the film, one of them dying a horrible death only minutes later; the horrifying sequence down in the well; the bone-chilling image of the dead child who crawls slowly out of the TV set to enter our real world) is aped almost letter perfect in the U.S. remake.

And here the Dreamworks release of *Ringu* is cause for celebration, as the letterboxed print including a remixed 5.1 Dolby Digital Surround soundtrack, subtitled, presents the Japanese original as it should be seen and heard. What makes *Ringu* so special is its reliance on the modern urban legend mythos (people who view the haunting videotape have one week to make a copy of the tape and show that copy to another person, or die) and its attention to classic ghost cinema. In the Japanese original the demon child Sadako (in a creepy performance by Rie Inou), possessing both ESP and telekinetic powers (of the *Carrie* variety), is savagely murdered (but not quite) and thrown down a well, where the child actually dies seven days later, a horrible death due to starvation and exposure to the elements. The videotape, a strange creation from beyond the grave, is Sadako's revenge by inflicting a one week death sentence on anyone who views the video (and after finishing watching the video, the phone always rings to signal the death sentence countdown is starting).

Talented director Hideo Nakata does a masterful job of creating both the sudden shock (the phone rings suddenly and loudly, the camera twists around and we see the contorted frightened-to-death face of the latest victim, an arm emerges from the muddy waters at the bottom of the well, etc.) and the atmospheric chill (the teenager at the film's beginning slowly walks to the kitchen and there, after several false starts, suddenly meets an abrupt ending; the sequence at the film's end where the TV suddenly turns itself on and the haunted video plays, in spastic video-cuts, leading to the living-dead zombie-like appearance of Sadako, who slowly emerges from the TV set and stalks her final victim, etc.). Simply stated, *Ringu*, like the American *The Ring* that followed, creeps us out from the playful but deadly initial sequence to the downbeat ending that follows the seemingly successful defeating of the ghostly curse. *Ringu* may not have the psychological depth to ever be considered a classic horror movie, but it does manage to chill the blood and make us think, one week later, as our time is running out, that perhaps maybe, just maybe, the curse might actually be real. Startling and upsetting as any effective horror movie is expected to be, *Ringu* deserves to be seen for being the original that it most definitely is.

### INVADERS FROM MARS
Movie: 3.5; Disc: 3.5 [Image Entertainment]

William Cameron Menzies' *Invaders from Mars* is one of the most eccentric and visually arresting low-budget classics of science fiction cinema. The movie, told from a 10-year-old boy's point of view, is a delight of nightmarish paranoia, foreshadowing the advent of the Pod People three years later in Don Siegel's *Invasion of the Body Snatchers*. Here, the horror becomes every child's worst nightmare… what if my father and mother are no longer Mom and Dad, but alien-controlled saboteurs intent on infiltrating and destroying America's military defense secrets!!! Even the little neighbor girl who lives next door has become "one of them" and the sand pit in the backyard now houses a mysterious flying saucer whose sand craters mysteriously deliver ordinary humans to the fate-worse-than-death alien operation theater below, to implant probes into the base of their skull reducing them to alien-controlled zombies. No one is safe, not parents, not the police, not even the military. Every authority figure is now suspected. The lumbering, evil aliens are giant green mutants who protect their leader, a disembodied head in a jar, the leader of Mars.

The movie, featuring an original 35mm CineColor print (like Technicolor, CineColor will not fade nor turn red; however, CineColor is only a two-color process, so the print's intensity is compromised by lacking the third color element), hasn't looked this good since its release to theaters during the late 1970s. Even the excellent laserdisc release did not feature this Wade Williams original 35mm print. CineColor does feature a soft focus, and unfortunately, the Wade Williams print has not been digitally cleaned (once in a while annoying scratches or lines appear, but these minor flaws do not take away from the intensity of the color-saturated print). But when this DVD is compared to any other home video release, this 50th Anniversary Image DVD leaves all the others in the dust. Concerning extras, included are the usual theatrical trailer and still gallery and a wonderful collector's booklet. However, to its credit, both the U.S. release print and the British

release print are included, and the British print is remarkably different from the American, mainly during the conclusion. The English print changes the final montage sequence now showing Jimmy Hunt and the military company running from the underground alien lair as the detonator is ready to explode an underground bomb. Instead of having Jimmy Hunt awaken from his nightmare, the British print has the flying saucer start to leave its lair, then exploding, with the aliens outright defeat providing the happy ending. As we all know, the American ending has Jimmy Hunt awakened later that night to again witness another flying saucer returning—dream or reality we never know. It is wonderful to see both versions side-by-side.

Image has provided fans with the best-possible versions of *Invaders from Mars* and the movie continues to intrigue with its imaginative set design and direction, making every kid in the audience the star of his or her own private nightmare. *Invaders from Mars* is a classic original and this DVD is absolutely the only way to revisit the film.

**RED DRAGON
(Collector's Edition)**
Movie: 3.0; Disc: 3.5
[Universal Home Video]

Everyone bemoans the fact that, beginning with the 1970s, the horror film market lost its star appeal—no Karloff, Lugosi, Lee, Cushing, Price for the modern generation. True, in the 1980s

we were bombarded with Robert Englund as Freddy Krueger, who became the horror personality by default. However, for the horror genre, the decade of the 1990s and the 2000s belongs to Anthony Hopkins' career-defining portrayal of Hannibal Lecter in his trilogy of films: *Silence of the Lambs* (1991), *Hannibal* (2001) and now the prequel *Red Dragon* (2002). Most people were highly critical of Ridley Scott's off-putting take on *Hannibal* (recasting Jodie Foster's Clarise in the person of Julianne Moore) using eccentric flourishes to emphasize the bizarre humor of Hannibal more so than his horrific intensity. And the European look of the second entry plays directly against the American *policier* look of the classic initial-entry *Silence of the Lambs*. For my mon-ey *Hannibal* was indeed quirky and over-the-top, but Anthony Hopkins was given the opportunity to place his character of Hannibal front and center. The tone, look and direction of *Hannibal* radically differed from *Silence of the Lambs*, but for my money, *Hannibal*, though inferior, was still an excellent hor-ror thriller. However, Brett Ratner's take on *Red Dragon*, a direct remake of Michael Mann's *Manhunter* (1986), seems to re-turn to the *Silence of the Lambs'* more familiar arena (even returning Ted Tally, the screenwriter of the original, to write *Red Dragon*). And while the results are still shy of Jonathan Demme's landmark original, *Red Dragon* does come closest in style and tone to the classic original recipe.

Even though Hannibal portrays a sidebar character in both *Manhunter* and *Silence of the Lambs*, Brett Ratner wisely beefs up the good doctor's role in *Red Dragon*, proving that Brian Cox's more insular portrayal of Hannibal in *Manhunter* is inferior to Anthony Hopkins' more flam-boyant portrayal. Just as Anthony Perkins, two generations before, demonstrated, Hopkins' classic portrayal of a screen psycho is inspired and gets beneath the skin because of its intensity and subtlety. Without doubt, Hopkins owns this role and it will remain the classic horror film performance of this generation.

While William Petersen's por-trayal of Will Graham in *Manhunter* is better than Edward Norton's portrayal here in *Red Dragon*, both men deliver intense perfor-mances that are more internal than external. Each is recovering from a savage attack by Hannibal which almost leaves the character of Graham dead but psychically scarred for life. *Red Dragon* clev-erly starts the movie off with the ultimate encounter between agent Graham and Hannibal, with the savage stiletto attack where Lecter rams the knife into Graham's gut, softly telling him his body is now going into shock, don't struggle, you won't feel any pain. But of course, mustering his last reserve of energy, Graham plunges arrows into Lecter's torso and then grabs his gun and shoots the maniac twice; however, the good doctor and Graham both survive.

The Tooth Fairy was por-trayed in *Manhunter* by weird-looking Tom Noonan, who seems to have, once again, the upper hand over the more recognizable Ralph Fiennes, whose hare-lipped quiet intensity never gets under the skin the way Noonan did in *Manhunter*. However, Fiennes' portrayal, fueled by a full body tattoo on his back and buttocks, allowing the performer to appear nude in several pivotal sequences, makes the actor an imposing pres-ence. Noonan has the eccentric look and intensity down, but Fi-ennes does a wonderful job with a characterization based upon a well-sculpted male physique.

Brett Ratner's direction is re-markably tense and in total control. Ratner likes to take a quietly in-tense shot, such as Norton rubbing his fingers over his face in deep concentration, and then a pound-ing musical crescendo (courtesy of a classic score by Danny Elfman) leads to a haunting flashback. Or when Norton visits Hopkins in prison, the fiend's hands chained in back, Lecter lunges with his mouth extended and teeth bared at the just-out-of-distance agent. Ratner is not quite the innovator that Jonathan Demme was in *Silence of the Lambs*, but his un-derstanding of atmospheric chills and the sudden shock proves that here is an artist whose talents would be best served within the horror genre.

Bottom line, although *Man-hunter* is a pivotal serial killer movie and was the first attempt to film Hannibal Lecter way back in 1986, I would have to give the artistic edge overall to *Red Dragon* for being the superior film, mainly based on Brett Ratner's sensitive direction and Anthony Hopkins' performance. I would love to see Anthony Hopkins go to the well one more time as Hannibal the Cannibal, for his performance is a credit to the horror film genre.

DVD extras include a private file dossier on Lecter (detailing his perverted history), an analysis of Lecter and serial killer profiling, audio commentary, alternative and deleted sequences. For extra money, a director's cut DVD may be purchased, but I opted for the less expensive Collector's Edition.

## JOURNEY TO THE CENTER OF THE EARTH
Movie: 3.0; Disc: 3.0
[20th Century Fox Home Video]

When we were kids back in 1959, *Journey to the Center of the Earth* was what action-adventure films were all about. Led by a fine cast featuring James Mason, Arlene Dahl and Pat Boone (who does exceedingly well as the romantic lead), the movie has an episodic sense of adventure. Basically, the story involves two rival teams' race to reach the center of the Earth, a journey made in the past by an explorer who never made it back. One team is scientifically motivated and these well-cultured people play according to the rules. The other team, more a duo, involves the quest of an affluent dandy who wants to win the exploration by any means possible. Leisurely paced but always exciting, the Mason/Boone expedition sing their way downward and are awestruck by the amazing things they find on their journey. Somehow they always find a way to circumvent all the problems they encounter. By the time they reach the center of the Earth, they find underground caverns with an actual lighted sky. They also find dinosaurs (portrayed by magnified lizards) and underground volcanic eruptions and lava flows which threaten their survival. But this widescreen color extravaganza is never less than thrilling, and the visuals were state-of-the-art at the time. The only thing lacking are Ray Harryhausen-created monsters, but the terrific musical score by Bernard Herrmann creates a somber bass-heavy mood that makes us almost forget about the lack of stop-motion animation.

The original source material used for this DVD release is in very good condition and the restoration captures the sense of the original production (whereby the Deluxe color approximates Technicolor hues). James Mason is both debonair and adventurous, and the supporting cast, including a hulking blonde-haired Hercules and his pet goose, creates a sense of fun that charmed youthful theater audiences back in the late 1950s. Surprisingly, the film holds up well today and proves it is one childhood film worth revisiting.

## THE DAY THE EARTH STOOD STILL
Movie: 3.0; Disc: 4.0
[20th Century Fox Home Video]

For 50 years people have been raving about 1951's *The Day the Earth Stood Still*, directed by acclaimed director Robert Wise. And on this Fox Home Video DVD, the movie has never looked nor sounded better, featuring a meticulously restored black-and-white 35mm print, with rich density and little grain. The package includes marvelous extras including a 70-minute making-of documentary featuring interviews with original cast and crew members, five still galleries, the shooting script, the theatrical trailer, Movietone newsreel and audio commentary by Robert Wise and Nicholas Meyer. This double-sided DVD contains everything anyone would hope to see included in the DVD package. And the package is affordably priced, as well.

However, this DVD only serves to drive home the fact that *The Day the Earth Stood Still* is vastly overrated, and as a true science fiction classic, does not really stand the test of time. For instance, the flying saucer hovering over landmarks in Washington, D.C. do not come close to touching Ray Harryhausen's similar special effects in *Earth vs. the Flying Saucers*, released about five years later. The presence of robot Gort is quite effective, but whenever he walks and his rubber-suited knees bend like rubber, this awe-inspiring effect is suddenly lost.

Even though Wise's direction has always been praised, I have always found the film to be quite slow moving and ponderous. The cast is at best adequate, with Michael Rennie's superior yet sensitive portrayal as the alien emissary the crowning performance of the film. Sam Jaffe's egghead professor is too stereotyped and by-the-numbers to be anything more than mediocre, Billy Gray as the little boy is typically obnoxious. Patricia Neal as Gray's mother is fairly standard, and Hugh Marlowe's trouble-making presence is always annoying. The alien-among-us plot wastes its balance on the mundane, and the terrific flying saucer set-piece scenes, with the military contingency and world leader delegations, are too few and far between. The moody nighttime photography featuring Neal confronting Gort, while played for tension and fright, feels almost lumbering and apathetic.

It seems this film always needs a kick in the creative butt and lacks that spark of both performance and directorial pacing to make it classic in any sense.

Most people will say its thesis idealogy is all the movie needs, but its message of a diplomat from the universe who warns Earthlings to get it together or face total destruction by the peacekeeping robots, of which Gort is only one example, seems almost hypocritical. The lame allusions of Rennie's alien (Mr. Carpenter) to Jesus Christ (his sacrifice at the hands of fools and his resurrection from the dead) are blatant and lack subtlety, and the message to accept peace or else face the release of monstrous robots against the human race seems to espouse a philosophy of succumbing to bullying threats rather than teaching a lesson of peace.

For me *The Day the Earth Stood Still* is neither a cinematic classic nor a particularly well done A production. Unlike other movie classics, this movie never resonates, for its simply told literal message is all the movie offers. The cinematography is workmanlike and the direction pedestrian. All this adds up to a good movie, but no aspect of this production seems great in any sense of the word. Isn't it about time we see this movie for what it is and stop trying to recast it as something it never was?

**SPIRITED AWAY**
Movie: 3.0; Disc: 4.0
[Buena Vista
Home Entertainment]

I have come late to the world of Japanese anime and haven't seen most of the classics of the animation genre, but when *Spirited Away* won the Academy Award for Best Animated Feature (winning over *Ice Age* and *Lilo and Stitch*), I became curious about this film that has garnered such positive press.

I subscribe to that arena of film criticism that holds that movies sometimes are great simply because they create a universe that has never been shown before and thus, by creating that totally original cinematic universe, such films deserve our attention. *Spirited Away*, written and directed by Hayao Miyazaki, would quite simply have been considered a "head" film back in the 1960s, its psychedelic visuals detailing two parallel worlds, one the world of human beings, the other a world of gods, spirits and imagination. The visual innovation inherent in *Spirited Away* makes it definitely one of the finest examples of animation in this generation. Where I have problems with the anime genre is in its lack of logic, relying mostly upon dream imagery and subconscious logic that tends to annoy me. Dream reality is fine for some, but I like my plot to tidy-up all loose ends by the film's conclusion. However, in the world of Japanese animation I have to accept the fact that I am experiencing something akin to the American world of David Lynch and accept the fantasy, at face value, for all that it offers.

I love the bridge between the mundane world where lead character and girl child Chihiro first appears as a spoiled brat, with little heroic qualities. In the car drive Chihiro appears very Westernized and her parents seem very Occidental in appearance (especially Dad's beer gut that hangs well over his belt). However, once the

parents have been transformed into pigs and Chihiro crosses the threshold tunnel into this parallel world, she suddenly seems more Asian and becomes more wide-eyed anime looking.

In this *Alice in Wonderland* world, Chihiro soon becomes Sen and meets the evil (yet, at the same time, not quite evil) Yubaba, whose matronly presence is haunting with her high-stacked gray hair, her large nose with pimple and her intense eyes and glasses. The various gods and spirits who frequent the bathhouse where Sen is required to work are always fascinating, with attention to rich detail (mostly involving the grime left in the tub by the stink demon). By movie's end, Sen has had encounters with a grotesque giant infant, a worm-like dragon, twin witch sisters, transparent no-face spirits and assorted netherworld creatures of the imagination. When Chi-hiro returns to the real world and is reunited with her parents, she has matured, becoming more self-sufficient and adult. Where her parents caution her concerning her adjustment to a new home (the family is moving to the suburbs) and new school, stating the change will be challenging, Chihiro confidently proclaims it's no big deal, and after all her adventures, she really means it.

The DVD double-disc set contains an absolutely gorgeous Dolby Surround 5.1 soundtrack (in dubbed English or original Japanese, with subtitles) and contains a second disc of fantastic extras including behind-the-scenes production documentaries and featurettes, as well as original Japanese trailers. It might take the unacquainted American eye a little time to adjust to the rich supernatural world created by Hayao Miyazaki, but it is a world definitely worth visiting and attempting to understand.

### FEMME FATALE
Movie: 3.5; Disc: 3.5
[Warner Bros. Home Video]

During the 1970s, the anticipation of the new Brian De Palma film was reason to celebrate, for his films evoked the spirit of Hitchcock and his approach was hip and cutting edge. Movies such as *Sisters, Obsession, Carrie, Dressed to Kill, Blow Out* became the *nouveau* marriage of sight and sound, but with the success of *The Untouchables*, things changed stylistically and De Palma became mainstream, more miss than hit and his creative energies appeared to be sputtering. His early and best work had an almost independent edge and seemed designed to make more an artistic than a commercial statement.

Brian De Palma's *Femme Fatale* again recaptures that quirky, artistic edge, returning to that creative spark of experimentation missing from most of his work for the last generation. At best,

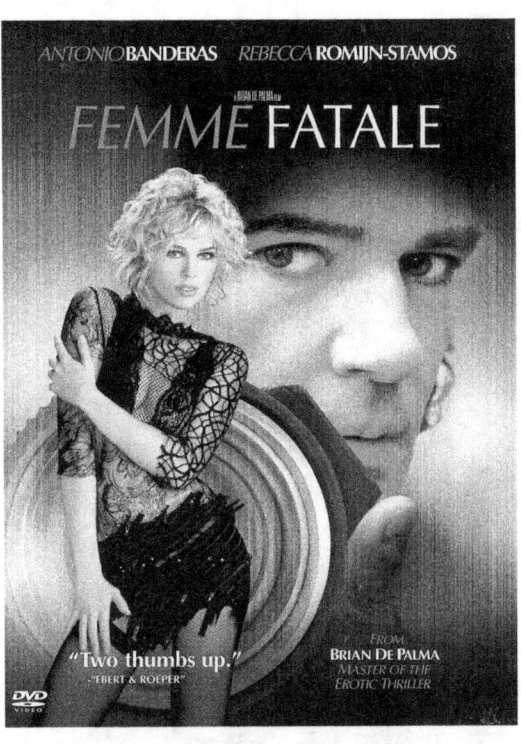

*Femme Fatale* is a flawed masterpiece, but it's a dazzling, visual virtuoso whose creative ambitions more than make up for the misfirings.

Imagine a self-confessed bad girl named Laure (Rebecca Romijn-Stamos), who opens the movie watching a French-subtitled version of *The Postman Always Rings Twice* almost totally nude in her hotel room. She is soon grilled about the heist she is about to undertake, involving the seduction of a model at the Cannes Film Festival who will be wearing 10 million dollars of gold jewelry. During the bathroom love-fest, Laure is supposed to undress the model and replace the jewelry originals with cheap imitations. However, the ruthless gang does not realize Laure is in cahoots with the model and the double-cross is underway. After the heist, Laure desperately tries to acquire a passport to escape to the United States, but she is mistaken for another woman, Lily, in whose apartment she is taking a relaxing bath when the original Lily abruptly returns home and soon commits

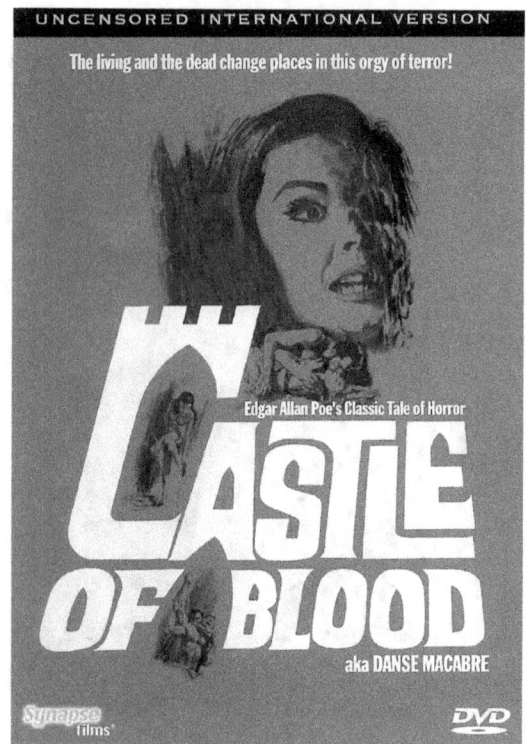

suicide by shooting herself in the head. From this point on the story plays out quite tragically, with many innocent deaths resulting. As Laure is abruptly dropped into the river, her nude, majestic form literally sparkles underwater as pulsing bubbles dissipate. Then she abruptly awakens in that same bathtub, having fallen asleep and *dreamed* her tragic film noir future. For the rest of the film, she methodically attempts to undo her "It's a Wonderful Life" nightmare, which leads to several visual sequences that are absolutely mind-blowing.

Interestingly, in her dream Laure tells photographer-for-hire buddy Nich-olas (Antonio Banderas) that in this hellhole life no good deed goes unpunished. But once she awakens, she is given a ride by a truck driver and, as a present, gives the driver a cheap necklace intended for a child, which he can place over his rearview mirror to always remember his daughter while he is away from her. Seven years later that trinket is responsible for saving the life of both Laure and her victimized female friend and punishing the two villains who have been stalking the ladies for seven years.

Every person, every sequence in the dream world has a counterpart in the world of reality, with imagery of overflowing water constantly invading the dream world, with *deja-vu* posters of women in bathtubs offering subtle hints that reality is not quite what it seems. Even a tumble over the railing from hotel room 214 to her supposed death (although she is saved by plunging two floors and landing on rolled-up installation padding, breaking her fall) parallels the tumble from the bridge and her nude descent into the water, thus awakening her from her dream state. *Femme Fatale* is a film rich in subtle visual imagery, and the film bears (and requires) repeated viewings to put all the pieces together.

Besides De Palma's quietly confident direction (perhaps his best-directed film ever), the film benefits from the subtle and mood-evoking musical score by Ryuichi Sakamoto and the tremendous cinematography by Thierry Arbogast. The gimmick of "oh no, it's only a dream" may alienate some viewers but invigorate others, but when the dream is tied to the *Christmas Carol* vision of a future that might be unless we change our life now, bad girl Laure can totally reinvent herself as morally cleansed and repentant, literally given what most of us seek... a new lease on life. *Femme Fatale* is often brilliant and it again proclaims the creative visual powers of Brian De Palma as one of the great directors of his time who, like Laure, has been given a new lease on his creative life.

The DVD package contains several helpful documentaries, many of which explain the imagery and help the viewer put all the pieces of the puzzle together. Both American and French trailers are included. The letterboxed Dolby 5.1 print looks and sounds awesome and invites frequent revisitings.

**CASTLE OF BLOOD**
**[aka Danse Macabre]**
Movie: 2.5; Disc: 3.0
[Synapse Films]

*Castle of Blood*, reedited and released in America in 1964 to the drive-in circuit, is here restored (using four different audio and video sources) as an uncensored International version, restoring a few erotically charged sequences of nudity and interrupted sexuality. Still, this Euro-horror mood piece, directed by Antonio Margheriti (who usually directed under the Americanized name of Anthony Dawson), is not a classic along the lines of Mario Bava's or Dario Argento's best. Working under a very low budget, Mar-gheriti does a marvelous job of controlling the photography and the atmosphere, most of it generated by slow-panning shots, well-dressed castle sets and lots of ambient sound effects with spooky musical score. Audiences could cut the mood in *Castle of Blood* with a knife, but unfortunately, the plot and characterization suffer.

The plot involves American author Edgar Allan Poe visiting London, insisting all his tales of horror are based in fact. In a bar Poe encounters a British journalist and his friend Sir Thomas Blackwood, who happens to own a haunted castle. They wager Poe cannot spend the night alone in the castle, and Poe, in need of money, accepts the bet.

Interestingly enough, the supposedly abandoned castle is filled to the gills with spirits of the dead, but to Poe, these ghosts appear to be regular people in need of help and release. As the plot unravels characters Poe meets in the castle returns to ghostly life one night each year on the anniversary of their interconnected deaths, literal crimes of passion, of lust and deceit. Barbara Steele, who portrays her typical tormented, sensual stereotyped role, falls in love with Poe, and while he wishes to take her away from the castle, in truth, she cannot ever leave the scene of the crime. By movie's end Poe is dead, and his spirit is then released to enjoy the ghostly company of Barbara Steele forever, a knockoff of *Wuthering Heights* for the Eurotrash set. By morning, when the journalist and Blackwood travel by coach to pick up Poe, they in fact find the author standing next to the steel gate, but upon closer examination, they discover the poor bastard is dead, impaled in an upright position, only inches away from surviving the most horrific night of his life. And this ironic undertone is one of the film's chief joys, reinforcing the darker underbelly the film tries desperately to project.

But for fans of Euro-horror, characterization and mood come secondary to cinematography and mood, and as stated earlier, *Castle of Blood* superbly demonstrates this dream reality that links the world of the living and the dead and the inability, sometimes, to distinguish between the two. The film does chill the blood with its ghostly plot which causes all the victims of the household to relive their tragic final night for eternity, never to escape their collected sins. American horror lovers may be bored, but Euro-horror fanatics might find *Castle of Blood* to be their cup of tea.

Extras on the DVD include a fine-grain letterboxed 35mm print (either dubbed in American or in French with English subtitles), restored to its original running time, insightful liner notes by Tim Lucas, still and poster gallery, American version title credits and trailers. The film lingered in my thoughts weeks after I saw it, and this alone is significant praise indeed.

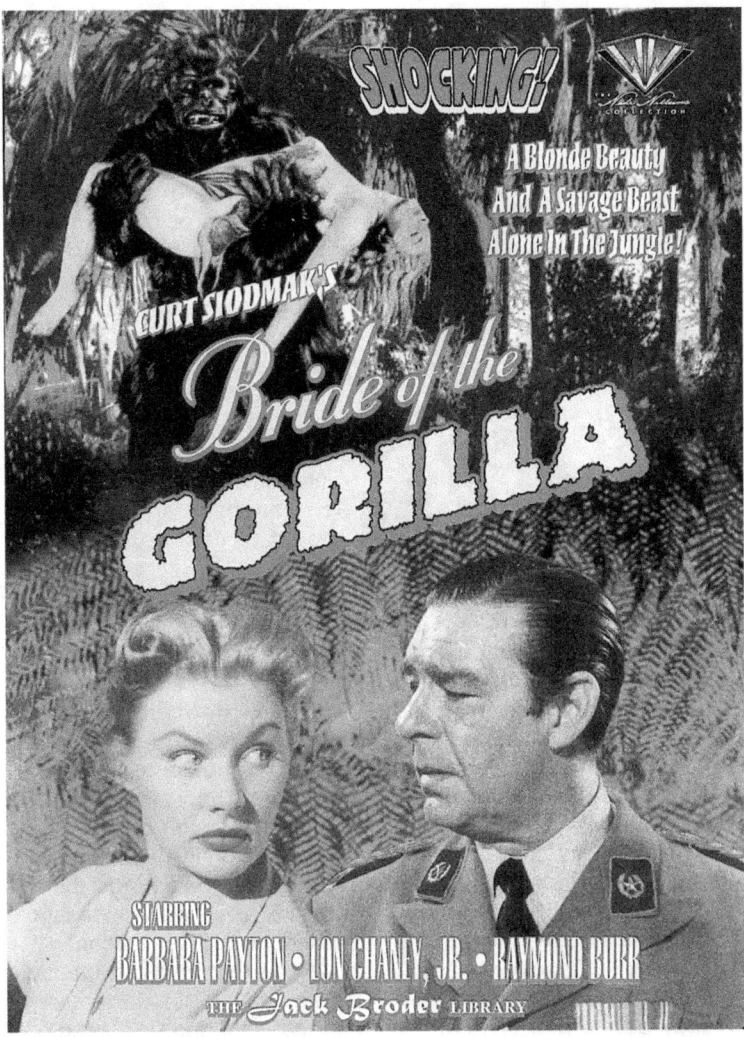

### BRIDE OF THE GORILLA
Movie: 2.5; Disc: 3.0
[Image Entertainment]

In 1948 Bela Lugosi portrayed Count Dracula in Universal's *Abbott and Costello Meet Frankenstein*, and four years later, in 1952, Lugosi, looking older and world-weary, starred in Jack Broder's production of *Bela Lugosi Meets a Brooklyn Gorilla*. However, back in 1948 Lon Chaney, Jr. portrayed a debonair Larry Talbot, leading man, in *A&C Meet Frankenstein*, while three years later he appeared in Jack Broder's *Bride of the Gorilla*, playing Commissioner Tara, a man with greasy slicked-back hair and a noticeable beer gut. Jack Broder might be credited with keeping movie careers alive, but his two gorilla low-budget epics certainly did not maintain much dignity for the former stars who each look at least 10 years older. However, *Bela Lugosi Meets a Brooklyn Gorilla*, as noted in these pages, is a great deal of fun, interesting for its Lugosi and Sammy Petrillo shenanigans and for its gorilla-on-the-loose thrills.

In 1951, a year earlier, Jack Broder hired Universal screenwriter Curt Siodmak (most known for his screenplay of *The Wolf Man*) to write and direct *Bride of the Gorilla*, a Val Lewtonesque

jungle horror Gothic filmed at the beginning of the emerging science fiction decade, almost becoming an anachronism by the time of its release. Strangely, in spite of a listless (yet name) cast, a cheapjack jungle setting (augmented with lots of wild animal footage from other productions) and a lethargic pace, *Bride of the Gorilla* is an interesting retake of *The Wolf Man* as seen filtered through the Val Lewton RKO factory.

First of all, we have Lon Chaney as narrator at both the film's beginning and ending, and while this former Larry Talbot here plays the jungle law, his man-into-gorilla counterpart is played by the always delightfully menacing Raymond Burr, himself starting to show a paunch. Siodmak loves to feature moody subjective shots where Burr looks at his darkening hands and arms turning simian and out-stretched gorilla arms lunging toward the sexy Barbara Payton, sprawled provocatively on her bed. These sequences are few and far between, but they are well worth the price of admission.

The Val Lewton touch comes from the sinister witchy performance of Gisela Werbisek as Al-long who purposely tries to gain revenge on the Raymond Burr character by using a poison plant (delivered via devious jungle-drink cocktails) to force Burr psychologically to believe he transforms into a gorilla, when in fact he is always human (of course the cinematography creates a sense of ambivalence). Perhaps the pivotal sequence occurs when Barney Chavey (Burr) goes to a mirror and sees a gorilla looking directly back at him. Then, in perfect unity, both the human and gorilla raise their fist and break the mirror in unison. Even borrowing another trick from *The Wolf Man*, Barney, out roaming the jungle, gets his leg caught in an animal trap meant to capture the demon animal.

Barbara Payton, looking more than a little like Elisha Cuthbert (the dim-witted Kim on TV's finest series, *24*), smolders as the temptress doomed to always marry the wrong man, her latest husband being Barney. We know something is very amiss when the smoldering Payton invites Barney to their bed on the wedding night, and he nervously pines that he needs to take a walk in the jungle and that he'll be back soon.

For a lost relic that attempts to keep the Val Lewton genre of horror alive during the atomic age, using many stars of the past, *Bride of the Gorilla* deserves kudos. The cinematography by Charles Van Enger with musical score by Raoul Kraushaar (he also scored *Invaders from Mars* two years later) keeps the visuals interesting and moody. Raymond Burr and Barbara Payton shine. The Wade Williams print is mostly excellent, containing some occasional scratches and a few replacement sections. Extras are only a theatrical trailer. But for an unassuming little B schlocker, *Bride of the Gorilla* is worth a watch.

**THE WICKER MAN**
Movie: 2.5; Disc: 3.0
[Anchor Bay Entertainment]
British Lion's 1973 release, *The Wicker Man*, has been called "the Citizen Kane of horror movies" in *Cinefantastique* and an entire issue was devoted to the film before its aborted U.S. release. Anchor Bay went back to the vaults and released a stunning 35mm letterboxed print of the original American theatrical release (88 minutes), and also, in a boxed set, released the so-called director's cut that was assembled from less than stellar print elements. Anchor Bay chose to send me only the theatrical reedited version, so I cannot judge the 11-minute-longer director's cut (which is discussed elsewhere this issue in *Forum/Against 'Em*).

In the extraordinary 35-minute documentary included called *The Wicker Man Enigma*, writer Anthony Shaffer, director Robin Hardy, Producer Peter Snell, editor Eric Boyd-Perkins, stars Edward Woodward, Christopher Lee and Ingrid Pitt, along with potential U.S. distributor Roger Corman, discuss the fascinating history of the movie, leading right up to the storage and disposal of the original negative elements of the uncut version. Fascinating and tragic.

Unfortunately, the so-called commercial art film discussed in this thoroughly interesting documentary cannot match the disappointment of the movie itself, a film that fails on almost every level. However, *The Wicker Man* is always an interesting failure, but interesting more in the discussion than the viewing.

First of all, Christopher Lee, attempting to break free of his Hammer Gothic-villain trappings, portrays a different-style villain, Lord Summerisle, the titular leader of a small remote Scottish island that believes in the "Old gods" of Paganism. Lee, at times sporting a mod "big hair" rug and by film's conclusion wearing a women's long black wig, complete with psychedelic flower-child dress, dancing up and down the countryside, has created a very interesting performance, one that goes completely counter to his then current onscreen image. Because of this eccentric performance that breaks through Lee's stereotypes, critics have branded the performance as exceptional, and while it might very well be one of Lee's finest, it is still a supporting performance. Lee always looks as though he is ready to break into a smile, and seems to feel so smug that he is in on the joke and can barely contain the secret.

For a self-professed art film, the director seems to be pandering to the exploitative audience, having Britt Ekland perform a musical seduction number and dance totally in the nude (and disappointingly we learn that the gyrating booty-twister is actually a body double when viewed full-frame nude from the rear). Actually, in the shorter version, this sequence, with the nude Ekland writhing and banging rhythmically on Officer Howie's bedroom wall, the policeman recoiling in absolute horror, becomes the only proof he is a virgin, a sexually repressed Christian. But later in the film, Officer Howie (Edward Woodward), while investigating village houses, comes nonchalantly upon the totally nude Ingrid Pitt who is bathing in a pot of water, her thumb very close to her mouth. Art film or exploitation film, humm??

The Wicker Man's lead character, Howie, is such a stick in the mud that the audience relates more to the Pagan villagers who play the stupid cop for the fool he most certainly is. It is only at the end, with the surprising introduction of the Wicker Man, that Howie earns our respect and sympathy. But that man of vision, commitment and inner strength, viewed in the film's fiery climax, is worlds apart from the prig we witnessed for well over an hour.

The Wicker Man, structured as a detective thriller as Officer Howie arrives by plane on this isolated Pagan island to find a child reported as missing, tries to recapture the eeriness of the first half of John Moxey's Horror Hotel (aka City of the Dead) as Venetia Stevenson visits a quaint village and soon disappears, only to have her brother search for her, while the village community one by one insists she never was there. In The Wicker Man, the entire village denies ever having seen the missing child, although evidence pops up to the contrary. Here, The Wicker Man is never able to maintain a consistent tone of malevolence because of the constant introduction of quirky characters or townspeople who break into song. And since Edward Woodward plays Howie as a police investigator who always has that plank up his ass, well, we almost wish he never solves the mystery because he's so unlikable.

Ultimately, The Wicker Man is offsetting and too quirky for its own good. Just like the smirks that everyone on the island wears, the plot is always a tad too cute and clever for its own good. Christopher Lee does submit a wonderful performance, but his ominous sequences early on, especially when he insults the logical inconsistencies of the Christian faith, are undermined by his glib frolicking in dress and wig through the Scottish countryside at the film's climax. And those off-putting musical interludes simply lead the viewer to question what exactly is the tone the director is striving for in this movie anyway? The Wicker Man is neither fish nor fowl, neither a horror chiller nor a philosophical thesis, neither a satire nor a free-love let's get naked and "do it" film. Bottom line, it is only quirky and odd and unsettling. I do not be-

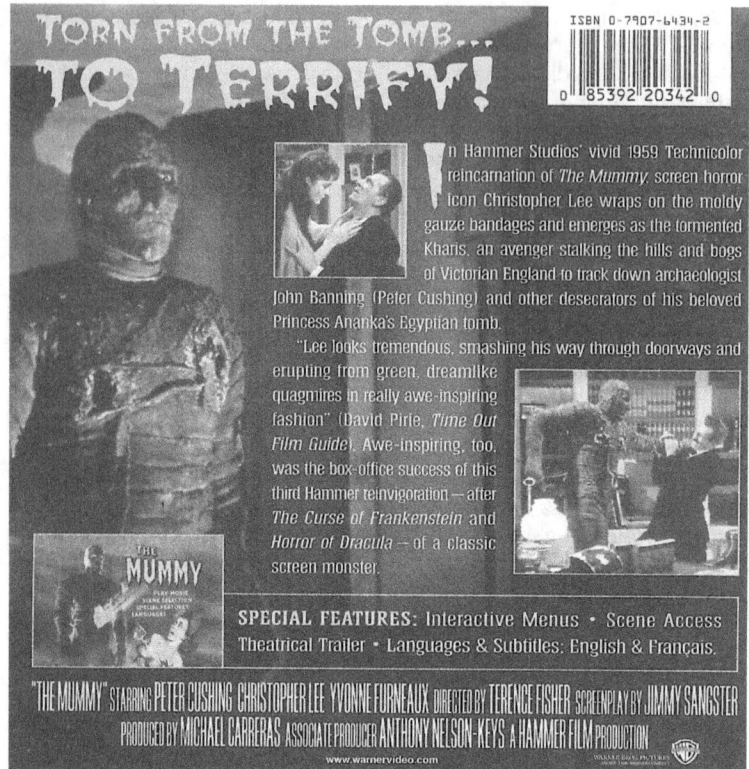

lieve 11 additional minutes would make this mess any better.

Anchor Bay is to be commended for delivering such a beautiful-looking letterboxed print that has been completely restored. For me the documentary extra is the main reason to own the film.

### THE MUMMY
Movie: 3.5; Disc: 3.0
[Warner Bros. Home Video]

Warner Brothers is at long last releasing the Universal-International Hammer productions to DVD, in restored deeply color-saturated letterboxed prints. As many fans note, these Hammer films were not anamorphic productions, but they were released theatrically in a slightly widescreen format. The problem here is that Warner Bros., rather than releasing the films in their true original aspect ratio, makes the films conform to a slightly more letterboxed format resulting in the tops of some heads being slightly clipped in some sequences. Shame on Warner Bros. for not truly duplicating the exact framing, but the effect is only sometimes annoying and distracting. The magnificent original source material, a deeply color-saturated 35mm print, is quite spectacular. However, having seen IB Technicolor 16mm prints of *The Mummy*, I can honestly say that this Warner Bros. DVD does not quite capture the intensity of the true Tech look of the Hammer classic. But it still delivers a fine-looking print. The only extra is a theatrical trailer.

What makes *The Mummy* one of the classic Hammer productions is the well-dressed though limited sets, and the classic performances of both Peter Cushing as Banning and Christopher Lee as Kharis the reanimated mummy. The screenplay by Jimmy Sangster is always intriguing and director Terence Fisher always keeps the action well-paced and moving forward.

Peter Cushing, nicknamed "Props," demonstrates the reason why in his very first scene, when he takes out a magnifying glass and intensely investigates a relic handled him. Cushing, starting the film with a broken leg that never receives proper medical attention, hobbles through the rest of the film, a very interesting aspect to his character. Later, back in America, marked for death by the Egyptian priest Mehemet Bey (Peter Pasco) who uses Kharis as his instrument for revenge, Cushing gets to jump backward over furniture, thrust a steel arrow through the mummy's body and, in his most famous gesture, allow Christopher Lee to strangle his prostrate body into unconsciousness and almost death. Let's not forgot the shot-gunned armed Cushing delivering both barrels point-blank into the mummy's rotting flesh.

And Christopher Lee, again submitting a mute performance (much as he did so successfully in *Curse of Frankenstein* and *Dracula—Prince of Darkness*), makes his performance as Kharis one of the best of his career. Unlike Boris Karloff and Lon Chaney, Lee creates his mummy as a speedy lumbering giant, a reanimated corpse that moves mechanically and soullessly; but like an animal prepared to corner and rip apart its prey, Lee's Kharis is always focused and bestial. The longing and human aspect of his soul comes through via his drooping eyes, eyes framing a face intense with his undying love for the Princess Ananka (here reincarnated into the beautiful Yvonne Furneaux whose performance is based more on her stance, her hair and her longing look). Remember, Karloff played a mummy for two seconds and Ardath Bey for the remainder of the 1932 classic movie. When it comes to the best mummy performance, Christopher Lee delivers the goods.

The truly classic Hammer films came and went within a decade, but *The Mummy* seems to feature all the essential ingredients (including a marvelous comic cameo by Michael Ripper as the Poacher) all done to the hilt of perfection. Perhaps the only missing ingredient is the lack of a James Bernard score. While I give the creative, dynamic edge to *Horror of Dracula* and *The Hound of the Baskervilles*, I must admit that *The Mummy* is one of the finest horror movies ever produced and showcases the one-two punch of Peter Cushing and Christopher Lee.

### STAKES
Movie: 2.5; Disc: 3.0
[Key East Entertainment]

Being a horror movie fan and living in Baltimore, the name Don Dohler is well known, he of *The Alien Factor* fame (his original 1977 indie film made, as are all his movies, in the Baltimore suburban area). After his original burst of creativity including *Fiend, Night Beast, Galaxy Invader* and *Blood Massacre*, Dohler took a 10-year or so hiatus from feature film production. Generally, Dohler was a beloved eccentric, writing, editing, producing and directing his own movies with his repertory crew of returning talent, both before and behind the camera. Dohler was infamous for retracing the same steps, recreating *The Alien Factor* as *Night Beast* and *Galaxy Invader* (and more recently as *Alien Rampage*). *Fiend* was his vampiric nod to horror, with Dohler's best actor Don Leifert portraying the energy-sucking "fiend" of the title. Short on ideas, Dohler was full of enthusiasm and became the ideal cheerleader for making monster movies in Baltimore. As George Stover always reminds me, Dohler's films are made for the working class guys who want to down a six pack and watch a bloody horror movie on a Friday night.

Returning to the wanderlust of feature filmmaking only a few years ago, Dohler's first misstep was *Alien Rampage*, simply more of the same and done less creatively with its minimal budget now blatantly showing. But then two important developments charged the creative battery of Dohler: First, discovering that high-res video cinematography looks almost as good as shooting in 16mm, his old tried and true method, and second, filming direct to video allows Adobe (and other) software programs to be used to create high-quality special effects on a budget. No longer did the film have to be shipped out to the lab where actual shooting was merged with laboratory-created visual effects. Finally, Dohler hooked up with his creative partner, Joe "The Cop" Ripple. Ripple wanted to become co-producer, co-writer and assume the position of director, a job that Dohler liked least of all. Ask anyone who worked with Dohler and they will say, Dohler loves the technical end, but he never offers much advice to his actors. Ripple's talent and enthusiasm freed Dohler to concentrate on what he liked doing the most, and Ripple was the man who could do technical things (being a Baltimore policeman, his experience with weapons becomes a plus in the latest batch of films, where gunfights and weapon handling look real) and work with the human element, the actors. Creatively, this was a marriage created in schlock film heaven, and it has proved to be a productive one improving the quality of the movies.

*Stakes* (not the latest Dohler film), Dohler/Ripple's film of 2002, is perhaps the best-realized film ever produced by Don Dohler, and

Joe Ripple's talent as director is developing by leaps and bounds.

Ostensibly a parallel world vampire thriller, Stakes has the most urban look of any Dohler movie, even though most of the action occurs in Perry Hall, returning to that old chestnut the Perry Inn (actually a neighborhood watering hole on Belair Road) and making good moody use of a rural greenhouse (lit with eerie blue light from both within and without). Stakes, running a tight 83 minutes, does not drag in the middle like many of Dohler's films, and the claustrophobic feel of the movie (the cellar sequences and warehouse sets are used for maximum horrific effect) actually generates some intense jolts, even causing me to fly out of my seat once (something I thought I would never say about a Dohler film). Since Don Dohler's resurgence, the Dohler/Ripple team is using professional actors and they put to shame the amateur talent inherent in movies such as The Alien Factor and Galaxy Invader. Perennial Dohler cult star George Stover, the only actor who appeared in every Dohler production (and starred in Blood Massacre and Harvesters), plays Father O'Grady, a kiss-ass priest who wears a beret with a cross embossed across the front. The actor's first appearance has the over-50 actor running full speed attempting to outrun the cult of vampires, and I must admit it was the fastest I ever saw Stover move in the almost 40 years I have known him. But Stover's grizzled intensity becomes the cornerstone of the movie, showing these young yahoos how to stomp vampire butt.

Special effects are handsomely mounted by Mitch Klein, who uses computer-generated effects to maximum effect, even adding that final puff of smoke after each vampire disintegration. The fight scenes are staged effectively and the concept of using frozen holy-water stakes to kill the pure-blood vampires is quite creative. The Night of the Living Dead steal, where both a mother's child and the mother herself become victims of vampires, is photographed quite cleverly, rapidly circling in on the child's fangs ("I got a secret to tell you") and then whipping back again to the mother, her fangs bared ("I know!"). And the film's ending with the vampire squad, armed with wooden stakes closing in for the kill, as the title and credits roll up, is a totally satisfying way to end this low-budget blood feast.

And to complete the package, Dohler includes a nifty "making-of" documentary that is very intriguing and funny and generally demonstrates the love these young professionals feel toward making quality backyard movies released directly to DVD. The usual standard Dohler blooper reel (here called "mis-Stakes") is included and shows the cast and crew having even more fun. Ripple and Dohler supply audio commentary as well.

For people who haven't seen a Don Dohler film since the late 1970s or early 1980s, you might be in for a pleasant surprise. Stakes is not the most original B production ever made, but it is an energetic vampire action adventure that is well worth 83 minutes of time. Stakes is obviously a labor of love, and here's hoping that Ripple and Dohler make many more films as good as this one in the years to come.

### INVISIBLE INVADERS/ JOURNEY TO THE SEVENTH PLANET

Movie: (Invaders 2.5; Journey 2.0); Disc: 3.0 [MGM Midnite Movies]

The latest batch of MGM Midnite Movies are light on horror and science fiction (we have to wait until the next round of releases in late August for more horror and science fiction), but for a $15 list price, this double-feature is a bargain. Interestingly enough, the only hook linking both features is that John Agar stars, yet the world of Sid Pink and Edward L. Cahn seem light-years apart.

First, for me, *Invisible Invaders* is the pick of this litter, for the 1959 Edward L. Cahn movie was seldom seen after its initial theatrical release and appeared infrequently on syndicated TV. Amazingly, the black and white source material used for this MGM release is outstanding, featuring a pristine high-contrast, deep-density 35mm print. The print looks as though it were stored in a vault since 1959. The movie itself is spotty, featuring some marvelous sequences, but it is not the best of its decade. The film runs a brisk 66 minutes and our hero John Agar does not enter the film until the 25-minute mark. Agar, looking slightly older than his Universal days, now sporting a military haircut, comes off as being cold-blooded and far less lovable. In an early sequence, Agar is escorting several people to his well-protected bunker when a citizen threatens him with a gun, claiming he wants the Jeep for his own escape. When the man's attention is diverted, Agar pumps a bullet into his head, instantly killing the pathetic aggressor. It seems a trace of the anti-hero 1960s was infiltrating the more innocent 1950s during its final year.

John Carradine plays a scientist who is blown up in his laboratory in the first few minutes of the movie, and it is his reanimated corpse and distinctive voice that stars in the movie. Those early sequences where the hedges move apart as the invisible alien lifeforce creates footprints in the dirt, shuffling along, as Carradine's disembodied voice emanates from his grave, are chillingly effective. And it is those sequences with our human survivors nestled in their caveside underground bunker that generates the horror. Outside, reanimated corpses, in various stages of early decay, walk Frankenstein-style, searching out

human survivors they desire to kill, in sequences that may have inspired George Romero when he made *Night of the Living Dead* (along with the plague sequence from *Things to Come*). The pivotal sequence occurs when Agar, wearing his radiation suit, lures one living-dead alien to fall into a pit of liquid acrylic that hardens rapidly, trapping the alien spirit inside. The corpse is taken back to a storage room in the bunker where the plastic coating is broken, allowing the alien spirit to be held captive in this small room. Experimenting with ways of destroying the alien threat, it is soon found that sound waves make the aliens become semi-visible, but also destroy them and their ships in the process.

*Invisible Invaders* is not classic in any sense, but it is far less familiar and seems to showcase an independent look that does not associate it with AIP or even other United Artist sci-fi monster classics (such as Cahn's *It! The Terror from Beyond Space*). *Invisible Invaders* is interesting B fodder and it is marvelous to see the film presented in such a gorgeous fashion after all these decades.

*Journey to the Seventh Planet*, co-scripted by Ib Melchior and Sid Pink, produced and directed by Sid Pink, was quite a colorful production when released by American International in 1962. It is juvenile B production fun featuring splashy color, miniature sets and miniature monsters and low-brow special effects that somehow work

much better than ever expected. John Agar is the American in this Danish production and he seems far too obsessed with sex and beautiful women to be a scientist aboard a UN-sponsored ship to explore Uranus (after systemically exploring all the closer planets in the solar system).

The Ib Melchior-Sid Pink screenplay is very intellectual for a playful exploitation B romp, and its premise has been used since in better productions. The movie concerns a dominant living brain on the planet Uranus who infiltrates the pysches of all the human crew members, learning their past, their weaknesses and strengths, and this brain intelligence can recreate vivid impressions of crew members' past lives here on Uranus. The movie-viewing audience can see that the planet's surface is rocky and dead appearing when the rocket first lands, but within moments, via time-lapse photography, a Danish forest and village is recreated, right down to a stream with a rock in the middle. John Agar, with only one thing on his mind, recreates Danish model Greta Thyssen as his blonde dream date, right here on Uranus. Other crew members see their past cherished memories brought to actual life millions of miles from Earth. Interestingly enough, Sid Pink was very clever... he filmed a movie situated on the surface of Uranus but makes Uranus appear very Earth-like.

Soon the rocket-crew members discover a huge wall, in actuality a force field that surrounds the center of the planet. One member dares to stick his arm through the force field wall and finds it is instantly frozen. Donning their space suits, the planetary explorers walk through the wall and discover the actual planet of Uranus inside, but all the rustic childhood memories are more fun, so they all return to the Uranus of their childhood and libido-driven dreams outside the wall.

By the film's end all monstrous one-eyed beasties and evil brains are destroyed, allowing the crew to return to a less exciting Earth, all to the strains of the classic theme song, *Journey to the Seventh Planet* (until now omitted from the laserdisc and other home video releases). Unfortunately, *Journey to the Seventh Planet* is very slow-paced and features underwhelming special effects. While the premise is intelligent and involving, the execution lacks the budget and imagination to effectively deliver the goods. The colorful widescreen print (unfortunately, not enhanced for 16:9 monitors) is beautiful looking, but the movie would be in higher resolution if the print were delivered anamorphically. The only extras on both movies are theatrical trailers.

Once again MGM has delivered two entertaining B productions with pristine prints for a very modest price. While neither movie is among John Agar's best, it is refreshing to see two low-profile genre pieces offered as a double-feature and at an affordable price.

### BEAST OF BLOOD
Movie: 2.0; Disc: 3.5
[Image Entertainment]

For me, it is hard to believe that people a generation younger love the *Beast of Blood* trilogy for the same reasons that I love, say, Richard Cunha's *Franken-stein's Daughter*. Schlock B programmers such as *Franken-stein's Daughter* offer a sense of fun and style, allowing me to relive a more innocent time from my past. Oddly enough, John Ashley, the actor who looks like a squat Elvis Presley, sneer and all, stars in both B productions, and Ashley still appears energetic and handsome in this Philippine cult classic.

What cheapens the appeal of *Beast of Blood* is its island location with its abundance of frightened natives looking gloomy and its too-often used long, dull treks through the jungle, over the rocky bluffs, across the beach. The plot is meandering and padded, but the monster attacks are numerous and, especially when the Ashley party finds and explores the deserted mansion of the evil Dr. Lorca (Eddie Garcia), the mood creepy and frightening. The shots of dead green-blooded monsters, maggots crawling over their decaying flesh, are unsettling. The other American cast member Celeste Yarnall (TV appearances include *Star Trek* and *It Takes a*

*Thief*) even has a gratuitous nude sequence and loves to parade around in her island jungle bikini, even after Lorca's men hold her captive.

This all leads to the ridiculous final third, when we finally come across the still-surviving Lorca (who was badly burned in the fiery conclusion of the previous entry) who has decapitated his beast of blood to attempt to control its killing instinct. Just like in *Re-Animator*, both the trunk and the head of the fiend are kept alive, and when the body breaks free of its straps, the head begins to moan menacingly, "Lorca, I will talk now," as the two-piece monster destroys the scientist's lab and again sets the island ablaze.

To be honest, when *Beast of Blood* is in its most creepy mode (such as the attack upon the sleeping Yarnall in her quarters as one of the green-blooded fiends slowly sneaks into the house, taking its time before attacking her), it is gripping and fun. The monsters are classic in the best 1950s sense, and Eddie Garcia's performance as Lorca is far too short but highly effective. If only the pacing were faster and the plot better constructed, this film might be its generation's *Frankenstein's Daughter*.

Extras on this Sam Sherman production are many, including the normal extras of audio commentary by Sherman, trailers of all the "Blood" series, a still gallery, etc. But most exceptional are current interviews with Celeste Yarnall (at the Chiller Theatre Expo 2000) and an in-depth chat with director Eddie Romero that is truly entertaining. Also included is a trailer for a horror spook show and the lost scenes missing from Sherman's Americanized version. The print used is full-frame and has occasional blemishes and wear, but the print is complete and the color deeply saturated. While never a favorite of mine, I must admit that *Beast of Blood* does have its moments.

### BRAIN OF BLOOD
Movie: 2.0; Disc: 3.0
[Image Entertainment]

In 1971 Hemisphere Pictures did not have a new Philippine monstrosity to loose upon the drive-in world, so Eddie Romero hired Sam Sherman and Al Adamson to produce a quickie drive-in feature that could fill the bill and satisfy the masses. What Sherman and Adamson loosed upon the unsuspecting masses was *Brain of Blood* (maintaining the profitable "blood" motif), a movie whose style is based upon generic low-budget ineptness. Once again we have a movie that screams it has no budget, but Sherman enjoyed giving old Hollywood veterans a chance to shine one more time. In this movie we have Kent Taylor as the maniacal mad scientist who wishes to prove that brain transplants are feasible, Grant Williams (the hero of *The Incredible Shrinking Man*) as another doctor (but Williams is hardly recognizable with his Beatles-style haircut and extra bulk added to his frame), Reed Hadley as the dying/transplanted Middle Eastern ruler and Angelo Rossitto as the dwarf medical assistant. The Sherman/Adamson team has concocted an homage to 1940s schlock but with a heavy dose of visceral violence.

In one delightful sequence in the dungeon, two girls are chained to the wall, both victims slowly being drained of their blood. The evil Angelo Rossitto comes down to drain another vial of blood and dangles the key ring in front of the ladies, ranting and raving, taunting them, laughing out of control. Instead of transplanting the Middle Eastern ruler's brain to a physically comparable human subject, the wily Kent Taylor uses his retarded burn-victim assistant, the giant, hulking John Bloom (he played the Frankenstein monster in *Dracula vs. Frankenstein*) as the recipient of the ruler's brain. Of course this will never work out, but by film's climax the poor unfortunate Grant Williams becomes the final resting place for the brain. Of course "big hair" Regina Carroll (the wife of Al Adamson) becomes the woman who needs to keep the ruler's brain alive so he can carry through with his promise to marry her and make her co-ruler of his nation.

The movie itself is slow-paced, predictable and mostly silly, but it does feature a few interesting sequences, and the cast of veterans is always interesting to watch, if sometimes in an embarrassing can-you-believe type of way. However, Sam Sherman and Al Adamson did deliver a Hemisphere product that was ready-made for the drive-in circuit and thus, for what it must have cost, was a success for all concerned.

The movie features a wealth of extras, but many of them also appear on the *Beast of Blood* DVD—an in-depth interview with Eddie Romero, the spook show trailer for *House of Terror*, theatrical trailers for all the Hemisphere "Blood" movies and a wonderful still gallery. What is new is the audio commentary delivered by Sam Sherman and another recent interview with Beverly Powers (Hills), star of *Brides of Blood*. The print used for *Brain of Blood* is a nice-looking 35mm 4:3 ratio print that shows some occasional wear (lacking outstanding color). Again, the film is not really my cup of tea, but for fans of low-budget 1970s exploitation, *Brain of Blood* has a cult following.

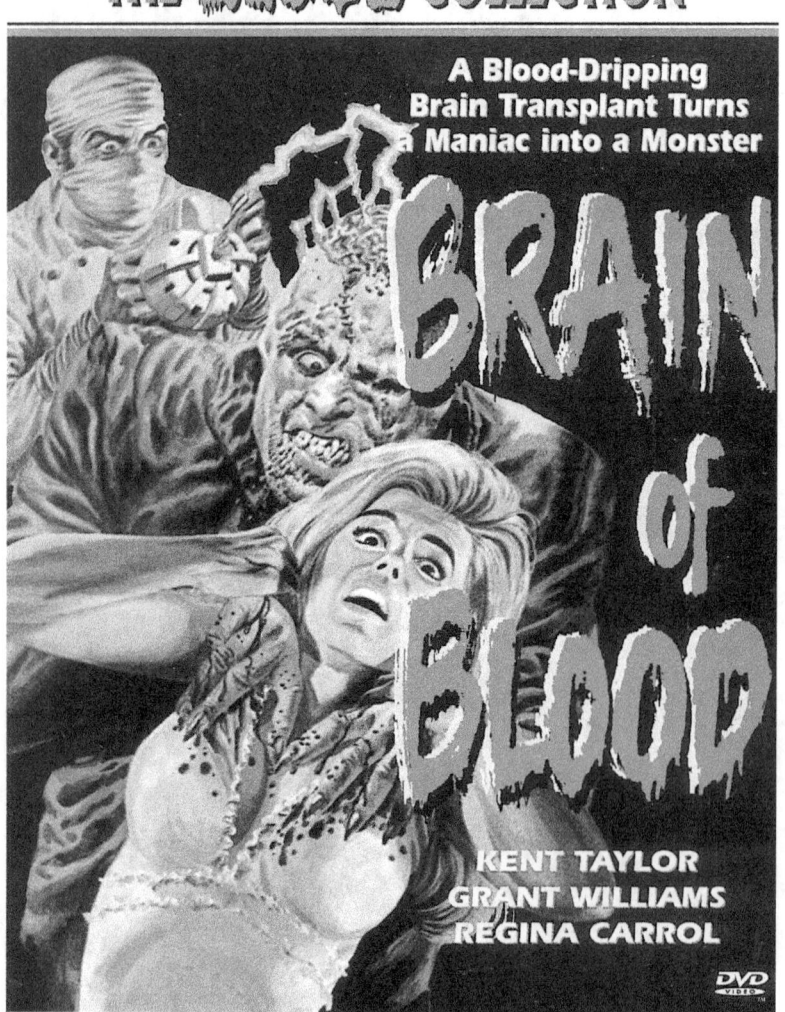

**20,000 LEAGUES UNDER THE SEA [SPECIAL EDITION]**
Movie: 3.0; Disc: 4.0
[Disney DVD]

Walt Disney's *20,000 Leagues Under the Sea* has always been critically lauded for its wonderful sense of adventure and groundbreaking special effects, and for 1954, the movie was cutting-edge. However, while I have always loved sections of this science fiction adventure more than others, overall, the film has always left me cold. For one thing, Richard Fleischer's direction doesn't possess a sense of pacing or tension, and with a running time of 127 minutes, the movie meanders and drifts when it needs to crescendo with suspense and anxiety. Too many shots are wasted filming undersea flora and fauna and slowly lumbering human sea divers. Also, the performances by James Mason (perhaps the finest performance of his career) and Paul Lukas are brooding, low-key and serious. Star Kirk

Douglas, energetic and the essence of the Disney hero, appears to be performing in a lighthearted adventure romp. His broad over-the-top adventurer is right out of a juvenile Disney production. Placed in the same movie, these performances clash. Peter Lorre, wonderful as always and a shining light in the production, tries to play his role somewhere between the playfulness of Douglas and the dramatic intensity of Lukas and Mason.

The film's strengths are its intense Technicolor photography and exciting special effects (ship-ram sinkings, pre-atomic explosions and giant squid attacks with dangling, floppy tentacles causing the audience to squeal). Judged by today's standards, the giant squid looks like a giant model, its quaint authority holds our attention.

James Mason as Captain Nemo, who may have discovered the power of the atom generations before mid-century America (this is based upon the novel by Jules Verne), shines in those sequences where he lovingly describes the beauty of the undersea world that he chooses over the actual one, and in the scene where he describes the torture and death of his wife and son, the audience can truly feel the captain's pain. His final noble sequence, after having been mortally wounded, as he lies writhing in pain, opening the portal to glance one more time at his undersea domain, is quite intense. But then we segue into scenes featuring Kirk Douglas strumming his guitar singing away, playing with the seal or rubbing Peter Lorre's hair the wrong way; all the dramatic tension is dissipated. But perhaps, appealing to a juvenile market, this is exactly what Richard Fleischer was told to do. Thus, ultimately, *20,000 Leagues Under the Sea* is a compromised vision, a film with great sequences and a few inspired performances that appears to have been a watered-down vision.

This two-disc Special Edition is the ultimate for fans of the movie. We have audio commentary with director Richard Fleischer, the ADR audio tracks of Peter Lorre, Radio Spots from 1954, documentaries on the making of the feature and another one on Disney and Verne. We have footage of the original squid, the sunset squid sequence, script excerpts, an animated short that ran with the feature, storyboards, unused animation, a tour of the *Nautilus*, a short on the actual Humbolt squid, etc. The actual print used (aspect ratio 2:55:1) is beautiful featuring intense Technicolor hues, but the only flaw is that the print appears to be a tad soft on focus. For lovers of this classic fantasy adventure, fans could not ask for more.

**STAR TREK: NEMESIS**
Movie: 3.0; Disc: 3.5
[Paramount Home Video]

Amazingly, the *Star Trek* fan base has now aged and most Trekkers have joined the legions of fans who love the classic Golden Age horror productions. Younger audiences no longer find the appeal of *Star Trek* as exciting as their parents did a generation before, as evidenced by the sagging ratings of the latest *Trek*-derived TV series.

The *Star Trek* film franchise, now controlled by Rick Berman in the wake of Gene Roddenberry's death over a decade ago, relies upon the second series, *Next Generation*, which is also viewed as a relic by younger sci-fi fans. Even though they look surprisingly chipper, stars Patrick Stewart, Jonathan Frakes, Brent Spiner and LeVar Burton are showing their maturity. Thus the *Star Trek* franchise appeals to a nostalgia audience of baby boomers and and graying Gen-X fans.

For these and other reasons, the box office generated by *Nemesis* was disappointing, and even worse, critics chewed up this latest entry in the *Star Trek* canon. Too bad, for *Star Trek: Nemesis* happens to be one of the best entries in the feature film series since the *Next Generation* cast replaced the original starship troopers. The direction by Stuart Baird, fortunately an outsider and not a member of the cast, brings a more objective and slick appearance to what is ultimately an action adventure movie. To the movie's strength, the action sequences (some of the best battle-in-outer-space ship-against-ship firefights ever staged) hold their own with the human performances (the mentoring humanity of Patrick Stewart's Picard and his tutelage of android Data, portrayed masterfully by Brent Spiner, is profoundly moving). As is true with the best *Star Trek* movies, this or the former generation, the story must not be dominated by intense action/special effects sequences. Such an action/adventure framework must be secondary to the human drama occurring between crew members. Besides the mentoring relationship between Picard and Data, the soul of this movie, we have the even more quirky relationship between Picard and his clone (yet much younger) double Shinzon, played by a powerful Tom Hardy, a man who pretends he wishes to make Romulan peace with the Federation but, in fact, he needs Picard's blood to stay alive. But the film subtly forwards the thesis that even genetically perfect matches do not produce the exact same human beings, that we are shaped more by environment than genes. As is true with all the best *Star Trek* movies, a beloved crew member dies in the final reel, sacrificing himself for the lives of the crew, and a life lesson is learned in the process. It's a formula, but when done as well as this film does it, the result is dramatic and emotionally moving.

The DVD features a wonderful letterboxed print with vibrant Dolby 5.1 sound and some outstanding extras including audio commentary by director Stuart Baird, several documentaries on filming the movie and deleted sequences. It is a pity that too many people dismiss *Star Trek: Nemesis*, for it is simply good science fiction with a core of sensitive human performances that teach lessons that all of us are better off having been exposed to.

### KRONOS
Movie: 2.0; Disc: 3.0
[Image Entertainment]

Science fiction B movies are beloved by generations of movie buffs, and while some fans love the cheap independents, others enjoy the major studio B programmers (Universal's *Monolith Monsters* or *Tarantula*; MGM's *Fiend Without a Face,* UAs' *Monster Who Challenged the World*,

etc.). 20th Century Fox entered the fray with the 1957 *Kronos*, a B movie filmed in widescreen Regalscope, which featured a noble cast consisting of Jeff Morrow, Morris Ankrum, Robert Shayne and was produced and directed by Kurt Neumann (director of *The Fly*). So why does this B film fail when so many others succeeded?

First of all, the movie is based on a story by Irving Block, one-third of the special effects team of Jack Rabin, Irving Block and Louis De Witt, who handle the principal special effects (along with Gene Warren and others) on the production. While the low-budget special effects created by the Rabin, Block, De Witt team are finally getting their due, perhaps the lesson learned here is don't let your special effects team write your script. While the basic script concept is very intellectual and scientifically curious, the resulting monster is little more than a giant black box that thumps along, piston-powered, and the result of creating a unique monster is pure tedium. Surprisingly, the special effects created by Rabin, Block and De Witt are hardly ever believable, sometimes having an animated component that is even less realistic. The concept of a two-part black box slowly stumping across grassy fields and rocky terrain is less dramatic than the ever-so- slow moving black monoliths from *The Monolith Monsters*. The giant black box hardly does anything except suck up all the energy used against it, so the most dramatic effects show stock footage of atomic explosions and electricity-based lightning bolts covering the box's surface.

Far more interesting is the subplot, occurring at military Lab-Central where a human being, taken over by the alien predators, infiltrates a scientist at the government lab and uses him to subvert the human efforts to defeat the alien invasion. The concept of how humans are alien-controlled with the fascinating energy-trans-

ference special effects are far more interesting than a giant black box lumbering through the countryside. Even Jeff Morrow's otherwise B-star charisma is wasted on a script that fails to do much with human interaction and acts of heroism. Running a lethargic 78 minutes, *Kronos* is one of the major disappointments of 1950s science fiction B cinema, and what was concocted as a novel idea was transformed into a dreary and dull programmer best forgotten.

**KISS OF THE VAMPIRE**
Movie: 3.0; Disc: 3.5
[Universal/Image DVD]

Hammer Film Productions peaked artistically by the time of *Kiss of the Vampire*, but the movie, arriving in 1963, offered an alternative to Terence Fisher's Hammer vampire mythos, and while I much prefer *Brides of Dracula*, *Horror of Dracula* and even *Dracula—Prince of Darkness*, Don Sharp's vision of vampirism is rather interesting, becoming more cult-based with sexual hedonism suggested by having vampires meet clandestinely wearing skimpy white robes with nothing underneath. This film more than a little reminds me of Terence Fisher's vision of the satanic cult in *The Devil Rides Out*.

The major deficiency of *Kiss of the Vampire* is failing to have either Peter Cushing as Van Helsing, the ultimate Hammer vampire hunter (instead, Clifford Evans portrays a drunken Professor Zimmer, the almost reluctant vampire slayer), or Christopher Lee as the featured vampire Dr. Ravna (here portrayed by aging and stately Noel Willman). Hammer does best with Byronic hero- style vampires, men of passion and fury (Christopher Lee in *Horror of Dracula* and David Peel in *Brides of Dracula*) and Noel Willman's performance is generally too low-key and underplayed. Willman's Dr. Ravna is subtle, regal and mannerly, but when we see the beast within, that beast is still rather stiff and regal.

Fortunately, the hero and heroine are played by talents who have passion and enthusiasm, chiefly Edward de Souza as Gerald who is honeymooning with wife Marianne, portrayed by Jennifer Daniel, essaying a performance that will be nailed by Barbara Shelley in *Dracula—Prince of Darkness* (a young innocent who is wooed to the dark side and loves the transformation that vampirism provides). Edward de Souza possesses the rugged good looks of a Hammer leading man, but he also submits a nuanced performance that makes him stand out. His performance as Gerald starts out with the young buck confident in his new married life, truly loving his beautiful wife. When she disappears at a masquerade party hosted by Rava and de Souza is compromised with a "mickey" in his drink, fueled by massive quantities of alcohol, he next submits the lovable-drunk performance. And finally awakening the next morning, suffering from a massive hangover, and being told that he does not have a wife, that no Marianne is here, de Souza next submits the fearfully panicked performance that stands out best of all. This morphs into the revengeful and resourceful hero role where he risks even the horrors of the undead to save Marianne from the sexually perverse world of vampirism. Transforming from confidence, to inebriated lout, to frightened, confused victim and finally the conquering hero, de Souza's acting is among the best of any Hammer leading male.

*Kiss of the Vampire* is often criticized for its climax showing low-budget bats attacking the castle of Ravna, biting and ripping out the throats of scantily clad vampires who scream for their lives. To be honest, such special effects, while they pale next to similar bird attacks from Hitchcock's *The Birds* released the same year, are still cozy and Hammeresque enough to earn my appreciation. The film's best sequence is when de Souza returns to Ravna's castle and is reintroduced to his wife Marianne, who splits in his face as a sexy young vampire girl begs to be able to initiate de Souza into the blood cult. This sequence portrays Hammer at its best.

*Kiss of the Vampire*, available for decades in faded pink 16mm prints (the film was printed in Eastmancolor, not Tech, so all available prints turned red or pink, losing their original luster), has been completely restored to its intense coloring of the original theatrical release, and the print here is presented with original aspect ratio (1:66:1) so the letterboxing makes this DVD presentation as close as possible to the original theatrical release. *Kiss of the Vampire* might not be *Horror of Dracula*, but it is a worthy addition to the Hammer vampire canon.

**BLUE SUNSHINE**
**(Special Limited Edition)**
Movie: 3.0; Disc: 3.5
[Synapse Films DVD]

In 1976, when the independent *Blue Sunshine* was given a

limited theatrical release, David Cronenberg and John Carpenter were ruling the horror film roost. Jeff Lieberman saw his debuting film *Squirm* released earlier that same year, which was a fun killer-worm B production. However, with *Blue Sunshine*, Lieberman's second production which he both wrote and directed, he was mining the same terrain as the more adventurous David Cronenberg. Cronenberg's cinematic style involved traumatic biochemical changes in human beings that create almost a new species. We see it in *Shivers* (aka *They Came from Within*) and *Rabid* where phallic parasites invade their human hosts, either killing them or causing them to transform into parasitic creatures. In *Scanners* women who receive an experimental drug give birth to telepathic children who seem a step or two further up the evolutionary scale. With *Blue Sunshine*, people attending college 10 years earlier all indulged in an LSD-style hallucinogenic that would profoundly change them 10 years later. The symptoms include schizophrenic/psychopathic rage coupled with a complete loss of hair (with a few ugly tufts remaining). Interestingly, the script is presented as a mystery with several significant characters introduced individually at the film's start whose lives crisscross as the plot unwinds.

Zalman King, before his soft-core porn days, stars as the tormented hero who witnesses his buddy freak out at a party and murder three women, burning their bodies in the fireplace. King is accused of the crime and must solve the mystery in order to clear himself. Along the way he encounters a doctor buddy who was a drug dealer in college, a state politician (Mark Goddard, star of *Lost in Space*) who indulged frequently in Blue Sunshine and becomes the loose cannon ready to explode when we least expect it. Another victim, a young woman, sees her hair slowly fall out as she finally morphs into the film's dominant horrific image… a bald psychopath wearing a bathrobe, who fights to the death before she is catapulted off the balcony of a high-rise and smashes against the pavement multiple stories below.

The film's climax is very exciting with the politico's now-deranged bodyguard confronting Zalman King after first destroying a disco (poetic justice or just another evil narcotic of modern civilization?), and the final climactic battle occurs in a deserted department store where mannequins become menacing and every shadow and creak causes audiences to rise in their seat. Lieberman shows his ability to generate subtle chills in this last sequence which is very frightening. Of course, once the last psychedelic madman is destroyed, the film's coda reveals that 250 tabs of Blue Sunshine were never accounted for, meaning more human time-bombs are ready to explode at any time.

Overall, *Blue Sunshine* lacks the visceral punch and the visionary imagination of David Cronenberg, but it is a solid horror feature of the 1970s and has been seldom seen for over a decade. The anamorphic widescreen print, created from the best surviving 35mm print (as the film's original negatives have been lost), is generally quite good with only a few blemishes. The film has been remixed in 5.1

Dolby and contains audio commentary by Lieberman, as well as the inclusion of his short anti-drug film *The Ringer*. We have a terrific 30-minute interview where Lieberman reflects on his career and his stylistic decisions. We also have a still gallery and theatrical trailer. The second disc is the original CD soundtrack of the movie, never before released.

Synapse Films has created quite a tidy little package with this overdue DVD release of *Blue Sunshine*, and for those fans of 1970s horror, this obscure little gem hasn't looked this spiffy since its original theatrical release.

### A VIRGIN AMONG THE LIVING DEAD
Movie: 2.0; Disc: 3.0
[Image Entertainment]

Many people claim that Jess Franco's movies improved as he moved from black and white to color, as he allowed his sexually perverse visions to dominate his movies and as the Euro-release of his movies during the 1970s and 1980s allowed him to put nightmares on film that surely would have been censored a decade before.

Others would say his early black-and-white films such as *Dr. Orlof's Monster* aimed more for horrific mood and mayhem and that his horror visions were unique and chilling and his plots more linear and focused. For me, those early Franco cheapies were his best, and once he allowed his dreams to dominate his cinematic vision, the movies became more self-indulgent and lost their power. Forsaking a coherent plot for extended dream sequences and sublimating the concept of character development, Franco's films have a keen visual style and a perverse sexuality that is only available in these uncut European release prints. However, erotic nudity is a pleasant deviation, but Franco again crosses the line by featuring shots of "uncle" John Vernon becoming obviously sexually aroused by niece Christina (von Blanc). And the film's climax is not horrific or supernatural but an extended rape sequence where the lovely lass is physically victimized. In his liner notes, Tim Lucas proclaims the merits of this film stating "mood supplants narrative" and *A Virgin Among the Living Dead* is "narratively more akin to macabre poetry than prose." To Tim Lucas this lack of plot and dependence upon visionary dream reality makes the film poetry and thus justifies its lack of character-motivated plot, one of the conventions of drama. For me, even in David Lynch-land where dream reality rules, movies such as *Mulholland Dr.* have tightly constructed plots (albeit difficult to figure out) and are character-driven. David Lynch uses the rules of conventional drama and then applies his idiosyncratic vision to create something quite Lynchian and innovative. But Jess Franco simply leaves me cold, and the sexual perversions that dominate his later films disturb me (they do not entertain me).

The widescreen director's cut of *A Virgin Among the Living Dead* is quite beautiful nonetheless and the disc contains alternate/deleted footage that is both perverse and sometimes interesting. A theatrical trailer is included, and to Image Entertainment's credit, the print is available with English subtitles.

I share Tim's joy that a seldom-seen and often butchered Franco supernatural horror film is at last available uncut, but I only wish the movie were worthy of such care and attention.

### TO THE DEVIL... A DAUGHTER
Movie: 3.0; Disc: 3.5
[Anchor Bay Entertainment]

Opinions certainly change in 25 years. Back in 1976, when *To the Devil... a Daughter* was released, I felt Christopher Lee's finest later performances were in *Rasputin—The Mad Monk* and *The Wicker Man*. While I agree that Lee is mostly stellar in *The Wicker Man*, his character is undermined by its foolish cross-dressing, prancing and dancing and silly-sung climax. Rasputin, one of his best performances that tried to stretch beyond his horror film persona, is interesting yet flawed. Lee tends to create a larger-than-life caricature and delivers a performance way over the top, bombastic throughout when it needs to be subtle. His Rasputin does have some marvelous sequences, but overall, the characterization does not stand the test of time.

However, *To the Devil... a Daughter*, sadly the final film Hammer ever released, co-stars Christopher Lee as Father Michael, a renegade priest (of a religion that worships Astaroth, or Satan), and while I did not think much of the movie upon its initial theatrical release, this wonderful Anchor Bay DVD totally changes my mind. While the film is very flawed, especially its final five minutes or so, the performance by Christopher Lee is one of his best, Hammer or otherwise. In the film's opening moments, Father Michael is excommunicated from the Christian church, and the film picks up his life two decades later as he now uses the black arts to resurrect the power of Satan. His 17-year-old "nun" Nastassja Kinski, in her first major role, will be used sexually for satanic purposes. She is rescued from Michael's henchman by her biological father (Denholm Elliott) and placed in the care of friend and occult author Richard Widmark (sleepwalking through a role tailor-made for Peter Cushing, in healthier days) who does not understand the evil inherent in the innocent-appearing young girl. Father Michael, wearing the mask of Astaroth, ritualistically impregnates a woman who will give birth to a monstrosity nine months later. Once her labor begins, Father Michael ties the unfortunate mother to the bed and binds her legs together, bending her legs at the knees so vaginal birth is impossible. As the woman writhes in pain, director Peter Sykes juxtaposes sequences of the sleeping Kinski writhing (but hers is more orgasmic) and thrusting her bare legs halfway back over her head, showing more than a few pubic hairs in the process. Ultimately, the doomed pregnant woman delivers her baby almost *Alien*-style (hmm, did Ridley Scott see this movie?), with the baby bursting forward through the woman's abdomen leaving the mother a blood-soaked mess who soon dies. Using many interesting camera angles, the few people attending this birth grimace in moral horror as the smiling face of Father Michael glares in the foreground. Christopher Lee's facial expressions alone, his perverse smiles especially, help to mold his performance as something special. His quiet smugness at knowing he has mastered the powers of darkness makes his performance beam with arrogance and self-confidence.

While *The Devil Rides Out*, the first Hammer film based upon Dennis Wheatley literature, was an artistic and commercial success, Hammer went to the well one more time with Wheatley's *To the Devil... a Daughter*. However, the script was in constant flux and after the ending was filmed (which was deemed too similar to the lightning/fire death of Lee's Dracula in *Scars of Dracula*), giving Christopher Lee's villain an explosive send-off, the climax was recut from already existing film. Now hero Widmark steps into the protective satanic circle, one created with human blood, and throws a rock at Father Michael, striking him square in the forehead, causing him to suddenly vanish from the film. Similar to *Scars of Dracula* or not, give me an ending worthy of disposing of such a villain that Lee has masterfully created, something that ends the movie dramatically by making Father Michael's dismissal worthy of the characterization Christopher Lee created. Also, during this final confrontation between Lee and Widmark, the Father Michael character offers Widmark the physical pleasures of Nastassja Kinski as diversion; she walks seductively toward the camera, sheds her sacrificial robe and displays full-frontal nudity. In today's cinematic arena, Kinski, with her normal God-given breasts, probably would not qualify for onscreen nudity because her natural body would be deemed in need of surgical enhancements.

Disappointing climax or not, *To the Devil... a Daughter* holds up surprisingly well in this uncut, uncensored version. It is sad to see the credits roll by and not recognize any of the personalities typically associated with Hammer in the glory days, but to be fair, *To the Devil... a Daughter* is a most fitting swan song for Hammer. The extras included on the disc include a 24-minute documentary containing interviews with Christopher Lee, Christopher Wicking, Roy Skeggs, Peter Sykes and Honor Blackman about the making and marketing of the movie. Talent bios, theatrical trailer and a poster and still gallery are also included. As is always expected from Anchor Bay, the letterboxed (enhanced 16:9) print used is superlative, encouraging one and all to give this often-maligned film a fresh reexamination.

### DIE ANOTHER DAY
Movie: 3.0; Disc: 3.5
[MGM Home Entertainment]

It is amazing that the James Bond franchise is alive and well 40 years after its original inception, making Sean Connery an international star overnight back in 1962 (*Darby O'Gill and the Little People* just did not do it for Connery). Pierce Brosnan, the best Bond since Roger Moore (whose reputation improves with age), here delivers his fourth outing as 007 and, without doubt, this is the best Bond movie since the finest from the Roger Moore era. Oh yes, this is the very type of film entertainment indie-snobs and people who attend film festivals detest; *Die Another Day* is supercharged, filled with kinetic action sequences, car chases, airplane destruction, underwater explosions, death rays, superficial sexual encounters, cartoon characters and a science fiction plot of world domination and destruction.

What's *not* to like?

For me *Die Another Day* is artistically so successful for several reasons. First of all, the scenario returns to the sci-fi arena with innovative new weapons of mass destruction, in this case a diamond-in-the-sky satellite that harnesses the sun's energy to produce a razor-accurate laser death ray. Next, we need the character of James Bond to be challenged and effectively threatened. In *Die Another Day*, the movie's required showstopper, the pre-credits sequence, is incorporated into the regular plot so that the pre-credits action segues directly into the main plot post-credits. In this action-packed audience grabber opening, James Bond impersonates an agent selling information for diamonds, but one of his own agents betrays him (whose identity is unknown until the end) and Bond ends up imprisoned in a North Korean death camp, tortured repeatedly (during the credits). Surprisingly, the agent who set up Bond makes it appear the British agent spilled his guts while being tortured, and his superiors, especially M (Judi Dench), believe he betrayed his nation. Thus, for a good part of the movie Bond is working alone, without protection or contacts, and Pierce Brosnan is required to demonstrate a wider range of acting than simply dressing in a tux and ordering martinis, shaken, not stirred.

We all know that Bonds sink or swim based upon the effectiveness of the villains, and here we have one major and two minor ones (no spoilers here... I won't reveal the identity of the double-agent). The first villain, Gustav Graves, is played sophisticatedly evil (yet suave) by Toby Stephens. Whether appearing in media exploitation campaigns as the dashing adventurer or unveiling his death ray and his actual identity, his performance is charismatic. Secondary villain Zao, acupuncture needles sticking out of one side of his face, his bald head shining, his eyes coolly intense, becomes the more monstrous presence in the Odd Job sense.

And while the Bond girls of late have been pretty bland and superficial, Halle Berry's character Jinx is the most sexy and energetic Bond girl in ages, and her clever bantering with Bond makes her almost his equal, truly a strong partner in the best sense.

Finally, the direction by Lee Tamahori keeps the plot moving forward in an interesting manner with pacing that allows characters to develop within the framework of an explosive cinematic universe. Tamahori keeps absolute tight control creatively, never allowing the film to slip out of his hands. The cinematography, stunts, fight sequences, battle hardware chase and crashes, etc. are all handled effectively with smoothness. I even love the electronically rendered Madonna title song (which most fans detest, instead preferring the bellowing theatrics of a Shirley Bassey).

The movie, letterboxed for 16:9 monitors, has both a Dolby Digital and DTS surround soundtrack available. The second disc includes music videos, mak-

ing-of documentary, storyboard comparisons, multi-angle access to action sequences, title designs, effects featurette, photo gallery, trailers/TV spots, etc.

When it comes to showing off my home theater this summer, the initial pre-title sequence of *Die Another Day* has all the bombast (both visually and sonically) to rattle the floors and get the blood pulsing. This is one Bond I can enjoy over and over again. Amazingly, after 40 years, the James Bond franchise can still rattle the universe.

## HORRORS OF THE BLACK MUSEUM
Movie: 3.0; Disc: 3.5
[VCI Entertainment]

One of my fondest childhood movie experiences was seeing the ultra-violent *Horrors of the Black Museum* in the theater when I was nine years old. However, in recent years, seeing the movie in faded and battered 16mm panned-and-scanned versions, the movie never holds up to that favorable memory. But this recent VCI DVD release is a revelation, for the film is presented in an anamorphic widescreen 2:35:1 aspect ratio print with restored Eastmancolor garishness. The print that VCI uses is absolutely pristine and visually stunning. And as a bonus, the American exploitative introduction short, *Hypno-Vista*, has been restored where optical illusions are presented live on film, spooky visual tricks that set the tone for the feature to follow. Seeing this mind-blowing VCI presentation, the magic of my first theatrical viewing has been restored.

*Horrors of the Black Museum* was probably producer/co-screenwriter Herman Cohen's biggest financial success for American International and it created the artistic green light for the studio to give Roger Corman a larger budget and the go-ahead to produce his Vincent Price/Poe series in widescreen and color. The true strength of *Horrors of the Black Museum* is the introduction of Michael Gough as a new horror film villain, a performance to be repeated in Cohen's *Konga, The Black Zoo* and *Trog*. Gough, who a year before played the doting brother, the reluctant hero, in Hammer's *Horror of Dracula*, is now recast with tri-color hair, a creepy limp with short cane (and personality to match) and the ability to deliver dramatically even the most trivial, inane dialogue. Gough chews up the scenery but does so in such a way that his performance makes him a truly memorable horror film villain. And he's never been more maniacal than his stellar performance in *Horrors of the Black Museum*. Following the basic story hook Cohen introduced in his teenage epics such as *I Was a Teenage Frankenstein* and *I Was a Teenage Werewolf*, we have an older, wizened madman who takes a young impressionable male under his wing, and after building up the sense of trust, abuses that trust and uses drugs to turn the young, innocent male

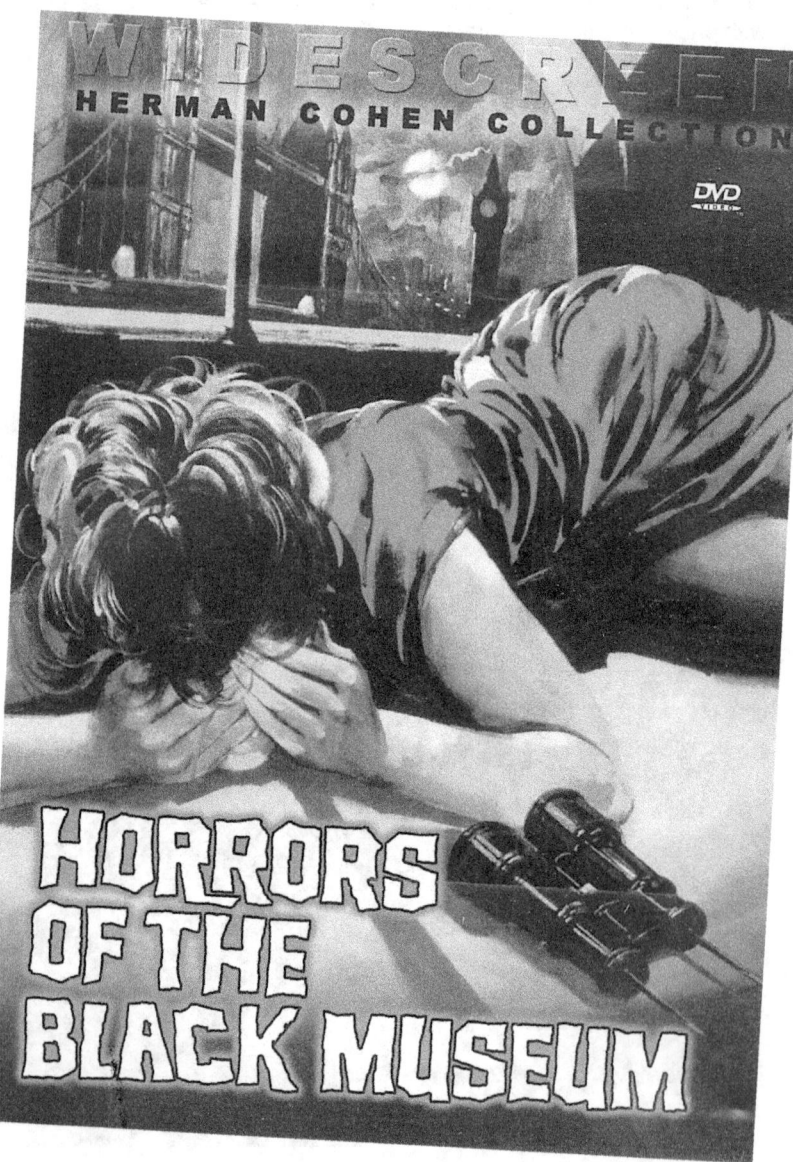

into a monster, one who does the elder's bidding.

Making full use of its gaudy Eastmancolor photography, *Horrors of the Black Museum* features a slew of grisly murders, mostly executed on beautiful, sexy young women—a woman has her eyeballs pierced by spiked binoculars, another blonde beauty is beheaded by a portable guillotine propped above her bed and an elderly woman (who runs a curio shop) gets her throat punctured by huge ice tongs (with Gough grimacing all the way), etc. Thrown in for good measure is a horrific ride through the tunnel of love at an amusement part, a maniac with a knife who jumps off the Ferris wheel, the dead body that is dipped into the vat of acid and reduced to bone. It's all sordid and overbaked, perfect for the youth horror market back in 1959. And while such mayhem might become dull and repetitive, Michael Gough's acting never allows that. Using the frame of Gough's Bancroft character, playing a newspaper writer whose column focuses on grisly crime, Gough becomes an annoying man who always haunts the offices of Scotland Yard to get gory details of the latest violent crime or murder. But unknown to Scotland Yard, Bancroft is a collector of esoteric weapons and presides over his hidden Black Museum where he displays his tribute to mayhem.

The extras on this disc are incredible. As mentioned, we have the *Hypno-Vista* opening, hosted by Emile Franchel; theatrical trailers; cast and director bios; a still/poster art gallery; audio commentary by the late Herman Cohen (prepared for the laserdisc release); a telephone interview with Cohen; and a Video Tribute to Herman Cohen by colleague and friend Didier Chatelain that touches upon all aspects of Cohen's career, including many marvelous behind-the-scenes photos.

Simply put, this is a loving tribute to a film held in high esteem by only a small number of people, and VCI has pulled out all the stops to make this release something special (including a fold-out full-color glossy poster). Forget those faded 16mm prints... this is the only way to enjoy *Horrors of the Black Museum*.

**TARGET EARTH**
Movie: 2.0; Disc: 3.0
[VCI Entertainment]

When it comes to the fantastic cinema produced by Herman Cohen, *Target Earth*, a very low-budget sci-fi programmer released in 1954, is the first film to mention, being Cohen's first independently produced effort. The movie, based upon the story *Deadly City*, becomes transformed into a screenplay co-written by James H. Nicholson, soon to head American International (and according to the DVD, Nicholson first asked Cohen to co-head the new studio, but when other commitments prevented Cohen from signing on, only then did Nicholson approach Sam Arkoff).

While *Target Earth* is an interesting movie, it is much too hampered by its low budget to be as effective as it should be. However, the minimal cast is quite effective. We meet rough and

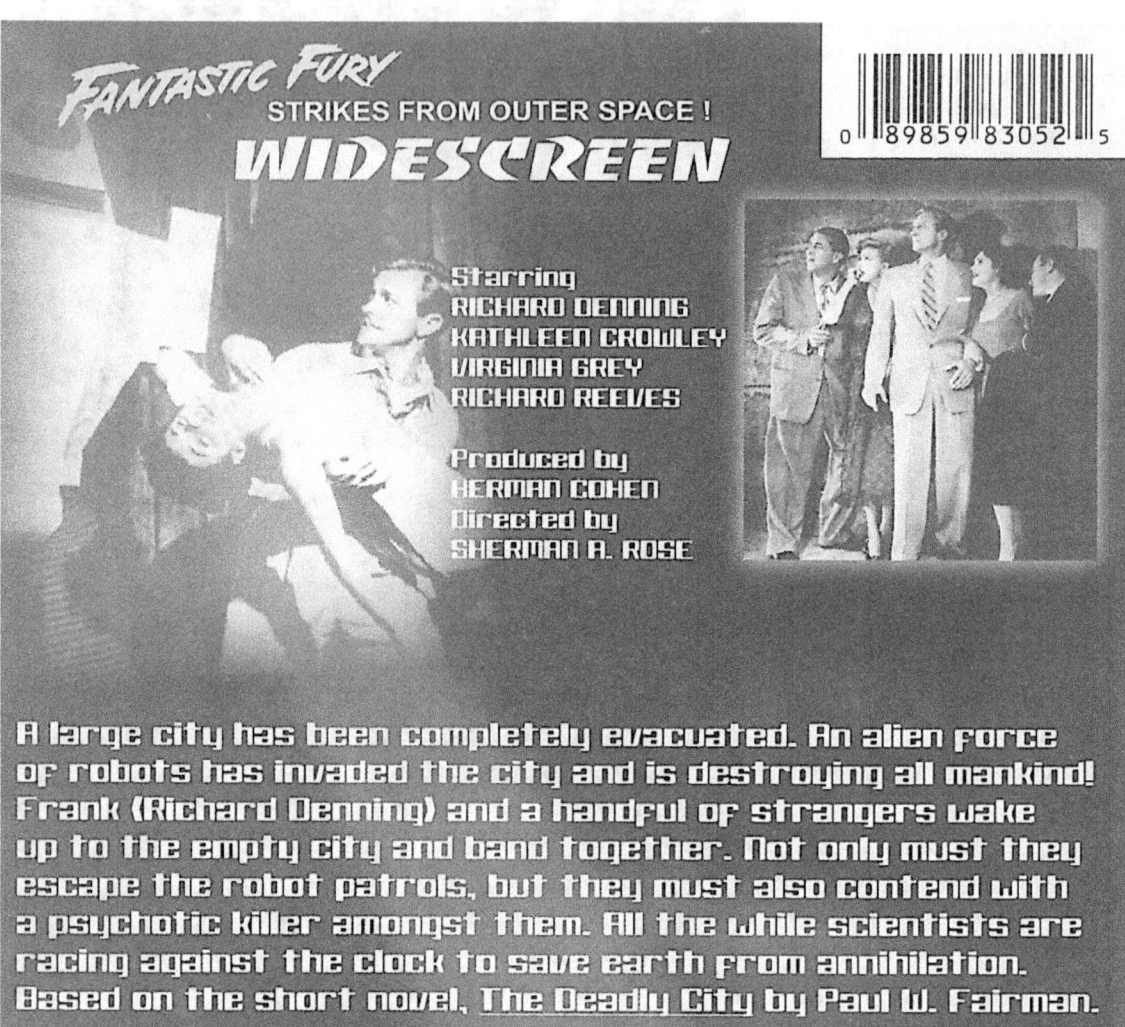

**FANTASTIC FURY STRIKES FROM OUTER SPACE!**

# WIDESCREEN

Starring
RICHARD DENNING
KATHLEEN CROWLEY
VIRGINIA GREY
RICHARD REEVES

Produced by HERMAN COHEN
Directed by SHERMAN A. ROSE

A large city has been completely evacuated. An alien force of robots has invaded the city and is destroying all mankind! Frank (Richard Denning) and a handful of strangers wake up to the empty city and band together. Not only must they escape the robot patrols, but they must also contend with a psychotic killer amongst them. All the while scientists are racing against the clock to save earth from annihilation. Based on the short novel, <u>The Deadly City</u> by Paul W. Fairman.

tough businessman Frank Brooks (Richard Denning), added as love interest is the suicidal sexpot Nora King (Kathleen Crowley) and we add comic relief with the "eat, drink and be merry; tomorrow we die" hedonist couple Jim Wilson (Richard Reeves) and Vicki Harris (Virginia Grey). The city of Los Angeles, eerily deserted (filming occurred early weekend mornings, without a permit), stars as Any City, U.S.A. where a massive evacuation has occurred and only people who were under the influence of heavy sleeping pills or robbed and knocked unconscious remain to face the alien invaders who are rampaging and killing all human life. Unfortunately, the only visible alien invasion force is one pretty cool-looking robot that keeps walking up and down the streets (although the robot's initial appearance, seen as only a giant silhouette on the side of a city building, is quite suspenseful). When the robot corners an unwary victim, it shoots a death ray from its helmet that kills him instantly.

What creates any type of suspense in the movie is the juxtaposing of sequences involving our trapped city-dwellers trying to hide from the invasion force with those sequences of the military analyzing one of the robots they captured, trying to discover the means by which to destroy such alien invaders. Just as the action gets heavy in the city, we segue to military scientist Whit Bissell using some sort of oscillator to create tones that will ultimately destroy the robot's cathode ray tube, rendering it a pile of scrap metal.

Those early initial sequences showing the deserted city streets, filmed at odd angles on hilly cityscapes, are mesmerizing in a strange sense, and the way that these left-of-center humans face their fate (Virginia Grey and Richard Reeves deciding to raid every juke joint between here and the ocean, partying until the day of doom vs. Crowley and Denning

who, understanding the invasion force is advancing from the north, decide if they travel south, they just may escape alien destruction, at least for the short term).

The movie's only suspenseful action sequence involves the lone robot breaking through the plate glass of the hotel in which the humans are hiding, as the few survivors are chased up the hotel steps and finally flee to the rooftop where the robot has Crowley and Denning cornered at the ledge, ready to jump to their deaths or be fried by the robot's death ray. In an earlier sequence, the original four survivors, held at bay by a criminal with a pistol, get the upper hand when heroic Virginia Grey stands up to the gunman and takes two shots at close range, allowing Denning to overpower the criminal (although Denning still takes a shot to the shoulder) before irate Richard Reeves strangles the formerly tough gunman to death. Up on the roof, Reeves lures the robot away from Denning and Crowley, sacrificing his own life as he dies by the robot's death ray. Lots of mood early on and far too little action later on make *Target Earth* a mediocre programmer, but one that is well worth viewing once or twice.

The special features on this VCI DVD include insightful liner notes by Eric Hoffman, commentary by the late Herman Cohen, a repeat of the Tribute to Herman Cohen by Didier Chatelain (as also seen on the *Horrors of the Black Museum* DVD), theatrical trailer (and bonus trailers) and cast and director bios. The 1:85:1 original widescreen print is in quite fine condition, very clean and splice-free. The contrast is very good, although the blacks are closer to gray and the focus is a tad on the soft side. However, for a low-budget film from 1954, the quality of the print is quite excellent. I must also add the DVD menu is most impressive and gives a sense of how the film would look if remade today. Once again VCI goes the extra mile to present its Herman Cohen Collection with the best quality prints and the largest amount of extras possible.

### DEAD OF NIGHT/ THE QUEEN OF SPADES
Movie: [*Dead*: 3.0; *Queen*: 3.0]
Disc: 3.5
[Anchor Bay Entertainment]

Anchor Bay, renowned for its archival releases on DVD of classic (and not so classic) Hammer films and uncut Euro-prints of the best of Dario Argento, generally has not released classics from the 1940s since its 1940 Hitch-cock releases were soon eclipsed by the superior Criterion releases in their wake. But DVD enthusiasts have been waiting patiently for the release of *Dead of Night*, the classic anthology chiller that has always been released in less than adequate-looking variations. But more about *Dead of Night* later. For this classic double-feature disc is blessed with the inclusion of a long-lost classic, *The Queen of Spades*, a British release of 1949 that has eluded me. While it is overly arty in execution and a tad staid in pacing, *The Queen* of Spades is an above-average horror entry marked by its carefully rendered art decoration, set design and period costuming. This is one movie that is better viewed in sequences (after the initial viewing), and when the mood gets creepy, the movie is terrifyingly horrific, suggesting Edgar Allan Poe.

The movie, based upon an 1834 novella by Alex-ander Pushkin, is a period piece occurring in Russia during the time when gambling and playing cards, particularly faro, was taking over the nation. Anton Walbrook stars as Herman Suvorin, the tragic protagonist of the story. He is obsessed with wealth and winning big at cards, but he doesn't wish to play any penny-ante game, he wants to amass his life's fortune and play one game for the ultimate payoff. However, he wants to make sure the deck is stacked in his favor. He hears of a Countess, superbly played by Dame Judith Evans in her sound screen debut, who supposedly sold her soul to Satan for luck (and resulting fortune) at the card table. Or so it states in a decaying book that details stories of people who sold their souls to the devil. To get closer to the Countess, to learn her secrets, Walbrook's character attempts to seduce the ward of the Countess (Yvonne Mitchell) merely to gain access to the old woman.

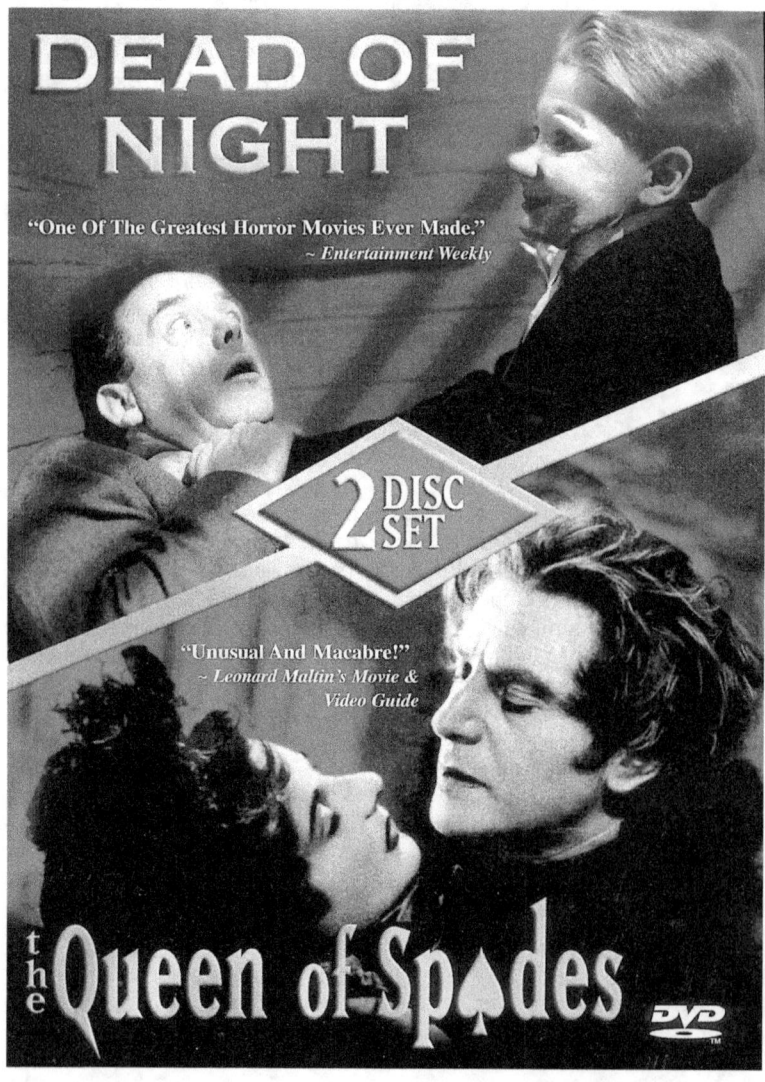

By movie's end, Wal-brook has descended into insanity with an ace slowly transforming into the queen of spades (the unluckiest of all cards).

The movie's pivotal, mesmerizing sequences involve both the faro card games at the beginning and end of the movie, well orchestrated with dancing Gypsy girls and singing. The sequence where Walbrook, hidden in the shadows, announces himself to the Countess and pleads with her to share her secrets, leading to her sudden heart-attack death when the young rogue terrifies her with a pistol, is classic in execution, with the Countess' mute reactions, conveying all emotion by her face and eyes. The sequence, a menagerie of blacks and grays and whites, is always focused on Anton Walbrook's intense line delivery. Then the supernatural merges with the distorted human psyche as voices bellow in the rustling wind. Atmospheric cinematography depicts curtains swinging and such an elaborate aristocratic setting becomes mired in frantic sounds and visions weaving a ghostly presence. Such sequences, combined with a closing montage focusing upon the dead, open eyes of the Countess, her lips almost smirking, reveals contentment in knowing she retained her secret until the end. Add all this with the suspense of the final card game, where Walbrook's character thinks he knows the three winning card number sequences, and wins through the first two. Only one final card stands in his way, and the manner in which the totally obsessive victim loses is masterful, a credit to Walbrook's acting talent and the ghostly cinematography.

The Queen of Spades drags on unnecessarily far too long, but such sequences of cinematic terror are a worthy payoff; the horror sequences remind me of Hurst's 1951 A Christmas Carol, with Alastair Sim as Scrooge, where the period set pieces remain austere and sophisticated until the horror sequences suddenly appear, radically changing the period mood. Director Thorold Dickinson (who helmed the original British version of *Gaslight*, also with Anton Walbrook) seems to desire to create a low-budget Charles Dickens world in Russia, dripping with period detail and opulence, and he only allows his expressionistic recreation of horror (photographed by Otto Heller, who started in silents and also filmed Michael Powell's *Peeping Tom*, among others) to emerge as punctuation to character-induced madness. It's as though Dickinson doesn't want his movie to sink to the level of a horror film, so the outstanding horror sequences are almost downplayed.

After all these years, it is almost amazing to consider that a supernatural Poe-inspired chiller (as in Poe's best fiction, the horror usually occurs inside the mind of the first-person narrator) of this magnitude has not been seen by so many. After repeated viewings of so many other horror classics, it is indeed a privilege to see *The Queen of Spades* for the very first time, and Anchor Bay does it up right. Slowly paced, *The Queen of Spades* is a movie driven by its wonderful performances and cinematography. The sequences of visual, moody horror more than make up for any flaws the production might contain.

As stated earlier, for years on home video it was impossible to find a decent 35mm print of *Dead of Night*, a film dependent upon a sharp, densely textured print that allows the nightmarish movie to properly weave its spell. Fortunately, the Anchor Bay DVD is the best print yet released to home video and many sequences are like seeing the film for the first time. Warning, some short sections of the film appear to be replacement footage (another generation removed from the original footage), slightly softer in focus

**Edith Evans as the Countess from *The Queen of Spades***

and with intense blacks changing to shades of gray. But such sequences are relatively brief. The soundtrack used is not as powerful as the soundtrack for *The Queen of Spades*, but the dialogue which tends to sound tinny is still quite adequate and powerful enough.

I have never been a fan of anthology horror movies, but *Dead of Night* is perhaps the best simply because the framing story remains front and center and because elements from each of the individual story sequences tie back to that framing story. The basic story has engineer Mervyn Johns journey to a country estate/farmhouse whose owners desire a renovation. As soon as he enters the household and meets a living room full of people, Johns has the sense of *deja-vu* declaring that he knows everyone assembled from his dreams and he soon predicts exactly what will happen, the pivotal moment to occur when the psychiatrist breaks his glasses—that's when the dream turns into nightmare, Johns states.

The individual sequences vary in quality, but fortunately, no

The Michael Redgrave "Dummy" sequence from *Dead of Night* is the best in the movie, along with the montage of horror at the film's end.

padding occurs so some sequences are relatively brief while others are more fully fleshed out. Some individual tales are *Twilight Zone*-style stories where a passenger is about to board a bus, experiences a sense of dread and refuses to board, and the bus crashes over the side of the hill within seconds. Others are more intense ghost stories, where a young girl playing hide-and-seek discovers a hidden nursery with a crying child who dreads that his half-sister wants to kill him. We soon find out that very thing occurred and that the crying child is indeed a ghost. We have *Thriller*-style chills as a newlywed couple is almost destroyed when a present, a mirror, the bride buys for the groom causes the husband to become suspicious of the wife's fidelity. The innocent wife and her marriage is saved when she violently shatters the mirror as her husband, in a rage, attempts to strangle her, driven to unfounded suspicion by the mirror. However, the best story, the classic story, is the ventriloquist dummy sequence starring Michael Redgrave as a man whose soul is taken over by his stage dummy, and in the final sequence, the Michael Redgrave character speaks with the dazed look and voice of the dummy, having lost his identity. Again, some sequences work better than others, but it is the climactic ending sequence, after the doctor's glasses are broken, where the terrifying montage sequence occurs, placing the now murderous Mervyn Johns into the major set pieces previously shown with the main characters of each individual story presenting key images or lines of dialogue that now relate to his current state of mind. Without doubt, the Michael Redgrave ventriloquist sequence, the framing story and the montage of horror at the end give *Dead of Night* its reputation of classic notoriety. However, when all is said and done, *Dead of Night* is a good horror film, but certainly not a classic one.

Extras on this essential Anchor Bay release include theatrical trailers and still galleries for each film (broken down into behind-the-scenes and regular still photos). An audio commentary might have been appreciated, as well as a documentary about British horror movies of the 1940s, but the simple fact that these movies, one of them quite rare, are presented with pristine prints, the best available, is reason enough to consider this double-feature DVD release to be one of the most important releases of the year.

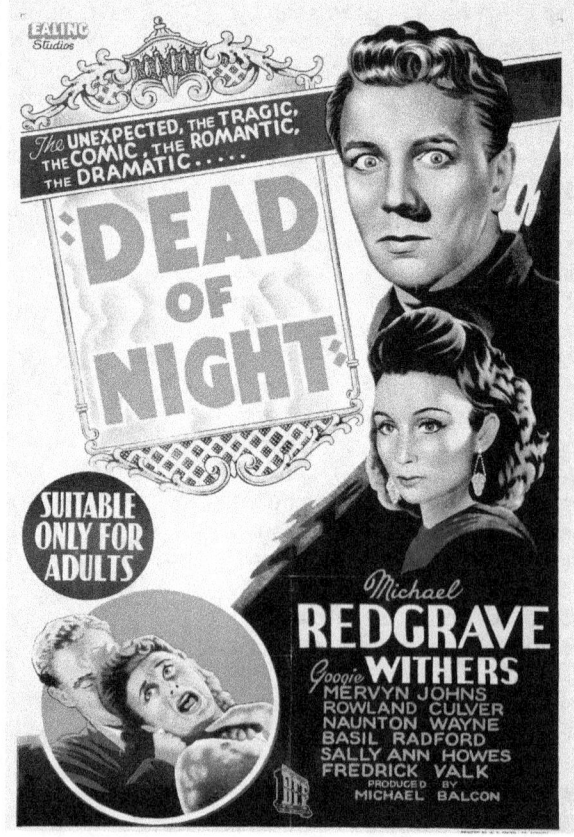

# GRAVE DIGGINGS

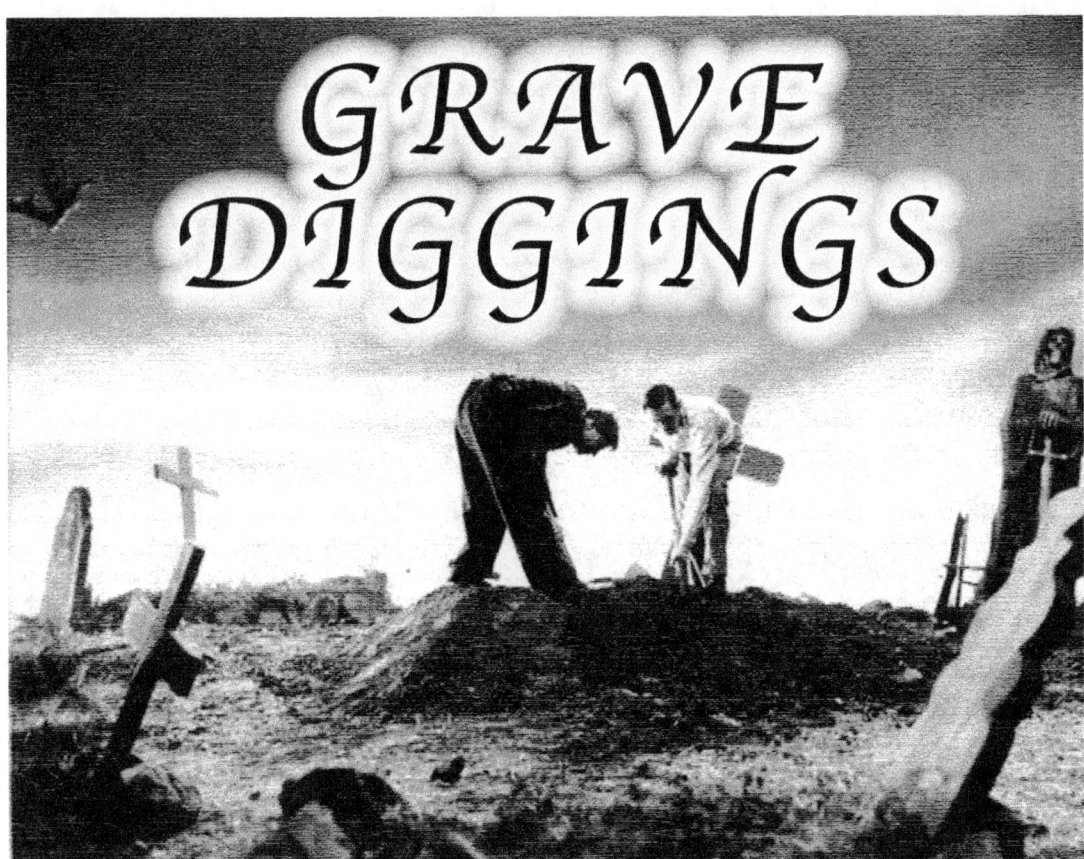

Dear Gary and Susan:

Thanks for another fine issue of *MidMar* (67/68), even though Gary's editorial bemoaning the shrinking number of classic movie buffs among younger folks was not exactly a day-brightener. I suppose us old fogies must keep the torch burning as long as possible, since there may not be anyone to pass it to.

"Overrated or Underrated Performances?" was, of course, very thought provoking, and here are two of the thoughts it provoked. It is difficult to see how Lon Chaney, Jr.'s performance in *Son of Dracula* can be called overrated, as I have heard of almost no one who has praised it. Virtually everyone who has written about the film in these past 60 years seems to agree that Chaney was miscast.

What really surprised me about the article was the absence of any mention of Anthony Hopkins' ridiculous performance as Dr. Van Helsing in *Bram Stoker's Dracula*, which gets my vote for the most outrageous overacting of the decade. It was not only over the top, but also all the way down the other side and up to the top again. I suppose director Francis Coppola, or perhaps Hopkins himself, thought it would be brilliantly original to portray Van Helsing as a wild and crazy guy rather than as the respectable, scholarly type he is in the novel and all previous film versions. Original, perhaps. Brilliant, no. The film's pretentious title (implying that this version is really faithful to the novel) made Hopkins' performance even more offensive.

As for the DVD reviews, although I disagree with Gary's opinion of *Teenage Monster*, he certainly deserves recognition for writing what may be the only favorable review that film has ever received!
Marc Russell

Dear Gary and Susan:

Congratulations on 40 years of publishing the best Horror-SFantasy film scholarship in the field. Those forty years flew by before we realized it. Gary, myself, and a lot of other *MidMar* readers were only very early in the second decade of our lives in 1963, so we're not all that old today. We just got started early. Still, 40 years is a long time, and those of us who can remember the state of Horror-SFantasy filmdom in 1963 have seen a lot of changes. Living in the U.S.A., I'm best able to comment on changes I've seen in American cinema during all these years. And, these changes have interacted to change not only our favorite genre, but also American cinema as a whole. Probably the most important change was the end of self-censorship by the major film studios and the establishment of their film rating system, with scenes of explicit violence becoming the norm in major releases. And, great improvements in special effects made the horrible scenes even more realistic, as well as making SFilms of outer space travel much

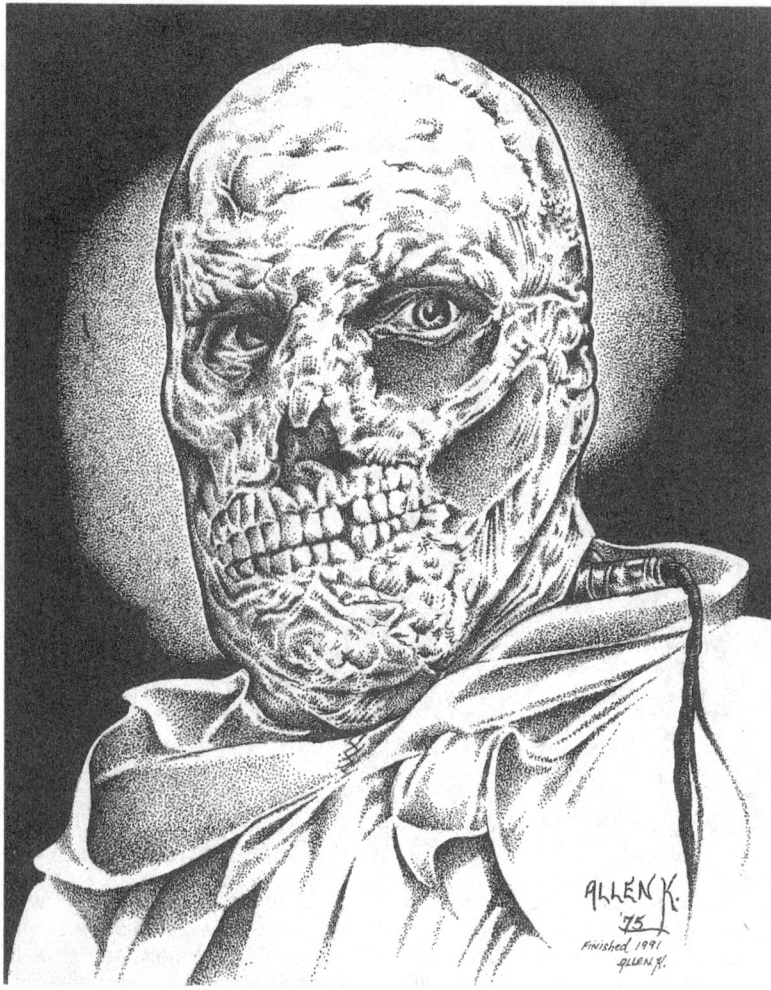

more spectacular. With their rating system, the majors pretty much put the old-fashioned independent exploitation filmmakers out of business. And, the drive-ins and grindhouses where the independent films were shown have disappeared from the American Scene.

Back in 1963, Horror-SFans ridiculed and derided low-budget, independent films, but in the years since then, an appreciation has developed for the art of such films. While most of them were pretty bad, there were some good ones made by talented filmmakers, despite having little money to work with. And, even expensive, major studio films could often times be pretty bad. Forty years ago, we had drive-ins and grindhouses offering us an alternative to major studio films. Today, expensive major studio films, with their spectacular special effects, dominate our genre. I suppose that videotape is one avenue whereby low-budget filmmakers can still develop their talents and offer us an alternative to the major studio stuff, but watching a video just isn't the same as seeing a film at a drive-in or grindhouse.

Well, that's my observation of changes in our genre since 1963. Although I don't think the changes are all that much for the better, there are still good films being made and to be made in the years to come. And, I hope *Midnight Marquee* continues for many more years.
Fred Hamilton

Dear Gary and Susan:
I was truly shocked when I saw a VHS double feature of two Universal monster films selling for $4.99. This was the actual cost, not a discount price. This was when Universal had recently pulled all their DVD monster classics from additional sales.

I just turned 50 back in March and I had this sinking feeling that the classic monster world was marching toward oblivion. Unless it is/was *I Love Lucy* or *Leave It to Beaver*, my now-adult kids would never watch anything in black and white. And there are no horror host weekly monster shows in the L.A. TV area. Not since Elvira and *MST3K* went off the air. Kids just aren't exposed to those great and not so great monster films of the past.

Now I read your editorial and you say it all. When you and Dennis Druktenis reported sluggish sales a couple of years ago, I knew it was the beginning of the end. Add high prices for magazines and collectibles and eBay sales bottoming out on these very items. You can't even give away VHS tapes on eBay now. I tried, two for one auctions. Had some success but when I relisted the second time, I got no bites whatsoever. Creepy Classics came to the rescue and I was able to trade VHS for DVDs.

Anyway, just wanted to comment on your editorial. Very sad.
Randy L Jepsen

Hello Gary and Susan:
Your analysis of the demise of Baby Boomer Nostalgia was upsetting, but I agree with it, unfortunately. If we were as honest as you, we would all admit that similar thoughts have come to us when we check out eBay or go to conventions and shows. But rather than rolling over and playing dead, we need to excite new audiences about our cherished actors and films, as you mentioned. I found some interesting vintage horror fans lately. As a member of our local board of education, I helped to interview candidates for a drama/English/speech position. One of them quoted from *The Black Cat*, *The Raven* and *The Invisible Ray*. Guess who got the job?

"Overrated or Underrated?" sent me trotting to the computer. Lover, surgeon, maniac and Poe expert all in one, how could Bela's Dr. Vollin be better? He tosses off kilter lines and takes over the movie with no apologies. The only thing I can't stomach is Vollin's passion for the judge's daughter! And maybe Bryan Senn could explain why Boris Karloff's Janos Rukh should be subtle when Radium X is slowly poisoning him? For my money, his portrayal is aces and is especially touching when he cannot kill his wife, Diane, even though she shows execrable taste in second husbands. Yes to Brian Smith's and nix to Anthony Ambrogio's opinions regarding Gloria Holden's Countess Zaleska who has a lot more going for her than marvelous cheekbones. Holden makes us weep that she can never be "one of us." Thank you to Jonathan Malcolm Lampley for his *Arsenic and Old Lace* paragraph. Karloff's absence is more than a crime; it's a sin! Steve Thornton is right about Jane Randolph's Alice in *Cat People*, but I hate her anyway for what she does to poor Irena. (Which of course proves his point.)

OOH, more comments about poor Stanley Ridges in *Black Friday*. What was Universal thinking? Would they have put Stanley Ridges between Abbott and Costello? Then why in blue blazes did they have the gall to do it here? All the advance hype about Karloff and Lugosi and then we get Stanley Ridges. And don't even start to say that Karloff couldn't have pulled off the love scenes. What about *The Mummy*, *The Black Room*, *The Man Who Lived Again*, *The Climax* and I *am* just getting warmed up here. Plus Boris' Hyde side would have been scarier than anything Ridges did. Never forget that Universal had Karloff and Lugosi and they gave us Stanley Ridges!

Thanks for everything. If you two did not exist, you would have to be invented.
Nathalie Yafet

Dear Gary:
A most poignant editorial appeared in issue *MidMar* #67-68. It's really true—names like Boris Karloff and Bela Lugosi mean about as much to the current generation of kids as Roman Navarro and Lillian Gish meant to our generation growing up.

Time passes and things change, but I always find it sad that the fact that something is old carries with it such a negative connotation. It's not the younger generation's fault for not having an interest in the past; it's our generation's fault for leading them to believe that the word "new" means "an improvement over something old."

There will always be film lovers who will seek out the past (I hope). But for the most part, everything we so passionately love about the genre —from the Universal Monsters, to the 1950s bug-eyed sci-fi, to the Little Rascals and on, will be largely forgotten.
Robert Billera

Dear Gary and Sue:
Just got around to commenting on *MidMar* #65/66.

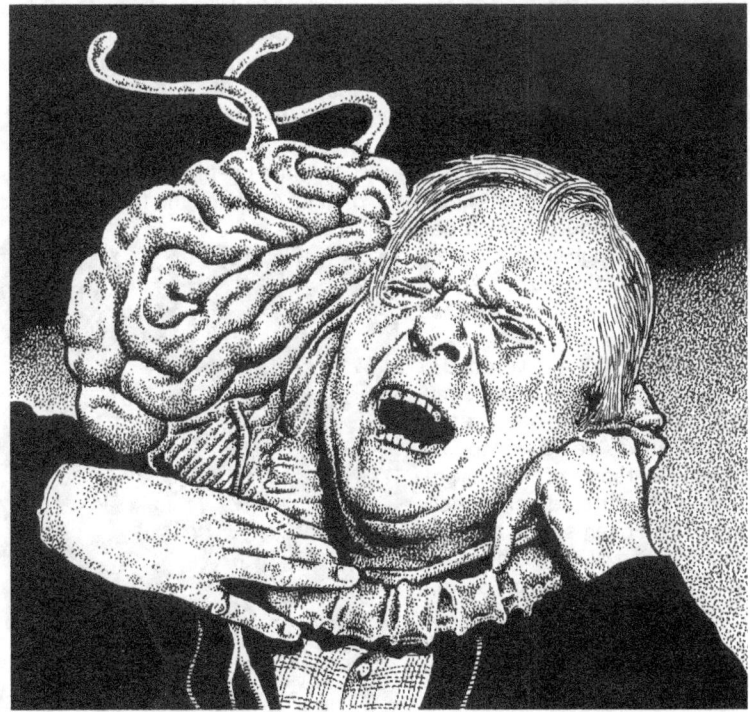

MIDNIGHT MARQUEE #69/70        125

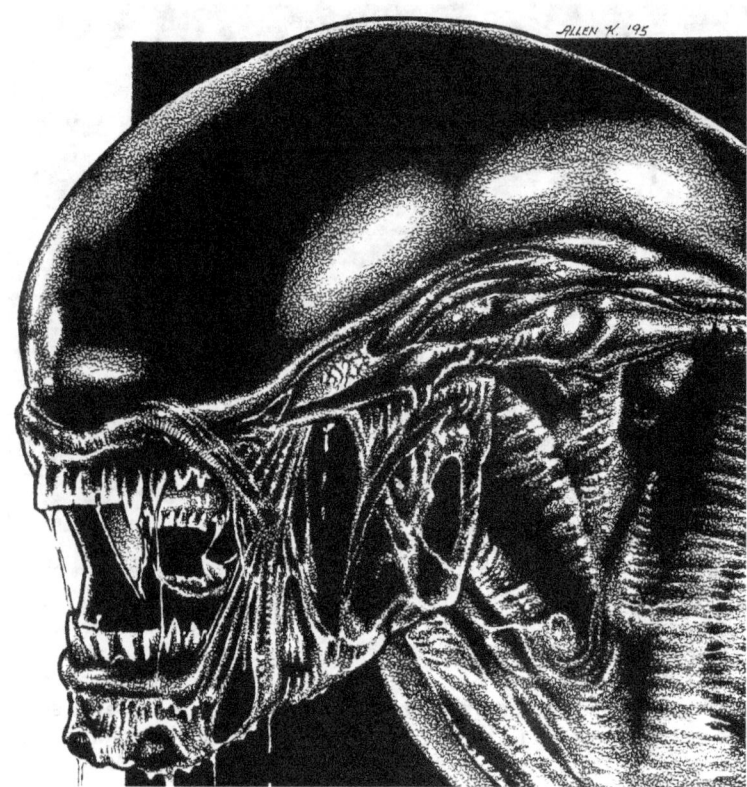

Once again your talented staff of writers continues to amaze with well-researched and well-versed articles that tackle new ground on old subjects. Case in point, "The Diary of Dracula" by Greg Mank and Gary Don Rhodes. This gave me the first-person perspective of actually being there during the time period when the film was unspooling before an unsuspecting public.

Equally fascinating was the "Battle-Scarred Horrors" piece by Arthur J. Lundquist, which had more than enough visuals to present its case of the Golden Age of Horror being influenced by the great world wars.

Regarding the "Overrated or Underrated?" article, I found myself more often than not agreeing with what was being written. I'm pleased that some of the films presented as overrated were exactly what I had been saying all these years, but now I have others who share the same opinion as me! I'm not alone anymore!

However, I have a few bones to pick on some of the selections, which boils down to personal taste, but then that's what makes each of us unique, no? I don't see *Horror of Dracula* as being overrated simply because it doesn't follow the book; it stands alone as a well-crafted film featuring Dracula, which is all it sets out to do in the first place. How many of the other film adaptations of Stoker's character completely follow his work? And while I agree completely with James J.J. Janis on the brilliance of the original *Godzilla*, the film has been re-discovered and re-established as the true classic it is over the years (especially in Japan) to break out of the underrated banner in my opinion (but with the disaster of the American *Godzilla* film, perhaps that does set things back). My picks for underrated Japanese monster movies would include *Matango* (*Attack of the Mushroom People*) for its brilliant take on the horrors of addiction done in a supremely creepy way, and the trilogy of Daimajin films about the giant stone God that comes to life when invoked which remains some of the best-acted, shot, scored serious movies to come out during the Golden Age of Kaiju flicks.

*The Conqueror Worm* works very well in its original form (seek out the import DVD under its original moniker, *Witchfinder General*, for the definitive package), and hardly rates as being overrated since many have not seen it as originally intended. Also *Psycho* is most certainly a horror film, since it established the character of Norman Bates as that shy, lonely guy just down the road who wouldn't even harm a fly. For most folks the realization that this could happen in your neighborhood, on your street, even next door, is terror of the highest order, and this is what makes *Psycho* arguably the most influential horror movie of all time. The idea that *Psycho* "transformed" the horror film is correct, but in a positive way, since the old monsters of yore just couldn't cut the mustard anymore in a world transfix-

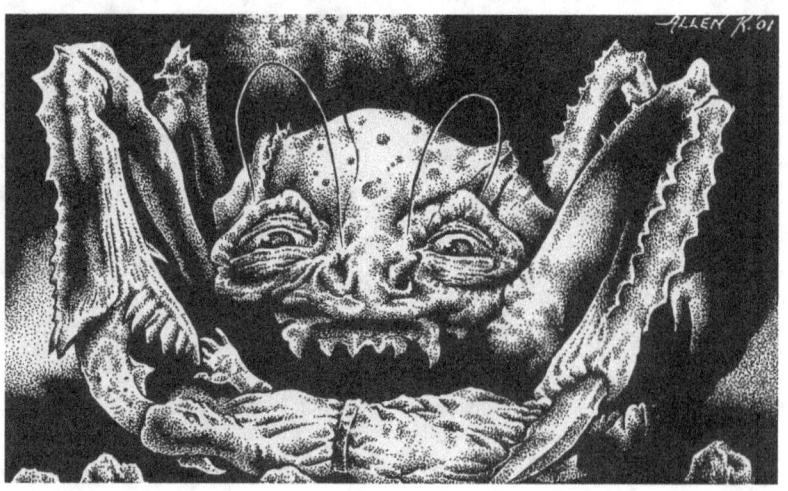

ing itself into an ever-winding cesspool of violence. This also holds true for *The Exorcist* and *Texas Chain Saw Massacre*, which brought reality into the proceedings, thus earning them high points for making the audience believe such terror could even happen to them!

James J.J. Janis' claim that *Friday the 13th* and *A Nightmare on Elm Street* are "glorified snuff films where murder is an occasion for funny one-liners and laughter" is only correct when discussing the sequels and not the original movies, since stupid one-liners and laughter do not exist in either.

Finally, I don't agree that John Carpenter's *The Thing* sacrificed the nail-biting pace of the original, instead it reinvented this pace by placing the viewers in total surprise because they never know who the actual thing is, which is where the tension comes from. It is this very ingredient which places Carpenter's version miles ahead of the original (brilliant film that it is), and in my opinion the funhouse ride of special effects as designed by Rob Bottin will never be surpassed in terms of sheer brilliance and execution in this age of lackluster CGI.

All in all, another round of applause for a job well done!
Dave Kosanke

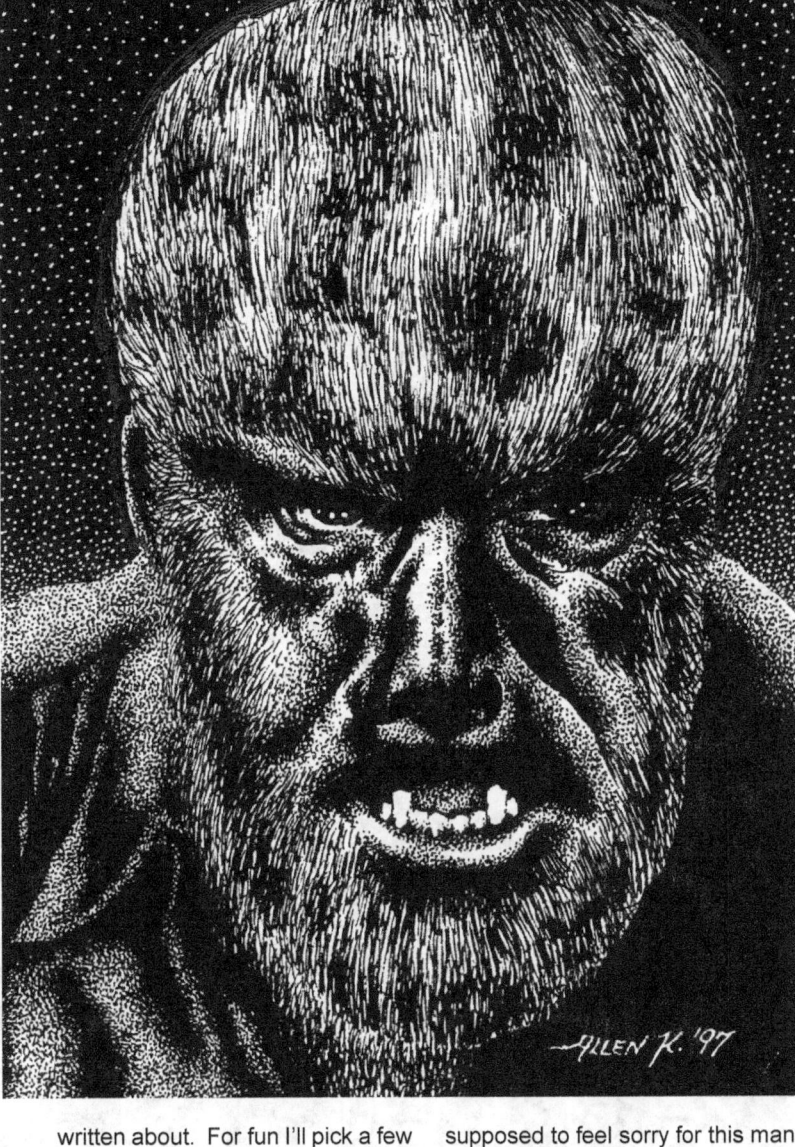

Dear Gary and Sue:

I've got to take Gary's side concerning *Bride of Frankenstein* in the Forum/Against 'Em debate. *Bride of Frankenstein* is not a "great horror film for people who don't like horror films." It's a great horror film, period. I think a lot of Mr. Ambrogio's comments about the film could be answered if the missing 45 minutes of the film could be found.

The "Overrated and Underrated?" section is a plus. I have never stopped to think about why I like certain performances before. On the ones that I have seen from the piece, I've had to take a second thought about these characters written about. For fun I'll pick a few where I agree and disagree and say why.

For example, Charles Laughton from *Island of Lost Souls*—I disagree on overrated. Here's a character who thinks he is God. He then decides that, through his abilities, he can perform god-like creation. No sir, he caught this madness perfectly. He did H.G. Wells proud in *Island of Lost Souls*. Henry Hull from *Werewolf of London*—I agree with his underrated performance in *Werewolf of London*. I agree that we all get caught up in Lon Chaney's portrayal of Larry Talbot in *The Wolf Man*, but in this case, we're supposed to feel sorry for this man who is a workaholic before the term was ever used. Yes, Valerie Hobson's character falls in love with an old friend from her youth, Mr. Hull; apparently from his character's point of view, never had to deal with feelings of jealousy before. It's a new feeling for him and, along with his realization of what has happened to him, he does a marvelous job.

Keep up the great work!
Don E. Wilhoite, Jr.

**Editor's Note**: Keep those cards, letters and emails coming. We appreciate your comments, suggestions and criticisms. Consider *Grave Diggings* your horror film forum.

   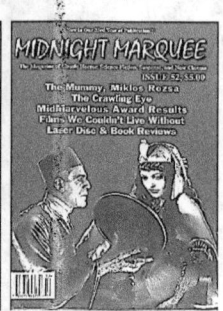 

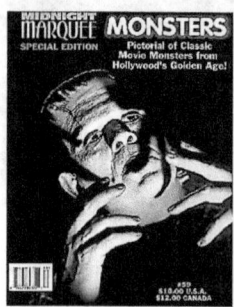    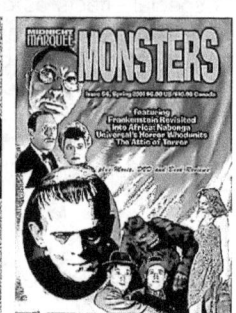
  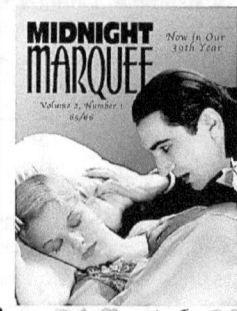

**Back Issue Blow Out Sale**
**$2 Each**
33, 37, 43, 46, 47, 50,
52, 53, 54, 55, 56, 57
58, 59, 60, 61, 63, 63
MAM 1 & 2

MidMar 65
$10

Minimum order $12, Shipping $4 first 6, 30 cents each additional mag
Midnight Marquee Press, 9721 Britinay Lane, Baltimore, MD 21234
410-665-1198, V/MC/AE/D

www.ingramcontent.com/pod-product-compliance
Lightning Source LLC
Chambersburg PA
CBHW081724100526

44591CB00016B/2495